ARCHAEOLOGIES OF TEXT

Joukowsky Institute Publications

ARCHAEOLOGIES OF TEXT

ARCHAEOLOGY, TECHNOLOGY, AND ETHICS

edited by

Matthew T. Rutz and Morag M. Kersel

Oxbow Books
Oxford and Philadelphia

Joukowsky Institute Publication 6

General series editor: Prof. John F. Cherry
Joukowsky Institute for Archaeology and the Ancient World
Brown University, Box 1837/60 George Street, Providence, RI 02912, USA

Published in the United Kingdom in 2014 by
OXBOW BOOKS
10 Hythe Bridge Street, Oxford OX1 2EW

and in the United States by
OXBOW BOOKS
908 Darby Road, Havertown, PA 19083

Published by Oxbow Books on behalf of the Joukowsky Institute

© Brown University, Oxbow Books and the individual contributors 2014

Paperback Edition: ISBN 978-1-78297-766-7
Digital Edition: ISBN 978-1-78297-767-4

A CIP record for this book is available from the British Library

Printed in the United Kingdom by Hobbs the Printers Ltd, Totton, Hampshire

For a complete list of Oxbow titles, please contact:

UNITED KINGDOM	UNITED STATES OF AMERICA
Oxbow Books	Oxbow Books
Telephone (01865) 241249	Telephone (800) 791-9354
Fax (01865) 794449	Fax (610) 853-9146
Email: oxbow@oxbowbooks.com	Email: queries@casemateacademic.com
www.oxbowbooks.com	www.casemateacademic.com/oxbow

Oxbow Books is part of the Casemate Group

Front cover: Cuneiform tablet PF 0694 (see p. 17, Figure 2.3) with Elamite text on the obverse (top
left) and on the reverse (top right) an impression of seal PFS 0093*, inscribed with name of
Cyrus of Anzan, son of Teispes (images courtesy of Persepolis Fortification Archive Project,
University of Chicago); detail (bottom) from the Greek inscription on the Rosetta Stone
(EA24, © Trustees of the British Museum).

Back cover: Excerpt from Mayan hieroglyphic inscriptions on Copan Stela 10 (see p. 37, Figure 3.2a);
drawing by Nicholas P. Carter after field sketches by David Stuart (images courtesy of
Nicholas P. Carter).

Contents

List of Figures

List of Tables

Notes on Contributors

Lisa Anderson (Ph.D., Brown University, 2009) is Frederick Randolph Grace Assistant Curator of Ancient Art in the Harvard Art Museums and former project manager of the U.S. Epigraphy Project, Brown University.

Neil J. Brodie (Ph.D., University of Liverpool, 1992) is Senior Research Fellow in the Scottish Centre for Crime and Justice Research at the University of Glasgow. Dr Brodie is an archaeologist by training and has held positions at the British School at Athens, the McDonald Institute for Archaeological Research at the University of Cambridge, where he was Research Director of the Illicit Antiquities Research Centre, and Stanford University's Archaeology Center. He was co-author (with Jennifer Doole and Peter Watson) of the report *Stealing History* (2000), commissioned by the Museums Association and ICOM-UK to advise upon the illicit trade in cultural material. He also co-edited (with Morag M. Kersel, Christina Luke, and Kathryn Walker Tubb) *Archaeology, Cultural Heritage, and the Antiquities Trade* (2006), (with Kathryn Walker Tubb) *Illicit Antiquities: The Theft of Culture and the Extinction of Archaeology* (2002), and (with Jennifer Doole and Colin Renfrew) *Trade in Illicit Antiquities: The Destruction of the World's Archaeological Heritage* (2001). He has worked on archaeological projects in the United Kingdom, Jordan, and Greece, where his work is ongoing.

Scott Bucking (Ph.D., University of Cambridge, 1998) is Associate Professor, Department of History, DePaul University. Professor Bucking's interests include the archaeology and epigraphy of late antique Egypt and Palestine, literacy and education in the ancient world, Greek and Coptic papyrology, and early Christianity and monasticism. His publications have appeared in the journals *Public Archaeology*, *Palestine Excavation Quarterly*, *Zeitschrift für Papyrologie und Epigraphik*, and *Journal of Coptic Studies*, and he is author of *Practice Makes Perfect: P. Cotsen-Princeton 1 and the Training of Scribes in Byzantine Egypt* (2011). He has two ongoing field projects: the Byzantine Cave Dwelling Project at Avdat, a UNESCO World Heritage Site in the Negev Desert of Israel, and the Beni Hasan in Late Antiquity Project in Middle Egypt, near Minya. He also currently serves on the Board of Trustees of the Albright Institute of Archaeological Research in Jerusalem.

Nicholas P. Carter (Ph.D., Brown University, 2014) is Adjunct Lecturer, Department of Anthropology, Brown University. Since 2006 he has worked with the El Zotz Archaeological Project, which has been excavating at the ancient Maya site of El Zotz in central Petén, Guatemala, and directs the Sierra Mazateca Archaeological Project. His research interests include anthropological archaeology; the origins, nature, and disintegration of complex polities; linguistic and semiotic anthropology; writing systems; ancient economies; and ceramic analysis. He has worked on the non-calendrical component of the Zapotec hieroglyphic writing system, as well as the networks of cultural and political influence behind the palaeographic and linguistic trends in Classic Maya inscriptions.

John F. Cherry (Ph.D., Southampton University, 1981) is Joukowsky Family Professor of Archaeology and Professor of Classics, Brown University. His teaching, research interests, and publications are eclectic and reflect a background in Classics, Anthropology, and Archaeology, as well as educational training on both sides of the Atlantic, and archaeological fieldwork experience in Great Britain, the United States, Yugoslav Macedonia, Italy, Armenia, and (especially) Greece and (currently) Montserrat. He is co-author (with A. Bernard Knapp) of *Provenience Studies and Bronze Age Cyprus: Production, Exchange and Politico-economic Change* (1994), as well as co-editor (with Lauren E. Talalay and Despina Margomenou) of *Prehistorians Round the Pond: Reflections on Aegean Prehistory as a Discipline* (2005), (with Susan E. Alcock) *Side-by-side Survey: Comparative Regional Studies in the Mediterranean World* (2004), (with Susan E. Alcock and Jaś Elsner) *Pausanias: Travel and Memory in Roman Greece* (2001), and (with Colin Renfrew) *Peer Polity Interaction and Socio-political Change* (1986). He has been co-editor of the *Journal of Mediterranean Archaeology* for almost 25 years and is the General Series Editor for *Joukowsky Institute Publications*.

Patty Gerstenblith (Ph.D., Harvard University, 1977; J.D., Northwestern University School of Law, 1983) is Distinguished Research Professor of Law at DePaul University and director of its Center for Art, Museum and Cultural Heritage Law. She is founding President of the Lawyers' Committee for Cultural Heritage Preservation (2005–2011), a Director of the U.S. Committee of the Blue Shield, and Co-Chair of the American Bar Association's Art and Cultural Heritage Law Committee. In 2011 she was appointed by President Obama to serve as the Chair of the President's Cultural Property Advisory Committee in the U.S. Department of State, on which she had previously served as a public representative in the Clinton administration. From 1995 to 2002, she was editor-in-chief of the *International Journal of Cultural Property*.

Her publications include the casebook *Art, Cultural Heritage and the Law* (2004; 3rd edition, 2012) and numerous articles. Before joining the DePaul faculty, Professor Gerstenblith clerked for the Honorable Richard D. Cudahy of the U.S. Court of Appeals for the Seventh Circuit.

Timothy P. Harrison (Ph.D., University of Chicago, 1995) is Chair of the Department of Near and Middle Eastern Civilizations, University of Toronto. Professor Harrison is the Director of the Tell Madaba Archaeological Project (Jordan) and the Tayinat Archaeological Project (Turkey) as well as a former President of the American Schools of Oriental Research (ASOR). He is the principal author of *Megiddo 3: Final Report on the Stratum VI Excavations* (2004), as well as numerous articles.

Morag M. Kersel (Ph.D., University of Cambridge, 2006) is Assistant Professor of Anthropology, DePaul University. Professor Kersel is Co-Director of two ongoing projects: Galilee Prehistory Project (Israel); "Follow the Pots" Project (Jordan). Her research interests include the Chalcolithic and Early Bronze Age of the eastern Mediterranean and Levant, cultural heritage protection, the built environment, object biographies, museums, and archaeological tourism. Her work combines archaeological, archival, and oral history research in order to understand the efficacy of cultural heritage law in protecting archaeological landscapes from looting. She is co-author (with Christina Luke) of *U.S. Cultural Diplomacy and Archaeology: Soft Power, Hard Heritage* (2013).

Eleanor Robson (D.Phil., Wolfson College, University of Oxford, 1995) is Reader in Ancient Near Eastern History in the Department of History, University College London. She was Co-Director (with Steve Tinney) of the Arts and Humanities Research Council-funded research project *The Geography of Knowledge in Assyria and Babylonia* (2007–2012) and is currently the British Institute for the Study of Iraq's voluntary Chair of Council. Dr Robson is the author or co-author of several books on Mesopotamian culture and the history of mathematics, most recently *Mathematics in Ancient Iraq: A Social History* (2008), which in 2011 won the History of Science Society's Pfizer Prize for the Best Scholarly Book. She co-edited (with Jacqueline Stedall) *The Oxford Handbook of the History of Mathematics* (2009) and (with Karen Radner) *The Oxford Handbook of Cuneiform Culture* (2011).

Christopher A. Rollston (Ph.D., The Johns Hopkins University, 1999) is Associate Professor of Northwest Semitic Languages and Literatures in the Department of Classical and Near Eastern Languages and Civilizations,

The George Washington University. Professor Rollston is the editor of the journal *MAARAV: A Journal for the Study of Northwest Semitic Languages and Literatures* and co-editor (with Eric Cline) of the *Bulletin of the American Schools of Oriental Research*. He was educated as a critical historian and a philologist of ancient Near Eastern languages, with Northwest Semitic epigraphy, ancient scribal education, literacy in the ancient Levant, Hebrew Bible, and Second Temple Jewish Literature as his strongest emphases. He works in more than a dozen ancient and modern languages, especially the biblical languages (Hebrew, Aramaic, and Greek), as well as Akkadian, Ugaritic, Phoenician, Ammonite, Moabite, and Sahidic Coptic. He has published widely in the area of Northwest Semitic epigraphy and is author of *Writing and Literacy in the World of Ancient Israel: Epigraphic Evidence from the Iron Age* (2010), which received the Frank Moore Cross Epigraphy Prize of the American Schools of Oriental Research.

Matthew T. Rutz (Ph.D., University of Pennsylvania, 2008) is Assistant Professor in the Department of Egyptology and Assyriology, Brown University. Professor Rutz works in the field of Assyriology with emphasis on Akkadian (Babylonian/Assyrian) and Sumerian documents from the late second and first millennia B.C., the social and political history of the Late Bronze Age, Babylonian literary and scholastic texts from the site of Nippur (Iraq), divination and medicine in ancient Mesopotamia, the textual transmission of cuneiform literature, and the study of ancient texts as archaeological objects. He is the author of *Bodies of Knowledge in Ancient Mesopotamia: The Diviners of Late Bronze Age Emar and Their Tablet Collection* (2013).

Adam Smith (Ph.D., University of California, Los Angeles, 2008) is Assistant Professor in the Department of East Asian Languages and Civilizations, University of Pennsylvania, where he is also Assistant Curator in the University of Pennsylvania Museum of Archaeology and Anthropology's Asian Section. Professor Smith's ongoing research focuses on the emergence and evolution of the Chinese writing system during the late second and first millennia B.C., and the early literate activities with which it was associated. He is currently working on a monograph on the topic of divination and its written record in early China.

Matthew W. Stolper (Ph.D., University of Michigan, 1974) is Emeritus Professor of Assyriology and John A. Wilson Professor Emeritus of Oriental Studies in the Oriental Institute and the Department of Near Eastern Languages and Civilizations of the University of Chicago. Professor Stolper has worked on Achaemenid Babylonian history and texts as well as on Elamite history and texts. As Director of the Persepolis Fortification Archive Project, his efforts are focused on Achaemenid administrative records excavated by the Oriental Institute in 1933 at Persepolis, the imperial residence in the Persian homeland, to be published in electronic and conventional forms. He is author of *Tall-i Malyan, I: Elamite Administrative Texts (1972–1974)* (1984), (with Elizabeth Carter) *Elam: Surveys of Political History and Archaeology* (1984), *Entrepreneurs and Empire: The Murašû Archive, the Murašû Firm, and Persian Rule in Babylonia* (1985), *Late Achaemenid, Early Macedonian and Early Seleucid Records of Deposit and Related Texts* (1993), and (with Veysel Donbaz) *Istanbul Murašû Texts* (1997), as well as numerous articles.

Heidi Wendt (Ph.D., Brown University, 2013) is Assistant Professor in the Departments of Religion, Philosophy, and Classics, Wright State University. Her interdisciplinary research focuses on religion in the Roman Empire, including early Christianity, and the activities of freelance religious experts and their significance for the emergence of Christians in the first century. Professor Wendt is interested in relationships between Roman and provincial religions, particularly in Roman strategies for negotiating the "foreign" ritual practices and spaces with which they came into contact through imperial expansion. In 2011 she was awarded the Emeline Hill Richardson Pre-Doctoral Rome Prize in Ancient Studies from the American Academy in Rome. She has worked on archaeological projects and conducted research throughout Italy, Greece, and Turkey.

Contributor Addresses

Lisa Anderson
Division of Asian and Mediterranean
    Art
Harvard Art Museums
32 Quincy St
Cambridge, MA 02138
lisa_anderson@harvard.edu

Neil J. Brodie
Scottish Centre for Crime and Justice
    Research
University of Glasgow
Ivy Lodge, 63 Gibson St
Glasgow G12 8LR
Scotland
Neil.Brodie@glasgow.ac.uk

Scott Bucking
Department of History
DePaul University
2320 N. Kenmore Ave
Chicago, IL 60614
sbucking@depaul.edu

Nicholas P. Carter
Department of Anthropology
Brown University, Box 1921
Providence, RI 02912
Nicholas_P_Carter@brown.edu

John F. Cherry
Joukowsky Institute for Archaeology
    and the Ancient World
Brown University, Box 1837
60 George St
Providence, RI 02912
John_Cherry@brown.edu

Patty Gerstenblith
DePaul University College of Law
25 E. Jackson Blvd
Chicago, IL 60604
pgerstcn@depaul.edu

Timothy P. Harrison
Department of Near and Middle
    Eastern Civilizations
University of Toronto
4 Bancroft Ave
Toronto, ON
Canada M5S 1C1
tim.harrison@utoronto.ca

Morag M. Kersel
Department of Anthropology
DePaul University
2343 North Racine Ave
Chicago, IL 60614
mkersel@depaul.edu

Eleanor Robson
Department of History
University College London
Gower St
London WC1E 6BT
United Kingdom
e.robson@ucl.ac.uk

Christopher A. Rollston
Department of Classical and Near
    Eastern Languages and Civilizations
The George Washington University
801 22nd St NW, Phillips Hall 345
Washington, DC 20052
rollston@gwu.edu

Matthew T. Rutz
Department of Egyptology
    and Assyriology
Brown University, Box 1899
2 Prospect St
Providence, RI 02912
Matthew_Rutz@brown.edu

Adam Smith
University of Pennsylvania Museum
    of Archaeology and Anthropology
3260 South St, Room 510
Philadelphia, PA 19104
adsmit@sas.upenn.edu

Matthew W. Stolper
Oriental Institute
University of Chicago
1155 E 58th St
Chicago, IL 60637
m-stolper@uchicago.edu

Heidi Wendt
Religion, Philosophy, and Classics
Wright State University
Millett Hall 370
3640 Colonel Glenn Hwy
Dayton, OH 45435
heidi.wendt@wright.edu

Acknowledgments

This volume grew out of a symposium hosted at Brown University on December 3–5, 2010, the purpose of which was to explore different perspectives on the interplay of archaeological and textual material from the ancient world – hence *archaeologies* of text. For the symposium we invited scholars who routinely engage with the archaeology of texts – archaeologists, classicists, epigraphers, papyrologists, philologists, Assyriologists, Egyptologists, Mayanists, ancient historians – to discuss current theoretical and practical problems that have grown out of their work on early inscriptions and archaeology, and we warmly thank all contributors and participants for their interest, energy, and thoughtful engagement with this perennially relevant, promising, and vexing topic. Our hope was that the variety and specificity of perspectives and methods under discussion would catalyze cross-disciplinary exchange as well as underscore the importance of reevaluating the well-established disciplinary practices and assumptions within our respective fields. We leave it to the reader to decide if we succeeded in our approach, even if only asymptotically.

The symposium was generously supported by several institutional sponsors that we are only too happy to thank: the Department of Egyptology and Assyriology (James P. Allen, then Chair), the Joukowsky Institute for Archaeology and the Ancient World (Susan E. Alcock, Director), the Program in Early Cultures, and The Colver Lectureship Fund at Brown University, and the Department of Anthropology at DePaul University. Additional funding for publishing this volume was provided by the Joukowsky Institute for Archaeology and the Ancient World and the Humanities Research Fund of Brown University's Office of the Vice President for Research.

Institutional support is essential, but it is people who give vitality and meaning to symposia such as ours. Over and above the authors of the individual chapters included herein and the many people who came to Brown to participate in the symposium, we gladly acknowledge a number of others by name. Bruce Zuckerman of the University of Southern California gave a stimulating presentation at the symposium, but due to personal reasons he was unable to contribute a chapter to this book. Sue Alcock and Jim Allen were pivotal in making the symposium a success. Claire Benson,

Diana Richardson, and Sarah Sharpe provided enthusiastic and capable administrative and logistical support. Doctoral students from a number of programs at Brown University served as session chairs: Bryan Brinkman, Kathryn Howley, Jessica Nowlin, Timothy Sandiford, Julia Troche, and Zackary Wainer. Subsequently a number of Brown graduate students (some of whom were also chairs) took a graduate seminar that grew out of the symposium: Emanuela Bocancea, Müge Durusu-Tanrıöver, Katherine Harrington, Ian Randall, Timothy Sandiford, and Alexander Smith (Archaeology and the Ancient World); Scott DiGiulio and Christopher Geggie (Classics); Christian Casey, Kathryn Howley, and Julia Troche (Egyptology); M. Willis Monroe and Zackary Wainer (Assyriology). Clive Vella, Ian Randall, and Magdelyne Christakis assisted with editing some of the individual chapters. John Cherry must also be singled out for a final word of thanks. He was a supporter of this enterprise from its inception and later took on a number of roles: as participant in the symposium, as thoughtful contributor to the volume, and as attentive series editor.

— 1 —

Introduction:
No Discipline is an Island

Morag M. Kersel and Matthew T. Rutz

As a discipline archaeology may be distinct, but it is hardly isolated: its scope is as broad as the disparate fields that inform its methods and perspectives, among them anthropology, art history, epigraphy, and the physical and biological sciences. Archaeology's object of study is as varied as the material traces of human behavior, from prehistory to recent history. In contrast the study of the premodern textual record is not a single discipline at all, but rather an array of fields and sub-fields loosely allied around a common purpose: to gain insight into the human past principally through written text, a powerful if relatively recent technology for visually and physically encoding natural language, storing and transmitting information, and extending, supporting, or subverting memory. Ancient texts bear witness to the multiple uses of writing, from mediating political and economic interactions to reproducing, reflecting, and refracting culture to both literate and non-literate audiences, both of whom would have encountered text albeit in powerfully unequal ways. Writing can be viewed as occupying a particular and peculiar niche among the rich repertoire of human communication technologies that are embedded literally as well as figuratively in frameworks of material culture and the built environment, squarely in the domain of anthropological archaeology (e.g., Andrássy et al. 2009; Glatz 2012; Houston 2004a).

However, even before the practice of archaeology, certain bodies of ancient literature were carefully transmitted across space and time, and some of these corpora even managed to survive down to the present in some form, be it complete or fragmentary (e.g., Reynolds and Wilson 2013; Tov 2012). Bearing witness to this long process are the anthologies that constitute the core of the traditional canons of the world's ancient literate cultures: classical works from Asia, Africa, Europe, and the Americas. The complex processes behind the transmission of ancient literature took many historical forms, but forces that were highly intentional as well as entirely random or accidental inevitably buffeted the texts that somehow survived. Similarly, other ancient texts survived on monuments that never quite slipped from view, but whose meanings were transformed or obscured by the interest or neglect of various shifting audiences over time. In either case, until the relatively recent advent of archaeology as a mode of inquiry (Trigger 2006 [1989]), vast bodies of text were excluded from reckonings of the distant past (e.g., Baines et al. 2008; Sanders 2006). Beginning in earnest in the fifteenth century, European antiquarians began uncovering ancient inscriptions in the classical Mediterranean world, and since that time countless premodern texts inscribed in many media have been found throughout Africa, the Americas, Asia, and beyond.

Perhaps surprisingly, archaeology and the study of the premodern textual record may be thought of as approaches that are interdependent and complementary as well as independent or even contradictory. The adoption of one of these views or the other has largely depended on a given scholar's training, disposition, research questions, and preferred interpretive lens. In historical perspective, from the eighteenth century on the archaeological discovery of previously unknown texts led to the adaptation of existing interpretive methods, such as classical philology, to deal with new epigraphic environments. In addition this glut of new data brought about the creation of entirely new fields, such as Assyriology, Egyptology, or Maya Studies, that are devoted to recording the epigraphic record, deciphering obsolete scripts, and reconstructing the lost languages and language families encoded in those scripts. For much of the twentieth century, archaeological and epigraphic research largely moved in different directions, sometimes in parallel or complementary configurations, sometimes at odds or simply mutually uninterested. This fragmentation of research programs prompts some fundamental theoretical questions and presents a number of practical problems, and thus the relationship between archaeology and textual study periodically needs to be revisited (e.g., Kohl 2006; Moreland 2001, 2006; Zettler 2003).

Despite this complicated, sometimes fraught history, archaeological and textual research trajectories intersect necessarily and unavoidably in a number of ways. In light of this entangled relationship, we may reasonably interrogate the roles ancient texts play in archaeological discourses. First, premodern texts suggest taxonomies, both explicit and implicit, that allow scholars to assign names: names to places (e.g., historical geography, urban/non-urban/cosmic topography), names to periods (including both emic and etic reckonings of time in a given sequence), names to people (e.g., ethnolinguistic identification, titles or epithets, and actual people, that is, names of specific persons and kinship groups), as well as names to objects, architecture, and features in the built and natural environments. In addition, texts can act as informants and provide descriptions, however limited or tendentious, of how objects, features, spaces, or landscapes functioned or were perceived in a variety of ancient social contexts. Alternatively, interpreting textual finds found in situ frequently provides the basis for making inferences about who inhabited or otherwise interacted with spaces, especially in the case of archives, libraries, or other inscribed remains found associated with architecture or environmental features, such as display inscriptions, graffiti, or textual deposits. Textual documentation sometimes suggests a chronological anchor, be it relative or absolute, explicitly stated in a dated record or inferred from palaeographic, grammatical, iconographic, prosopographic, or other markers associated with a text. In terms of ancient written records' analytical effects on academic discourses, the technology of writing itself is often ascribed as a correlate of social complexity or an attribute of civilization (e.g., Powell 2009), which in turn necessarily informs how researchers construct narratives about the past. Some ancient texts espouse specific narratives of ancient events; others are swept up in modern scholars' narrativized reconstructions of the past. For both of these reasons, ancient writings can also act as a tether that connects the past to the present, with profound effects on popular interest in archaeological and historical research, the amount of funding available to support research, tourism and economic development or exploitation, identity politics, as well as nationalism and modern state-craft. Finally, textual research can and does recover meaningful information about the past from otherwise contextless ancient texts, either from the received canons that have a complex or scarcely known transmission history as material objects, or from more recently rediscovered textual artifacts that were dislodged from their archaeological context by whatever means.

Looked at from the opposite perspective, what role does archaeology play in discourses focused on ancient texts? In the case of some textual traditions, archaeological investigation is responsible for the creation of the corpus itself, in the sense that archaeological excavation or survey has recovered scripts, languages, and text corpora that had otherwise been lost to history. It may even be argued that the proper study of the origins of the world's writing systems is as much a problem of prehistory (i.e., the domain of archaeology) as it is one of epigraphic and historical research (e.g., Darnell et al. 2005; Goldwasser 2011; Houston 2004b; Sanders 2006). In addition, the emphasis of archaeological research on context effectively circumscribes textual sources from any period in analytically productive ways: there are innumerable examples of excavated textual artifacts that cohere archaeologically in ways that are not apparent in the contents of the texts themselves (e.g., Cohen et al. 2010; Rutz 2013; Stocker and Davis 2004; Zettler 2008). The archaeological sequence also has the ability to provide a chronological anchor that can support, undermine, or problematize any chronological scheme suggested in the textual record. Similarly, archaeological research can affirm, contradict, or complicate the assumptions and received wisdom of living cultural traditions or purely historical modes of inquiry. Above all, archaeology can and does shed light on facets of human life around or outside the purview of even the most robustly diverse array of ancient textual documentation. Because of archaeology's focus on the material traces of the human past, textual studies have been enriched by thinking about materials and materiality in relation to the social practice and products of ancient writing. On the one hand, archaeological research helps to place texts (ancient narratives or descriptions, as well as physical manuscripts or inscribed objects) in a world of other things, schemes of value, and webs of cultural meaning; on the other hand, textual studies have grown to include the material analysis of inscribed objects in order to understand their physical properties and composition, which in turn can elucidate textual production as a craft (a technological, cultural, and socio-economic practice) with material correlates in the archaeological record (e.g., Houston 2012; Payne 2008; Piquette and Whitehouse 2013; Taylor and Cartwright 2011). A closer analysis of inscribed materials has also made it possible to source individual inscribed objects or groups of objects (e.g., Goren et al. 2004, 2006, 2009, 2011; Powers et al. 2009). Current practices in the imaging, documentation, dissemination, and conservation of ancient inscriptions have all undergone radical transformation in recent decades (e.g., Bodel 2012; Gütschow 2012; Hahn et al. 2007; Hameeuw and Willems 2011; van Peursen et al. 2010; Powers et al. 2005; Zuckerman 2010a, 2010b). Though not solely a contribution of archaeological science, at least some of these developments were arguably catalyzed by concurrent developments in archaeological research. Finally, archaeological modes of analysis have played a central role in how scholars of all stripes conceive of and handle contextless or undocumented inscriptions. Two fundamental dimensions of this engagement are the authentication of contextless objects through non-textual means and the proposition that inscribed objects that lack context pose serious intellectual and ethical problems that cannot be ignored.

The interplay between textual research and archaeology is not only a function of a shared interest in the past, but also a common purpose: concern for the fundamental issues surrounding our access to and perceptions of the past. The purpose of this volume is to scrutinize the relationship between textual and archaeological approaches by moving beyond the tendency to treat texts and archaeological remains as independent or even casually interdependent sources of information. Central to this discussion is a concern with the ways in which the two discourses inform each other, the ways in which their results are disseminated, and the intellectual and ethical issues that arise from the functional fragmentation of research agendas that ultimately share a common goal.

The relationship between text-based research and archaeology is clearly not without its challenges, especially concerning artifacts with missing or incomplete object histories. Scholars tend to split into two opposing camps. One side maintains that archaeological items found on the antiquities market with no accompanying background documents, or those from unauthorized archaeological excavations, should be ignored, flagged, or otherwise marginalized in academic discourses. The other side holds that historical data can and do hold value that should be preserved, disseminated, and integrated into historical syntheses regardless of how such data came into view, a position encapsulated in the following quotation, which refers to the 1970 UNESCO Convention on the Means of Prohibiting and Preventing the Illicit Import, Export and Transfer of Ownership of Cultural Property: "A policy that disregards essential data, excluded after some arbitrary date imposed by a patently political body and enforced by academic censorship, is objectionable to scholarship and should be rejected outright" (Owen 2013a: 6; cf. Owen 2013b: 335–356). The nature and evolution of the gulf that separates these perspectives has a complex history that we will not rehash, but it seems likely that a genealogy of mentalities and practices in each discipline ought to be significant: archaeologists view the issue through the lens of anthropological ethics, while philologists, epigraphers, or text-based researchers have no unifying agenda or guidelines to regulate intellectual practice beyond accurately and thoroughly representing the historical record — and surely it is also telling that scholars who work mainly with texts cannot be conveniently labeled under one rubric, but are rather divided up among numerous fields and subfields of area studies.

At least in part, the chapters in this volume seek to respond to this current disciplinary divide by addressing one or more of the following three principal aims: (1) to confront the bifurcation of archaeology and the study of early textual sources; (2) to rethink the fragmentation of the various specialized disciplines that ask questions about the interface between archaeology and the textual record; and (3) to discuss the best practices in archaeological and epigraphic methods, documentation and dissemination technologies, and ethical practices for dealing with early inscriptions.

This synthetic volume brings together archaeologists and those who study premodern texts to once again draw attention to the importance of the topic and to stimulate discussion of a number of perennial questions:

Do ancient documents speak for themselves or do they require contextual information that can only be supplied by archaeology? What are the limits of contextual analysis? What are the major archaeological and conservational problems confronting the study of the epigraphic record? What technologies are the best at recovering and preserving the information encoded in ancient inscriptions, and what are the analytical payoffs of such technologies? How should scholars deal with the long-term big data challenges of access, preservation, and stability presented by the proliferation of new technologies for non-print-based dissemination and storage? What methods do the least harm in documenting inscriptions? What are the most effective ways to publish and disseminate ancient texts for the benefit of researchers and other interested communities? What are the particular complications of using ancient textual sources to access the past? Are texts unique or privileged as types of communication embedded in the archaeological record, or do texts fall somewhere on a spectrum of symbolic, figural, and material data? How are forgeries, both ancient and modern, to be detected and dealt with, and how serious a threat do forgeries pose to the scholarly production of knowledge about the past? What are the major intellectual and ethical issues of either utilizing or ignoring contextless or undocumented inscriptions? At the symposium from which this volume derives we asked scholars who routinely engage with the archaeology of texts – ancient historians, archaeologists, Assyriologists, classicists, Egyptologists, epigraphers, lawyers, Mayanists, papyrologists, philologists – to take up these and other pertinent questions and to reflect on how their work interacts with textual, historical, and archaeological problems. Our aim throughout has been to be selective and representative, not exhaustive or comprehensive.

In his contribution on the Persepolis Fortification Archive, Matthew Stolper interweaves the themes of archaeology, ethics, and technology in a fascinating case study of how history can be written using the tiniest of fragments, providing invaluable insights into the imperial city of Persepolis between 509 and 493 B.C. Using new and innovative imaging and publishing technologies, Stolper highlights the importance of these tablets, excavated in the early twentieth century, in the past and in the present for our understanding of ancient daily life.

Drawing from the Mesoamerican, Egyptian, and Anatolian worlds, Nicholas Carter, Scott Bucking, and Timothy Harrison examine texts in landscapes, each in turn illustrating the conclusive consequences of the importance of text in context. Discussing the Classic Maya hieroglyphic record – text from pots, text from wall paintings, text on paper codices, text on buildings and monuments – Carter illustrates the link between those texts and the built and ecological environments of the ancient Maya. He demonstrates the importance of archaeological context in shedding light on the textual record. Through an examination of graffiti at the Egyptian sites of Beni Hasan and the temple of Queen Hatshepsut at Deir el-Bahri, Bucking illustrates the human and natural agencies that contribute both negatively and positively to the functional aspects of archaeological and epigraphic landscapes. The "marks" of the sixth century monks left on the even older Egyptian landscape, the effects of the subsequent archaeological excavations, and the forces of nature demonstrate the importance of having the complete history of texts in spatial and architectural contexts in order to produce a meaningful comprehensive narrative. The archaeological excavations at Tell Tayinat undertaken by Harrison and his colleagues have produced some of the richest evidence for how texts and material culture, when examined together, produce unexpected insights into the complex social and historical experiences of the ancient past. In the recent discovery of a cache of cuneiform tablets dating to the late eighth–seventh centuries B.C. Harrison makes a persuasive case for the need to consider epigraphic and archaeological evidence jointly, which in this example may point to the intersecting roles played by divine authority and religious ritual in framing our understanding of the ideological world that the texts inhabit.

The two chapters dealing specifically with text and interpretation present case studies from Mesopotamia and China, each concerned with ancient divination. In discussing the ancient meaning, theory, and practice of divination, Matthew Rutz provides a description of the importance of the intellectual curiosity of nineteenth century travellers and explorers in Mesopotamia. Their early "archaeological" and commercial pursuits brought to light evidence for ancient Mesopotamian life-ways and practices, but just as important are the lingering assumptions and interpretations that can come to be the received wisdom of a relatively young field like Assyriology. While Rutz illustrates the importance and usefulness of artifacts that may not have a secure archaeological documentation, he makes a contribution to discussions on missing knowledge when the tablet does not go hand-in-hand with its archaeological find spot. In this case the different sources for understanding Mesopotamian extispicy in the early second millennium B.C. have a very uneven archaeological distribution, with significant impact on the contextual analysis of the corpus as a whole.

In his chapter on a collection of Late Shang (ca. 1300–1050 B.C.) divination inscriptions from Anyang acquired in the 1930s and now in the C.V. Starr East Asian Library at Columbia University, Adam Smith recounts an overlooked aspect of a single bovine scapula, which he argues is indicative of ancient scribal education. In this instance the texts do appear to speak for themselves, for while they have no recorded associated archaeological findspot, the inscribed material does provide a precise site of origin. However, according to Smith it is the combination of the archaeological context and the writing style that leads to the conclusion that most of the inscriptions are by scribal trainees, suggesting that the Anyang divination workshops instructed their own scribes, an overlooked aspect of this important corpus. These two chapters focusing on divinatory texts from different areas of the world and different time periods illustrate the significance of obtaining the complete object biographies for the inscribed materials: text and context are inextricably linked and are interdependent. Together they can and do provide a greater understanding of people in the past.

The contributions on the technological aspects of text and archaeology, with specific examples of digital recording, archives, databases, and access, provide exemplary models of best practice, collegiality, and knowledge dissemination about ancient inscriptions. In her contribution, Eleanor Robson showcases three innovative technologies that are encouraging the development of a comprehensive cuneiform corpus. Oracc (*The Open, Richly Annotated Cuneiform Corpus*) and its core project *GKAB* (*The Geography of Knowledge in Assyria and Babylonia, 700–200 B.C.*), and Google Earth offer new features for the widest possible range of users, complementing the Cuneiform Digital Library Initiative's aspiration to be a comprehensive archive of digital images of original objects inscribed in cuneiform characters, occasionally with transliteration and translation, as well as a repository for older, published hand drawings of inscriptions in the cuneiform script. In her discussion Robson illustrates how writing systems come to life through the newest technologies for communication and interpretation.

In their chapter Lisa Anderson and Heidi Wendt discuss the U.S. Epigraphy Project (USEP), a digital record of over 3,000 Greek and Latin inscribed objects housed in more than 80 museum, university, and private collections of ancient art and artifacts in North America. Through the lens of the project's historical development Anderson and Wendt provide a basic orientation to the practical and intellectual advantages of digital humanities scholarship. In particular, they emphasize innovative possibilities for engaging with epigraphic materials at multiple levels of academic inquiry. They reinforce the contributions of Robson and Stolper by highlighting the need for participation in digital and academic peer communities: collaboration and knowledge exchange are integral to demonstrating affinities not only between texts represented in single collections of epigraphic materials, as in the Persepolis Fortification Archive, but also in comparing epigraphic data points to other forms of ancient evidence (e.g., tablets made of clay, wood, or stone, parchment manuscripts, papyri, and ostraca).

In the final section of the book, scholars were asked to contribute case studies and insights on intellectual and ethical issues associated with the forgery of ancient texts and the publication of undocumented textual materials. A goal of the symposium and the subsequent volume was to move beyond the "us vs. them" paradigm encapsulated by the constricting publication policies of some journals dealing with ancient inscriptions. Christopher Rollston tackles the always fascinating and ever thorny issue of forged inscriptions. Through a discussion of the basic content, probable purposes and motivations, putative dates, and the means of detection of various forgeries from antiquity up to the present day, Rollston demonstrates that, while there have been some recent high-profile cases like the James ossuary and the Jehoash inscription, forgeries are not a new phenomenon. Rollston's chapter is also a cautionary tale. He asserts that most recent forgeries (i.e., since the time of the Renaissance) have appeared on the antiquities market, leading to the conclusion that scholars who rely on artifacts from the market should beware: a lack of documentation immediately raises questions of authenticity, which may lead to a skewed academic understanding of the material. In their contribution Neil Brodie and Morag Kersel also present a cautionary tale involving incantation bowls, WikiLeaks, and the problems presented by lost archaeological context. They reveal how scholarly debate over the importance of documentation has deteriorated into sometimes-rancorous disagreement, with occasional legal consequences. Using a WikiLeaks published report on a private collection of incantation bowls, Brodie and Kersel raise questions surrounding documentation and evidence in the social lives of objects, in this case mundane objects inscribed with culturally potent textual material. This chapter echoes the sentiments expressed by Cherry and Gerstenblith that undocumented textual materials should only be studied with the permission of their rightful owner, affirming the significance of the law in the intersection of archaeological ethics and historical research on textual artifacts.

Patty Gerstenblith offers some explanation of the development of a publication policy that might satisfy both sides of the clash over undocumented artifacts. She articulates the policies of some of the key organizations whose membership is comprised of advocates for each side of the debate. Complementing this is John Cherry's chapter, which begins with a fascinating case study involving September 11, 2001, the World Trade Center, a group of cuneiform tablets and plaques looted from somewhere in southern Iraq, repatriation efforts, the conservation and academic study of this corpus of material, and finally finding a suitable place of publication for this important but undocumented group of tablets. Examining the editorial position of 19 leading academic journals Cherry attempts to answer his salient question "don't these artifacts deserve a little love?" Undocumented collections of texts present a unique set of opportunities and challenges for scholars in the twenty-first century. While ethically and legally problematic, these collections hold significant value for our understanding of the ancient world.

Examining the archaeology-text nexus from multiple perspectives, contributors to this volume discuss current theoretical and practical problems that have grown out of their work at the boundary of the division between archaeology and the study of early inscriptions. In the twelve representative case studies drawn from research in Asia, Africa, the Mediterranean, and Mesoamerica, scholars use various lenses to examine critically the interface between archaeology and the study of ancient texts, rethink the fragmentation of their various specialized disciplines, and illustrate the best in current approaches to contextual analysis. The collection of essays also highlights recent trends in the development of documentation and dissemination technologies, engages with the ethical and intellectual quandaries presented by ancient inscriptions that lack archaeological context, and sets out to find profitable future directions for interdisciplinary research. Chapters in this volume illustrate both the value of studying undocumented texts and the importance of texts in context, suggesting a closer look at the practice of ignoring potential benefits of undocumented material and the benefits of archaeological context in presenting a comprehensive picture of the past. We hope that this is the beginning of a rapprochement in the divide over archaeology and textual study.

References

Andrássy, Petra, Julia Budka, and Frank Kammerzell (editors)
    2009   *Non-Textual Marking Systems, Writing and Pseudo Script from Prehistory to Modern Times.* Lingua Aegyptia Studia Monographica Vol. 8. Seminar für Ägyptologie und Koptologie, Göttingen, Germany.
Baines, John, John Bennet, and Stephen D. Houston (editors)
    2008   *The Disappearance of Writing Systems: Perspectives on Literacy and Communication.* Equinox Publishing, London.
Bodel, John
    2012   Latin Epigraphy and the IT Revolution. In *Epigraphy and the Historical Sciences,* edited by John Davies and John Wilkes, pp. 275–296. Proceedings of the British Academy Vol. 177. Oxford University Press, Oxford.
Cohen, Chaim, Joseph Maran, and Melissa Vetters
    2010   An Ivory Rod with a Cuneiform Inscription, Most Probably Ugaritic, from a Final Palatial Workshop in the Lower Citadel of Tiryns. *Archäologischer Anzeiger* 2010(2): 1–22.

Darnell, John Coleman, F.W. Dobbs-Allsopp, Marilyn J. Lundberg, P. Kyle McCarter, and Bruce Zuckerman

2005 *Two Early Alphabetic Inscriptions from the Wadi el-Ḥôl: New Evidence for the Origin of the Alphabet from the Western Desert of Egypt*. Annual of the American Schools of Oriental Research 59, Part II. American Schools of Oriental Research, Boston.

Glatz, Claudia

2012 Bearing the Marks of Control? Reassessing Pot Marks in Late Bronze Age Anatolia. *American Journal of Archaeology* 116: 5–38.

Goldwasser, Orly

2011 The Advantage of Cultural Periphery: The Invention of the Alphabet in Sinai (Circa 1840 B.C.E.). In *Culture Contacts and the Making of Cultures: Papers in Homage to Itamar Even- Zohar*, edited by Rakefet Sela-Sheffy and Gideon Toury, pp. 255–321. Tel Aviv University, Tel Aviv.

Goren, Yuval, Israel Finkelstein, and Nadav Na'aman

2004 *Inscribed in Clay: Provenance Studies of the Amarna Letters and Other Ancient Near Eastern Texts*. Monograph Series, Number 23. Emery and Claire Yass Publications in Archaeology, Institute of Archaeology, Tel Aviv University, Tel Aviv.

Goren, Yuval, Hans Mommsen, Israel Finkelstein, and Nadav Na'aman

2009 A Provenance Study of the Gilgamesh Fragment from Megiddo. *Archaeometry* 51: 763–773.

Goren, Yuval, Hans Mommsen, and Jörg Klinger

2011 Non-destructive Provenance Study of Cuneiform Tablets Using Portable X-ray Fluorescence (pXRF). *Journal of Archaeological Science* 38: 684–696.

Goren, Yuval, Nadav Na'aman, Hans Mommsen, and Israel Finkelstein

2006 Provenance Study and Re-evaluation of the Cuneiform Documents from the Egyptian Residency at Tel Aphek. *Ägypten und Levante / Egypt and the Levant* 16: 161–171.

Gütschow, Carmen

2012 *Methoden zur Restaurierung von ungebrannten und gebrannten Keilschrifttafeln – Gestern und Heute*. Berliner Beiträge zum Vorderen Orient Vol. 22. PeWe-Verlag, Gladbeck, Germany.

Hahn, Daniel V., Kevin C. Baldwin, and Donald D. Duncan

2007 Non-Laser-Based Scanner for Three-Dimensional Digitization of Historical Artifacts. *Applied Optics* 46: 2838–2850.

Hameeuw, Hendrik, and Geert Willems

2011 New Visualization Techniques for Cuneiform Texts and Sealings. *Akkadica* 132: 163–178.

Houston, Stephen D.

2004a The Archaeology of Communication Technologies. *Annual Review of Anthropology* 33: 223–250.

Houston, Stephen D. (editor)

2004b *The First Writing: Script Invention as History and Process*. Cambridge University Press, Cambridge.

2012   *The Shape of Script: How and Why Writing Systems Change*. School for Advanced Research Press, Santa Fe.

Kohl, Philip L.

2006   The Materiality of History: Reflections on the Strengths of the Archaeological Record. In *Excavating Asian History: Interdisciplinary Studies in Archaeology and History*, edited by Norman Yoffee and Bradley L. Crowell, pp. 327–338. The University of Arizona Press, Tucson.

Moreland, John

2001   *Archaeology and Text*. Duckworth, London.

2006   Archaeology and Texts: Subservience or Enlightenment. *Annual Review of Anthropology* 35: 135–151.

Owen, David I.

2013a   Of Dogs and (Kennel) Men. *Cuneiform Digital Library Bulletin* 2013(2): 1–7. Electronic document, http://cdli.ucla.edu/pubs/cdlb/2013/cdlb2013_002.html, accessed December 13, 2013.

2013b   *Cuneiform Texts Primarily from Iri-Saĝrig/Āl-Šarrākī and the History of the Ur III Period*. Vol. I, Commentary and Indexes. NISABA Vol. 15. CDL Press, Bethesda, Maryland.

Payne, Annick

2008   Writing Systems and Identity. In *Anatolian Interfaces: Hittites, Greeks and their Neighbours*, edited by Billie Jean Collins, Mary R. Bachvarova, and Ian C. Rutherford, pp. 117–122. Oxbow Books, Oxford.

van Peursen, Wido, Ernst D. Thoutenhoofd, and Adriaan van der Weel (editors)

2010   *Text Comparison and Digital Creativity: The Production of Presence and Meaning in Digital Text Scholarship*. Scholarly Communication Vol. 1. Brill, Leiden.

Piquette, Kathryn E., and Ruth D. Whitehouse (editors)

2013   *Writing as Material Practice: Substance, Surface and Medium*. Ubiquity Press, London. Electronic document, DOI: http://dx.doi.org/10.5334/bai, accessed December 23, 2013.

Powell, Barry B.

2009   *Writing: Theory and History of the Technology of Civilization*. Wiley-Blackwell, Chichester, U.K.

Powers, J., N. Dimitrova, R. Huang, D.-M. Smilgies, D.H. Bilderback, K. Clinton, and Robert E. Thorne

2005   X-ray Fluorescence Recovers Writing from Ancient Inscriptions. *Zeitschrift für Papyrologie und Epigraphik* 152: 221–227.

Powers, J., D.M. Smilgies, E.C. Geil, K. Clinton, N. Dimitrova, M. Peachin, and Robert E. Thorne

2009   X-ray Fluorescence Imaging Analysis of Inscription Provenance. *Journal of Archaeological Science* 36: 343–350.

Reynolds, L.D., and N.G. Wilson

2013   *Scribes and Scholars: A Guide to the Transmission of Greek and Latin Literature*. 4th ed. Oxford University Press, Oxford.

Rutz, Matthew T.

    2013 *Bodies of Knowledge in Ancient Mesopotamia: The Diviners of Late Bronze Age Emar and Their Tablet Collection.* Ancient Magic and Divination Vol. 9. Brill, Leiden.

Sanders, Seth L. (editor)

    2006 *Margins of Writing, Origins of Cultures.* Oriental Institute Seminars Vol. 2. The Oriental Institute of the University of Chicago, Chicago.

Stocker, Sharon R., and Jack L. Davis

    2004 Animal Sacrifice, Archives, and Feasting at the Palace of Nestor. *Hesperia* 73: 179–195.

Taylor, Jon, and Caroline Cartwright

    2011 The Making and Re-making of Clay Tablets. *Scienze dell'Antichità* 17: 297–324.

Tov, Emanuel

    2012 *Textual Criticism of the Hebrew Bible.* 3rd revised and expanded ed. Fortress Press, Minneapolis.

Trigger, Bruce G.

    2006 [1989] *A History of Archaeological Thought.* 2nd ed. Cambridge University Press, Cambridge.

Zettler, Richard L.

    2003 Reconstructing the World of Ancient Mesopotamia: Divided Beginnings and Holistic History. *Journal of the Economic and Social History of the Orient* 46: 3–45.

    2008 Context and Text: Nippur Area TB Level IV and the "Archive" of Lama-palil. In *On the Third Dynasty of Ur: Studies in Honor of Marcel Sigrist,* edited by Piotr Michalowski, pp. 287–301. Journal of Cuneiform Studies Supplemental Series Vol. 1. American Schools of Oriental Research, Boston.

Zuckerman, Bruce

    2010a The Dynamics of Change in the Computer Imaging of the Dead Sea Scrolls and Other Ancient Inscriptions. In *Rediscovering the Dead Sea Scrolls: An Assessment of Old and New Approaches,* edited by Maxine L. Grosman, pp. 69–88. Eerdmans, Grand Rapids, Michigan.

    2010b The Dynamics of Change in the Computer Imaging of the Dead Sea Scrolls and Other Ancient Inscriptions. Digital design by Tara Waugh. Electronic document, http://www.usc.edu/dept/LAS/wsrp/information/DynamicsDSS/, accessed February 1, 2014.

Case in Point:
The Persepolis Fortification Archive

Matthew W. Stolper

Like many cuneiformists, I work on small pieces of information and their immediate implications. This is the price and the pleasure of acting in a data-rich field, as some empirical scientists do, rather than focusing on the interpretation and transmission of a canon, as some humanists do. I examine little bricks and infer their bonds. Occasionally I can glimpse a stretch of wall. Only rarely can I say something about larger structures. So it comes as a surprise that what consumes my attention now, the Persepolis Fortification Archive, illustrates most of the rubrics under which the proceedings of this symposium are arranged.

Excavating Texts

The Achaemenid Persian Empire was founded by Cyrus II, called "the Great," in the years after 550 B.C. By 500 B.C., it reached from the Indus to the Nile. It incorporated almost every literate complex society of the ancient old world and had profound effects on the identity and history of those that it did not incorporate.

Soon after 518 B.C., Darius I, also called "the Great," established a complex of palaces, public buildings, and support facilities in the Persian heartland, in southwestern Iran. In Old Persian, the complex was called simply Pārsa, "Persia." Later, in Greek, and then in other European languages, it was called Persepolis. Darius's Achaemenid successors built, maintained, renovated, and extended Persepolis for almost two centuries, until Alexander III, also called "the Great," looted and burned it in 330 B.C.

The ruins of Persepolis were a focal point in the European rediscovery of Near Eastern antiquity. They were visited by travelers from Odoric of Pordenone in the fourteenth century through Pietro della Valle in the seventeenth, Cornelis De Bruijn and Carsten Niebuhr in the eighteenth,

Figure 2.1. Photograph of the site of Persepolis indicating where the Persepolis
Fortification Archive was found. The aerial photograph (altitude 2,440m) made
by Erich Schmidt shows the status of the Persian Expedition's clearance of the
site as of April, 1936. (AE 252, image courtesy of Oriental Institute, University
of Chicago).

and many others in the nineteenth (Sancisi-Weerdenburg and Drijvers 1991),
but they were not seriously excavated before Reza Shah took power in 1925
and introduced a new antiquities law that ended a French monopoly on
archaeology in Iran after 1930 (Anonymous 1932).

Ernst Herzfeld, on leave from a professorship of oriental studies at the
University of Berlin (Renger 2005), helped draft the new antiquities law
(Mousavi 2005: 452–465). For years, he had urged the complete excavation
and conservation of Persepolis as one of the highest priorities of ancient
Near Eastern research and of Iranian cultural heritage (Herzfeld 1929), but
in the depth of the Great Depression he could not find German backing. He
obtained a concession for the Oriental Institute of the University of Chicago.
The director of the Oriental Institute, James Henry Breasted, found a donor
to fund the work. The concession was later revised to include a 10-km radius
around Persepolis and the aims of the project were expanded to include the
pre- and post-Achaemenid history of human occupation in Persia (Breasted
1933: 320). From 1931 to 1939, Herzfeld and his successor, Erich Schmidt, made
spectacular discoveries at and around Persepolis that brought international
attention (Figures 2.1 and 2.2).

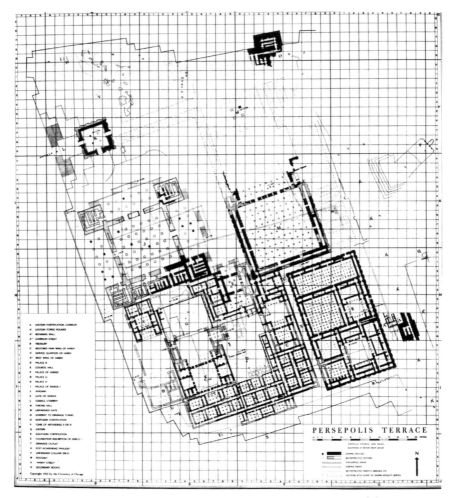

Figure 2.2. Plan of the site of Persepolis. The plan shows the final status of the Persian
     Expedition's work at the end of the 1939 season. (Image courtesy of Oriental
     Institute, University of Chicago).

On March 4, 1933, the same day that Franklin Roosevelt was inaugurated
for the first time as President of the United States, Herzfeld cabled the
director of the Oriental Institute, James Henry Breasted, about one such
startling discovery, saying, in the telegraphic prose of the time and medium,
"Hundreds Probably thousands business Tablets Elamite Discovered On
terrace." The tablets were in two rooms of a gatehouse in the fortification wall
around the terrace of Persepolis (Figure 2.1) – hence the name, "Fortification
tablets" (Garrison and Root 2001: 24–29). The discovery was fortuitous, a

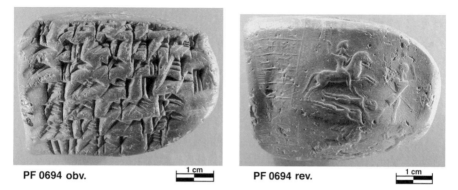

PF 0694 obv.   1 cm   **PF 0694 rev.**   1 cm

Figure 2.3. Elamite document PF 0694, with impression of seal PFS 0093*, inscribed
with name of Cyrus of Anzan, son of Teispes. (Images courtesy of Persepolis
Fortification Archive Project, University of Chicago).

byproduct of constructing a ramp for truck access to the Persepolis terrace. It
was unparalleled; only one other tablet of this kind had been found before in
Iran. And it was overwhelming; six months later Herzfeld was not speaking
of hundreds or thousands, but of an estimated thirty thousand tablets and
fragments, and not all in Elamite (Anonymous 1934: 231–232). In fact, there
were four main kinds of tablets (Figures 2.3–2.6; Jones and Stolper 2008):

1. Documents with cuneiform texts in Elamite language, most of them with
   impressions of cylinder seals or stamp seals, remains of about 10,000–15,000
   original documents, dominating the Archive (e.g., Figure 2.3).
2. Documents with texts in Aramaic script and Aramaic language, inked (e.g.,
   Figure 2.4), incised, or both, all of them with impressions of seals, remains
   of about 1,000 or fewer original documents.
3. Documents with impressions of seals but with no texts at all, about 4,000–
   6,000 items, perhaps a fifth or more of the entire find (e.g., Figure 2.5).
4. Miscellany and unique items, including one tablet in Greek script and
   language, one in Old Persian script and language (Figure 2.6), one in
   Babylonian, one probably in Phrygian, and tablets with impressions of Persian
   or Athenian coins instead of seals.

There were myriads of fragments, flakes, and crumbs, some with recoverable
information, some with information that might be recovered after careful
conservation and/or cleaning, some with information that might be recovered
with better technologies, but many that will probably never yield useful
information. There are tens of thousands of pieces, but they are all pieces of
one thing. They are records of one organization, recording activities around
Persepolis during only 16 years, 509–493 B.C. They were stored together
and found together. They have linked contents and common purpose. They

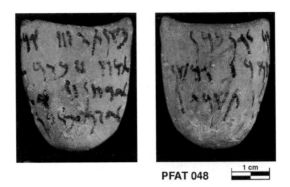

PFAT 048

Figure 2.4. Aramaic document PFAT 0048 with inked text. (Image courtesy of Persepolis Fortification Archive Project, University of Chicago).

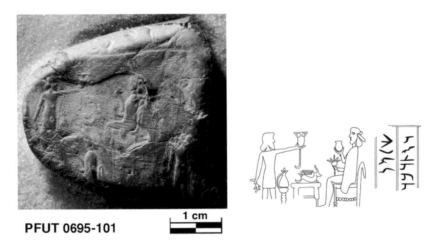

PFUT 0695-101

Figure 2.5. Uninscribed, sealed document PFUT 0695–101, with impression of seal PFS 0535. (Image courtesy of Persepolis Fortification Archive Project, University of Chicago; drawing of seal impression PFS 0535 by Mark B. Garrison).

are elements of a system through which information flowed, reflecting an administrative system through which commodities flowed. The different kinds of documents fit together systematically, in the same way that thousands of bones of different shapes and functions fit together as pieces of one ancient animal, shaped in a way that tells about the environment in which it acted.

Still, they are not about the characters of kings, the deeds of commanders, or the plots of eunuchs and queens. In short, they are not about the things that Hellenistic novels, Roman and European art, or American films look for in the Persian Empire. They are about the most ordinary thing in the world

Fort. 1208-101   1 cm

Figure 2.6. Unique Old Persian document Fort. 1208–0101. (Image courtesy of Persepolis
Fortification Archive Project, University of Chicago).

after death and taxes. They record food – grain and fruit, beer and wine,
sheep and goats – that was stored, moved, and paid out to people, animals,
and other entities on government payrolls.

Days after he received Herzfeld's telegram, Breasted put a hopeful face
on this disappointing circumstance. He wrote to Henri Frankfort, who was
directing the Oriental Institute's excavations in Iraq, that the discovery of
these tablets:

> gives us just ground for hoping, or even expecting, that tablet documents from the
> State Archives of the Persian Kings are still lying under the rubbish of the Terrace.
> If so, a new period in the history of the East has begun. Even these <u>business</u> tablets
> should contribute essentially to a full understanding of the Elamite language
> [unpublished letter from Breasted to Frankfort 1933: emphasis in original].

Interpreting Texts

To be sure, each of the Fortification tablets has a complex information load
with modest consequences. Each text fascinates a few cuneiformists. Each
seal impression fascinates a few art historians. Breasted's disappointment was
too hasty and his hopes for better sources were misdirected. When the many
pieces and kinds of pieces of the Fortification find fit together as a system of
information that represents systems of ancient behavior and circumstance,
the whole is much more than the parts. It is the largest, densest, most
complex, best dated, and best contextualized source of information from
inside Persia on languages, art, society, religion, institutions, and history
of the Persian Empire at its zenith. The published fraction of the Archive

(Garrison and Root 2001; Hallock 1969, 1976) has transformed every aspect of serious Achaemenid studies. To ignore this source risks cultural blindness, historical chauvinism, or outright error; examples abound.

Most of these Persian records are not in Persian language, but in Elamite or Aramaic. Elamite is a linguistic isolate, with no known relatives or survivors. It was the written language of western Iran from the earliest records, for more than a thousand years before Iranian-speakers arrived, and the Persians continued to use it as the written language of the region. The Elamite Fortification texts are the largest single corpus of Achaemenid Elamite, indeed, the largest single known corpus of Elamite texts of any kind. Aramaic, a Semitic language still spoken today, was widely used in the Assyrian and Babylonian empires, especially for communication among regions with different local languages, and the Persians continued that usage, too, spreading it to regions as far apart as Central Asia and southern Egypt in largely consistent form. The Aramaic Fortification texts are one of the largest and best contextualized known corpora of this Imperial Aramaic dialect. All of the texts were written by and for speakers of Persian and other Old Iranian dialects, and so they are also the largest single source of information on Old Iranian lexicon, phonology, and variation transcribed and transmitted through other languages.

At the heart of the empire that royal inscriptions described with the Old Persian word *vispazana*, "(composed) of all kinds of people," was functionally polyglot literacy. Just as the inscriptions on Achaemenid monuments display three languages that were linguistically unrelated but culturally comprehensive to represent the rhetorical claims of kings, this Archive shows the interplay of three languages that were linguistically unrelated but socially intimate, used at the most basic level of operations by people the Greeks deigned to call "barbarians," for the way they spoke.

Surprisingly, one of the documents *is* in Old Persian (see Figure 2.6; Stolper and Tavernier 2007). We know Old Persian from Achaemenid royal inscriptions, but this is the first and only everyday Old Persian text for practical use. At least one Persian in Persia wrote Persian language in Persian script, and expected at least one other to know where to file it. That comes as a surprise, one that could not be interpreted without the context of the whole Persepolis Fortification Archive.

Most of the tablets have impressions of cylinder seals or stamp seals, often of two seals or more. The seal impressions represent the concurrence of individuals or offices in the transactions recorded, so even before they are records of ancient art they are records of ancient behavior. Some of the seals resemble miniature versions of royal imagery carved on mountainsides and buildings, but most do not. They show a range of images and styles that cannot be found in monumental art, and they represent the hands and eyes of many craftsmen and the wishes and status of many clients. As of 2014 more than 3,300 distinct seals have been identified from their impressions, The extrapolated total of 3,500 analytically legible seals to be recorded in the Archive constitutes one of the biggest coherent sets of images from anywhere in the ancient world.

Like all art, the seal impressions show visualizations of the invisible conceptual world around the people who owned the seals. They also depict features of contemporary reality that are not described in the written sources, for example, scenes of religious or court ceremonial (e.g., Figure 2.5). Unlike monumental art, they represent the needs, choices, aims, and behaviors not just of the king, but also of thousands of individuals around the king related to each other in ways that can be discerned from associated texts.

That is one view of ancient society that these documents offer. Another view comes from considering the people who handled and consumed the food that the documents track. They range from gangs of workers drawing subsistence rations, through overseers, auditors, district officials, travelers passing through Persepolis, even the king's wives, children, and in-laws, some known, others new to the historical record. Some are described by the kind of work they do (agricultural, craft, administrative), by national origin (Indian, East Iranian, Lydian, Egyptian, Babylonian), by status (gentlemen, servants), by age and sex (men and women, boys and girls), by the names of the people in charge of them. This narrow window, the view from the lunchbox, shows a cross-section through almost the entire range of society around the Persian court, and describes it with many variables that reveal a complex social texture.

These kinds of revelation of the past have two things in common. First, they do not come from single documents; they depend on treating the whole corpus as a coherent system. Second, no other ancient sources offer this information in such volume and with such context, not scriptures, not royal inscriptions, not narrative histories, not monumental art. The Persepolis Fortification Archive is unique in that sense, but also in another sense: there were other ancient Achaemenid archives like this, and they may still survive to be found, but they have not been found, and for now the Persepolis Fortification Archive is the only one of its kind.

Texts and Ethics

The fact that this unique combination of complexity and coherence has been preserved is remarkable in itself. The new antiquities law of Iran that was in effect in 1933 provided for a division of finds between the host country and the sponsoring institutions. In Iran and elsewhere it became common practice to treat individual cuneiform tablets as distinct objects. Excavated clusters of tablets might be divided, so that some items stayed in Iran and others went to America or elsewhere, potentially to more than one sponsoring institution. The tablets excavated in the Treasury of Persepolis between 1934 and 1938 were treated in this way (Cameron 1948, 1958, 1965), but the first tablets discovered under the new law were not. The Persepolis Fortification Archive was treated as an indivisible find. The entire excavated Archive was sent to the Oriental Institute in Chicago in 1936 on indefinite loan for conservation, study, recording, and publication.

That statement glosses over difficult negotiations. The parties involved included representatives of the Iranian regime, representatives of the Oriental Institute, American diplomats acting for the Oriental Institute, Herzfeld's deputies, Herzfeld's successor, Herzfeld's archaeological rivals, and Herzfeld's professional and political enemies, not only in Iran but also in Germany, where the Nazis had come to power. Some of them despised Herzfeld, and some detested each other. Yet the outcome was an act of trust with few if any precedents. A unique discovery of great size and complexity, from the foremost ancient site in Iran, charged with particular importance by a nationalistic regime, was loaned to an American research institution, and it was loaned all together, not broken up into many pieces.

The fact that it was intact made it comprehensible, and after years of painstaking work it became the basis for prolific research with transformative results. The fact that it was loaned made it vulnerable to legal action that may cripple or extinguish continuing research. U.S. Federal courts have awarded judgments against the Islamic Republic of Iran to survivors and families of victims of bombings in Jerusalem and Beirut. The judgments amount to more than three billion dollars. With a legal basis for claiming Iranian property up to that amount, the holders of these awards seek to take the Persepolis Fortification Archive as partial satisfaction (Blair 2008).

This is not a repatriation dispute. All parties stipulate that the Persepolis Fortification Archive belongs to Iran. This is also not a heedless assault on cultural heritage. The plaintiffs are men and women whose lives have been devastated by atrocious acts, seeking redress offered by American law, though whatever redress this litigation brings may not include much money for any of them.

What is at issue includes not only continuing research access to the tablets, and not only the integrity of the Archive that is essential to continuing research, and not only the Oriental Institute's ability to redeem the trust that the loan of the Archive entailed. The issue also touches relationships that are fundamental to much modern work on cultural heritage materials by other institutions, whether research and publication by universities or loans and exhibitions by museums. This has been observed explicitly in connection with obstacles to loans of objects for the exhibition "Beyond Babylon" at the Metropolitan Museum of Art (Baker 2010; Heath and Schwartz 2009), and it is implicit in legal issues touching other loans (e.g., Vogel and Levy 2011).

The stakeholders also include cultural heirs, people for whose perceived identity these artifacts have particular meaning. Those heirs include not only citizens of the Islamic Republic, but also Iranians of the diaspora, and their children and grandchildren who are citizens of many countries, including the United States (e.g., National Iranian American Council 2011).

In these circumstances, the priorities of the Persepolis Fortification Archive Project (http://oi.uchicago.edu/research/projects/persepolis-fortification-archive) at the Oriental Institute of the University of Chicago correspond to two other rubrics of this volume: making useful records of as much of the Archive as possible to enable future research, that is, documenting texts; and distributing useful records quickly, continuously, and freely to enable current research, that is, disseminating texts. Thanks to electronic media, specialists can do much of the necessary cataloging, editing, and analysis remotely, punctuating work at widely separated institutions with frequent visits to the original artifacts in Chicago. Thanks also to electronic media, they can resist the centrifugal forces of specialization that would tend to separate the components of the Archive – Elamite, Aramaic, glyptic – in ways that would violate the integrity and coherence of the Archive.

Documenting Texts

Among other kinds of recording, the Persepolis Fortification Archive Project makes pictures of tablets, texts, and seal impressions. These include not only conventional digital photographs, but also high-quality images produced by two processes brought to the Archive by the West Semitic Research Project at the University of California (http://www.usc.edu/dept/LAS/wsrp/).

One of these processes uses a BetterLight scanning camera with a large-format high-resolution scanner, where a photoplate would once have been, to record images under daylight, polarized light, and yellow, orange, red, and infrared filtered light. These techniques, inherited from film photography, are especially good for recording inked text and for dealing with surface interference like glare, stains, or surface discoloration. The results can be dramatic, to the point that images made with filtered light are actually more legible than the original object is in natural light (e.g., Stolper 2009: 104, figure 1).

What makes these images useful, however, is not only their high resolution and high degree of legibility. Because they are electronic images presented in applications on the Internet, users can download them and then manipulate them, in ways that film, paper prints, and publications in book form would not enable. Members of the Project's editorial team find their ability to read texts and seal images improved, for example, by altering foreground and background tones, or by overlaying a negative image on a color image and manipulating the transparency of the layers.

User control is still greater with images produced by a second process, Polynomial Texture Mapping (PTM), a kind of Reflectance Transformation Imaging (RTI). The apparatus is a digital camera mounted on a dome wired with 32 lights (see Stolper 2010: 84, figure 2). A control box runs the lights and camera through a sequence of 32 images. Post-processing combines these images for delivery by an application that allows the viewer to manipulate the direction, angle, distance, intensity, and focus of one or two apparent light sources, as well as the apparent surface reflectivity of the object. The effect resembles having the object on a table and moving dominant and fill lights to highlight or shade parts of the surface as desired. This is especially useful for looking at information that is in low relief, including the strokes of a pen in an Aramaic text, the impressions of a stylus in a cuneiform text, and especially the impressions of seals. A single PTM set of a text and/or seal impression on a curved or irregular surface takes the place of many differently lit still images. The legibility of the image depends less on the linguistic, artistic, or epigraphic skill of the person making it than is true of still images. The decisive skills are the viewer's, and viewers with different skills can use the same image for different purposes, to examine texts under one range of lighting conditions, for example, and seal impressions under another, or to read an Aramaic word or phrase under one range of lighting conditions and to examine the order of strokes in the letters under another (e.g., Stolper 2008: 110, figure 2; 2010: 87, figure 6).

As of the end of 2010, the Persepolis Fortification Archive Project had made about 13,000 BetterLight scans, about 22,000 PTM sets and about 40,000 conventional digital pictures, records of more than 7,000 tablets and fragments (as of mid-2014 these figures have reached about 15,000, 40,000, 80,000, and 11,000, respectively). Whether they will be useful not only for preservation but also for research depends on dissemination.

Disseminating Texts

The first vehicles for disseminating the work of the Persepolis Fortification Archive Project are the on-line applications InscriptiFact and OCHRE, applications that respond to the urgency of the Archive's situation by making results public as the work progresses, without the delays that conventional publication requires, even if the results are incomplete and/or sometimes without the editorial polish that conventional publication demands.

InscriptiFact (http://www.inscriptifact.com/) is the robust on-line application of the West Semitic Research Project at the University of

Southern California. As of the end of 2010, about 20,000 high-quality images of about 750 Persepolis documents were available on InscriptiFact (and now, as of 2014, about 45,000 images of about 2,700 documents). Objects are illustrated both with BetterLight scans made with daylight, polarized light, and filtered light, and with PTM/RTI images. Users can crop, magnify, and compare images on line or download images for local use. Early entries have static images printed from PTM sets, but in 2010 InscriptiFact introduced a utility that allows users to display and manipulate high-resolution PTM sets on line. Users can also download a stand-alone version of the PTM viewer and download PTM sets for local use (see Stolper 2009: 108, figure 6).

OCHRE, the Online Cultural and Historical Research Environment (http://www.ochre.uchicago.edu, formerly Online Cultural Heritage Resource Environment), is an xml-based database and presentation environment developed by Sandra and David Schloen at the Oriental Institute of the University of Chicago, and designed to record and present many kinds of textual and archaeological information in compatible forms. Several excavations use it as a field database, and the Electronic Chicago Hittite Dictionary (The Oriental Institute of the University of Chicago 2010) uses it as a publication vehicle. The flexibility with which it organizes and displays many kinds of artifactual and textual information serves the Persepolis Fortification Archive (PFA) Project's need to represent the Archive's complexity without violating its integrity. OCHRE connects the several kinds of records (images, editions, catalogs, autographs) of the several classes of information (Elamite, Aramaic, and other texts, glyptic) at various levels of abstraction (paleography, lexicon, grammar, iconography, style). OCHRE allows the PFA Project to serve the specialized needs of distinct academic constituencies (art history, cuneiform studies, Semitic epigraphy) without separating the constituent elements of the Archive. It accommodates the modern reality of academic organization without distorting the ancient reality of the Archive's complexity and coherence.

OCHRE can display an Elamite document, for example, with combinations of cataloging and descriptive information, conventional digital images, transliteration, translation, and a click-through glossary that opens another text along with similar information and images (e.g., Figure 2.7, and see Stolper 2008: 113, figure 7; 2009: 107, figure 5; 2010: 88, figure 7; 2011: 108–109, figures 6–7). Many of the images are tagged and linked to the transliteration sign-by-sign. The display can be synchronized, to show the same word or phrase highlighted in the image, transliteration, and translation. The forms in the glossary are parsed and tagged to the morpheme level, and the text can be displayed with interlinear grammatical structure. Similar presentations of uninscribed and Aramaic tablets include selected BetterLight

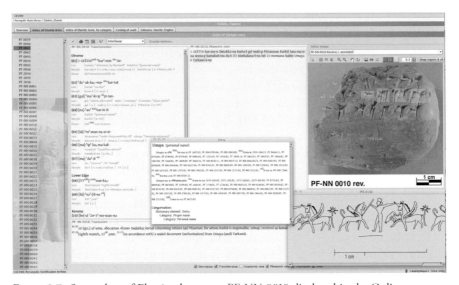

Figure 2.7. Screenshot of Elamite document PF-NN 0010 displayed in the Online
          Cultural and Historical Research Environment (OCHRE): open windows and
          frames show list of available documents (left); transliteration with interlinear
          grammatical parse (center left, top); normalized transcription (center right,
          top); translation (center, bottom); glossary entry for personal name Umaya,
          mentioned at end of text (center); digital image of reverse with overlaid
          identification of seal impression (PFS 0130) and overlaid transliteration with
          glossed personal name, Umaya, highlighted (upper right); collated drawing of
          seal PFS 0130, based on collation of all available impressions (lower right).

images available at screen resolution or high resolution, and PTM images at
screen resolution only. More than 1,200 Persepolis documents were public on
OCHRE by the end of 2010 (and, as of mid-2014, more than 4,000).

The PFA Project also shares data with other on-line venues, including the
Cuneiform Digital Archive Library Initiative at the University of California,
Los Angeles (http://cdli.ucla.edu/) and Achemenet (http://www.achemenet.
com/) and its companion Musée Achéménide (http://www.museum-
achemenet.college-de-france.fr/) at the Collège de France. This redundancy
has two motives. It reflects the zookeeper's strategy of preserving a collection
by distributing it. It also acknowledges growth and change; these sites have
different histories and structures, serve different audiences now, and, as on-line
practices and standards change, they will probably have different sequels.

Concern about the fragility of electronic media is eclipsed by the
expectation that electronic dissemination will transform the ways in which
research can be framed and pursued. Instead of looking at grammar or
paleography, for example, in terms of a template of forms and rules and an

array of instantiations that depart more or less from the template, it will be possible to examine them as continuums from the most abstract paradigmatic level to the most concrete behavioral level – from grammatical parse to marks in clay – in ways that printed reference works like grammars, dictionaries, and sign-lists do not facilitate.

The Persepolis Fortification Archive Project uses these means of dissemination to represent the attributes that give the Archive its greatest value: complexity, meaning that the Archive includes many pieces that served different ancient functions and convey different sorts of modern knowledge; and integrity, meaning that enough of the pieces are preserved to reveal the shape and structure of the whole in rich detail. A first measure of the Project's success is surprising results that reach surprising audiences (e.g., Chrisomalis 2010: 257). A second will be the ability to preserve and distribute an almost complete record of the contents of the Archive (for progress reports see Stolper 2007, 2008, 2009, 2010, 2011, 2012, 2013). A third will come when our colleagues begin to correct us or refute us, as the results make the transition from data to evidence, from matters of discovery to matters of argument. A fourth will come when our successors begin to laugh at us or condescend to us for our primitive conceptions of the capabilities of this extraordinary data set, and as they refine and replace the tools that the Project makes available for investigating the society, the art, the utterances, and the lives to which the Persepolis Fortification Archive is the only surviving witness.

Some Keynotes

Experience with the particular circumstances of the Persepolis Fortification Archive and the Persepolis Fortification Archive Project gives rise to some more general thoughts on the themes of this volume.

Excavating: for cuneiformists, all texts are excavated in some sense, but not many are excavated in a meaningful sense. Today politics, cost, and changing techniques make excavation a diminishing part of archaeology. The cuneiform world may have reached the Peak Tablet era. Future archaeology of cuneiform texts is likely to be more inferential than empirical. Future excavations of cuneiform texts are likely to be even less archaeological, and even less often legal than they have been. That will probably exacerbate and possibly refine arguments over research methods and standards.

Interpreting: cuneiformists often use "text" and "tablet" as synonyms, confusing the manuscript with the content, the material artifact with the linguistic artifact. That sloppiness might be a good thing if it encourages thinking of documents *as* artifacts like pots or tools, things whose shape and substance are evidence of the purposes for which they were made, the cultural processes that led to particular ways of serving those purposes, and the behaviors that led to their deposition and preservation. Like other artifacts, texts best convey such evidence when they can be considered as elements of assemblages.

Technology: electronic technologies narrow the separation among successive steps in the editorial process, recording, analysis, dissemination, and interpretation. They have changed working methods and they will change research agendas. That is at least in part because they can do some things very well that books cannot do as well or at all. That is one reason that electronic technologies are not yet a comfortable fit with academic scholarship. A bigger reason, which many foundations and consortia now contemplate, is the frequent incompatibility and general fragility of the products, and the lack of a coherent model for preserving them in forms as practical and universal as shelves full of books. This is academic scholarship's version of the greater crisis of Old Media, not specific to texts and/or archaeology, but looming.

Ethics: in the past, legal excavations and compliance with existing antiquities laws have been considered sufficient measures of ethical practice. Museums and academic archaeologists were once united in fieldwork and *partage*, but divided over collections and collectors. Now, museums and academic archaeologists sometimes divide even more sharply over the nature of cultural heritage and the identity of cultural heirs. These disputes are perhaps more complicated in law than previously and they are certainly more complicated in political and social expressions. Texts, which academic scholars have often treated less fastidiously than pots or statues, have an especially complicated status because the commercial or cultural values of the exemplars depend not on the objects, but on the contents, statements that can be claimed but cannot be possessed.

Acknowledgments

The Persepolis Fortification Archive Project has received timely and generous support, even during straitened times, from the Andrew W. Mellon Foundation, the Farhang Foundation, the Getty Foundation, the Iran Heritage Foundation, the National Endowment for the Humanities, the National Geographic Society Committee for Research and Exploration, the PARSA Community Foundation, the Roshan Cultural Heritage Institute, the University of Chicago Women's Board, the Friends of the Persepolis Fortification Archive Project, and many private donors and organizations.

References

Anonymous

    1932   Persien. *Archiv für Orientforschung* 7: 64–65.

    1934   Recent Discoveries at Persepolis. *Journal of the Royal Asiatic Society* 1934: 226–232.

Baker, Heather D.

    2010   Review of *Beyond Babylon: Art, Trade and Diplomacy in the Second Millennium B.C.*, edited by Joan Aruz, Kim Benzel, and Jean M. Evans, *Antiquity* 84(323): 261–262.

Blair, Gwenda

    2008   Paying With the Past. *Chicago* 57(12) (December): 90–95, 110–113. Electronic document, http://www.chicagomag.com/Chicago-Magazine/December-2008/Paying-with-the-Past/, accessed September 17, 2013.

Breasted, James Henry

    1933   *The Oriental Institute*. The University of Chicago Survey Vol. 12. University of Chicago Press, Chicago.

Cameron, George G.

    1948   *Persepolis Treasury Tablets*. Oriental Institute Publications Vol. 65. University of Chicago Press, Chicago.

    1958   Persepolis Treasury Tablets Old and New. *Journal of Near Eastern Studies* 17: 161–176.

    1965   New Tablets from the Persepolis Treasury. *Journal of Near Eastern Studies* 24: 167–192.

Chrisomalis, Stephen

    2010   *Numerical Notation: A Comparative History*. Cambridge University Press, New York.

Garrison, Mark B., and Margaret Cool Root

    2001   *Seals on the Persepolis Fortification Tablets, I: Images of the Heroic Encounter*. Oriental Institute Publications Vol. 117. The Oriental Institute of the University of Chicago, Chicago.

Hallock, Richard T.

    1969   *Persepolis Fortification Tablets*. Oriental Institute Publications Vol. 92. University of Chicago Press, Chicago.

    1976   Selected Fortification Texts. *Cahiers de la Délégation Archéologique Française en Iran* 8: 109–136.

Heath, Sebastian, and Glenn M. Schwarz

    2009   Legal Threats to Cultural Exchange of Archaeological Materials. *American Journal of Archaeology* 113: 459–462.

Herzfeld, Ernst E.

    1929   Rapport sur l'état actuel des ruines de Persépolis et propositions pour leur conservation. *Archaeologische Mitteilungen aus Iran* 1: 17–40 (French section) and 3–24 (Persian section).

Jones, Charles E., and Matthew W. Stolper

    2008   How many Persepolis Fortification tablets are there? In *L'archive des Fortifications de Persépolis: État des questions et perspectives de recherches*, edited by Pierre Briant, Wouter Henkelman, and Matthew Stolper, pp. 27–50. Persika Vol. 12. Boccard, Paris.

Mousavi, Ali
  2005 Ernst Herzfeld, Politics, and Antiquities Legislation in Iran. In *Ernst Herzfeld and the Development of Near Eastern Studies, 1900–1950*, edited by Ann C. Gunter and Stefan R. Hauser, pp. 445–475. Brill, Leiden.

National Iranian American Council
  2014 Persepolis Center. Electronic document, http://www.niacouncil.org/persepolis-tablets-resource-center, accessed September 4, 2014.

The Oriental Institute of the University of Chicago
  2010 The Chicago Hittite Dictionary Project. Electronic document, http://ochre.lib.uchicago.edu/eCHD/, accessed September 17, 2013.

Renger, Johannes
  2005 Ernst Herzfeld in Context: Gleanings from His Personnel File and Other Sources. In *Ernst Herzfeld and the Development of Near Eastern Studies, 1900–1950*, edited by Ann C. Gunter and Stefan R. Hauser, pp. 561–582. Brill, Leiden.

Sancisi-Weerdenburg, Heleen, and Jan Willem Drijvers (editors)
  1991 *Through Travellers' Eyes: European Travellers on the Iranian Monuments*. Achaemenid History Vol. 7. Nederlands Instituut voor het Nabije Oosten, Leiden.

Stolper, Matthew W.
  2007 Persepolis Fortification Archive Project. In *The Oriental Institute 2006–2007 Annual Report*, pp. 92–103. The Oriental Institute of the University of Chicago, Chicago.
  2008 The Persepolis Fortification Archive Project. In *The Oriental Institute 2007–2008 Annual Report*, pp. 110–115. The Oriental Institute of the University of Chicago, Chicago.
  2009 Persepolis Fortification Archive Project. In *The Oriental Institute 2008–2009 Annual Report*, pp. 104–111. The Oriental Institute of the University of Chicago, Chicago.
  2010 Persepolis Fortification Archive Project. In *The Oriental Institute 2009–2010 Annual Report*, pp. 83–91. The Oriental Institute of the University of Chicago, Chicago.
  2011 Persepolis Fortification Archive Project. In *The Oriental Institute 2010–2011 Annual Report*, pp. 102–111. The Oriental Institute of the University of Chicago, Chicago.
  2012 Persepolis Fortification Archive Project. In *The Oriental Institute 2011–2012 Annual Report*, pp. 145–152. The Oriental Institute of the University of Chicago, Chicago.
  2013 Persepolis Fortification Archive Project. In *The Oriental Institute 2012–2013 Annual Report*, pp. 105–112. The Oriental Institute of the University of Chicago, Chicago.

Stolper, Matthew W., and Jan Tavernier
  2007 From the Persepolis Fortification Archive Project, 1: An Old Persian Administrative Tablet from the Persepolis Fortification. *Arta: Achaemenid Research on Texts and Archaeology* 2007.001. Electronic document, http://www.achemenet.com/document/2007.001-Stolper-Tavernier.pdf, accessed September 4, 2014.

Vogel, Carol, and Clifford J. Levy
  2011 Dispute over Jewish Archive Derails Russian Art Loans. *New York Times*, 3 February: C1. New York.

— 3 —

Space, Time, and Texts:
A Landscape Approach to the
Classic Maya Hieroglyphic Record

Nicholas P. Carter

Landscapes and Texts

The indigenous Maya writing system – the best-attested and most structurally complex in the Americas – was employed throughout the Maya Lowlands of present-day Mexico, Guatemala, Belize, and Honduras (Figure 3.1) between about 300 B.C. and the late seventeenth century. Four bark-paper codices in Maya script survive, all dating to the Late Postclassic or early Colonial periods, but the vast majority of hieroglyphic texts are found on imperishable artifacts produced during the Classic era, between A.D. 150 and 1000. Most Classic-period monumental texts, whatever their historical and mythological content, have as their rhetorical focus the dedication of the architectural features – buildings or free-standing monuments – on which they are inscribed (Stuart 1998). Texts on portable objects, too, tend to deal with the dedication of those objects and the identities of the rulers or aristocrats who owned or commissioned them (Houston et al. 1989; Stuart 1989, 1994: 374). Even the texts painted on the walls of the Naj Tunich cave in modern Belize emphasize the cavern's importance as a pilgrimage site for potentates in the region, including lords from Caracol (Stone 1995). The surviving Classic corpus, then, is explicitly linked to ancient Maya built and ecological environments (Rapoport 1990; Webster 1994: 5), to local and translocal political relationships, and to landscapes incorporating natural and cultural features.

For Adam T. Smith, space is "that philosophical rubric under which all problems related to extension and the parameters of synchronic relation may be discussed" (Smith 2003: 32). Places, as opposed to spaces, are culturally defined spatial features produced as socially shared meanings are

Figure 3.1. A map of the Maya area showing sites mentioned in this chapter.
Map by Katharine Lukach and Thomas Garrison.

attached to them, reinterpreted, and forgotten over time. Landscapes, in
Smith's terms, are assemblages of places and the relationships among them
– spatial, political, representational, and aesthetic – structured according to
culturally and historically specific perspectives (Smith 2003: 32). As linked
places, landscapes are composed in part of accumulated, socially constituted

meanings, to which landscapes of text add the meanings that those texts generate and the language ideologies current in the societies which produce and experience them (Gorter 2006a: 82). Although almost all the meanings not committed to paint or stone in ancient times are inaccessible to present-day scholars, a study of inscriptions in context can point us toward a partial reconstruction of ancient Maya linguistic landscapes. Given the subject matter of most Classic Maya inscriptions, which emphasize the military and ceremonial deeds of a tiny, elite segment of society, the Maya epigraphic record constitutes a rich source of information about two such structures in particular: political and ritual landscapes.

Political landscapes shape the experience of persons as political subjects by guiding their movement through culturally produced environments, by evoking affective responses to perceived spaces, and by guiding the imaginative creation of a "sense of place" laden with social and political values (Smith 2003: 6–10). As such, political landscapes must be distinguished from territorial claims and diplomatic relationships, even though the three concepts are mutually inextricable in practice. Inasmuch as the political and the ceremonial are inseparable in ancient Mesoamerica, the same can be said of sacred landscapes, which connected living people with a mythic past and provided elites a stage on which to perform their political authority (e.g., Aguilar-Moreno 2009; Carrasco 1999; Demarest 1992; Guernsey Kappelman 2001; Reese-Taylor and Koontz 2001; Schele and Guernsey Kappelman 2001; Stuart 1997). Mesoamerican ritual landscapes incorporated an additional diachronic factor integrating place and time: ritual visits and pilgrimages to sacred destinations near and far (e.g., Ashmore and Blackmore 2008; Brady 2003: 89; Carrasco 1991; Houston 2010: 201; Kubler 1985; Stone 1995).

A number of scholars have discussed the ways in which Classic Maya texts mapped political institutions and mythic cosmology onto built and natural landscapes, although not all work along those lines has dealt explicitly with landscapes in the sense meant here. Joyce Marcus (1976) interpreted the inclusion of four Emblem Glyphs (now known to be dynastic titles) in a long, poetic passage on Copan Stela A as a reference to four large, regional states centered at Copan, Calakmul, Tikal, and Palenque. Subsequent decipherments revealed that kings of those sites – among numerous others – did at times exercise suzerainty over other lords, but such hegemonic systems were unstable and usually not internally integrated in the manner of territorial states (Martin and Grube 1994, 1995, 2008; Mathews 1985; Mathews and Justeson 1984). Linda Schele and Peter Mathews (1998) intensively explored relationships among place, mythology, and text at sites including Tikal, Palenque, Copan, Seibal, and Chichen Itza. David Stuart (1998) elucidated the intersection of place, political authority, and ritual activity in architectural dedicatory texts, the most common genre of Classic inscription; in subsequent works, Stuart has addressed the accretion of mythological and political meanings in the ritual-historical texts of that site's Cross Group (Stuart 2005a; Stuart and Stuart 2008). At Copan, William and Barbara Fash (B. Fash 2004, 2005; B. Fash et al. 1992; W. Fash 2005) and other scholars (e.g., Andrews and Bill 2005; Schele and Looper 2005; Sharer et al. 2005; Stuart 1992, 2004; 2005b; Taube 2004) have connected persons and places named in the hieroglyphic record to supernatural locations and to physical areas and buildings – both nearby and, occasionally, as far away as Central Mexico.

A third type of landscape about which Maya inscriptions, taken in context, have much to tell us is the linguistic landscape. Language has been addressed in terms of landscapes in recent years by a number of social scientists (e.g., Bourhis and Landry 2002; Gorter, ed. 2006; Hicks 2002; Kreslins 2003; Labov and Boberg 1997; Landry and Bourhis 1997; Shohamy and Waksman 2009). While their work has tended to focus on issues of contemporary language politics, sociolinguistics, and multilingualism in postmodern urban environments (Gorter, ed. 2006), the linguistic landscape approach is a natural one for epigraphers studying the public inscriptions of past societies. As used by some authors (e.g., Labov and Boberg 1997; Sciriha and Vassallo 2001), the term "linguistic landscape" is basically synonymous with existing terms, like the "linguistic market" or the "linguistic situation," having to do with the social contexts of linguistic variation. As defined by Landry and Bourhis (1997: 25), however, the linguistic landscape has primarily to do with written texts in public places (cf. Shohamy and Waksman 2009 for a broader definition).

The goal of the present chapter is to draw attention to the insights that considerations of hieroglyphic inscriptions in their spatio-temporal contexts have already provided into Classic Maya ceremonial, linguistic, and political landscapes, and to suggest potential avenues for future research along similar lines. I begin by considering a program of monumental texts at a single site, Copan, dedicated by a single king and dealing with a series of ceremonies carried out over a period of about five years. Next, I discuss the role of a single toponym, *chiik nahb*, in reconstructions of Classic Maya sociopolitical landscapes at two scales: that of the urban center of Calakmul and that of the broader Maya Lowlands. Finally, moving to an exclusively macroregional scale, I discuss the results, and the often conflicting theoretical underpinnings, of efforts to use the spatiotemporal distribution of textual themes and scribal practices to reconstruct the shifting linguistic geographies of the Classic Maya Lowlands.

The Edges of the World at Copan, Honduras

For modern visitors to the Classic Maya city of Copan, in present-day Honduras – and, surely, for the polity's ancient inhabitants – the carved stelae for which the site has long been noted are vital parts of its landscape. Besides the 13 stelae in Copan's Main Group, at least seven stelae stand in the hills bounding the Copan Valley. These include Stelae 10 and 19, located in the hills west of the site center; Stela 12, on a hill just east of the Acropolis; Stela 13, about 6.5 km northeast of the site center; the uncarved Stelae A13 and A14, both located within .5 km of Stela 13; and Stela 23, which originally stood in what is now the plaza of the town of Santa Rita, in the far northeast of the valley. Stelae 2 and 3, whose texts connect them to the programs of the outlying stelae, stand in the Middle Court of the Main Group. Of these monuments, all those with inscriptions are united by their subject matter: all deal with the end of the eleventh 20-year *k'atun*, in the ninth *bak'tun* of 20 *k'atuns* since the beginning of the current era (October 9, A.D. 652), and with the ceremonies in which the Late Classic ruler K'ahk' U Ti' Witz' K'awiil participated on that day and on other significant dates before and after it.

Herbert Spinden (1913) was the first to note this pattern of dates, suggesting that the outlying monuments marked the extent of Copan's political territory at the time of their planting. Sylvanus Morley (1920) suggested that their placement relative to one another and to the setting sun on certain days created a kind of solar calendar to assist in swidden agriculture. Tatiana Proskouriakoff (1973) proposed that the hills on which the stelae were placed had special religious significance to the Copanec dynasty, and that the presence of the stelae associated venerated ancestors with those sites. Finally, William Fash (2001: 104) suggests that at least the eastern stelae could, in addition to their religious functions, have been of use in a valley-wide communications system employing beacons or smoke signals, possibly for defensive purposes.

Whatever their other applications, it has long been clear that at least two of the outliers – Stelae 10 and 12 – were astronomically aligned. Based on data collected by Morley, R.W. Willson (personal communication to Sylvanus Morley, 1916) calculated that, as observed from Stela 12, the sun would be seen to set behind Stela 10 "20.3 days after the vernal equinox and 20.6 days before the autumnal equinox." As Morley (1920: 143) pointed out, any observations of the position of the sun relative to one of the two stelae from the other would have to have been made of Stela 10 from the vantage point of Stela 12, since Stela 10 stands about 40 m higher above the valley floor and, unlike Stela 12, is visible against the sky. It may seem strange to contemporary sensibilities that the stelae were not placed to produce solar alignments on the equinoxes themselves. As it happens, however, 20 days is the length of one *winal* in the Maya Long Count calendar, and there are 20 named days in the *tuk* cycle, which combine with 13 numbers to generate a ritual "year" (called the *tzolk'in* by contemporary scholars) of 260 days. The days on which the alignments occurred would have shared ritually significant day-names – and thus, to an extent, identities – with those of the equinoxes.

Such metaphysical echoes, created through the repetition of similar events at meaningful intervals of time, are a consistent feature of Classic-period monuments at Copan and, indeed, throughout the Maya Lowlands. In particular, they are an important part of the story told in the texts on Stelae 10, 12, and a third monument, Stela 2, in Copan's Main Plaza, which repeats large sections of the Stela 12 text verbatim. Stela 12 opens with a reference to a ritual on 9.10.15.0.0 6 Ajaw 13 Mak (November 5, A.D. 647) – five 360-day *tun* years before the 9.11.0.0.0 *k'atun* ending, and 15 *tuns* since the last *k'atun* ending. Stela 2 records an identical ritual 260 days later, on 9.10.15.13.0 6 Ajaw 9 Mol,[1] a date whose only significance appears to be that it shares a *tzolk'in* date (6 Ajaw) with 9.10.15.0.0.

The narrative then skips ahead nearly four *tuns*, to 9.10.19.5.0 12 Ajaw 13 K'ayab (January 23, A.D. 652), 260 days *before* the upcoming *k'atun* ending. The text on Stela 10 once dwelt at some length on the rites conducted on that day, but the glyphs are now too badly damaged to read. The same inscription moves on to another "echo" date: 9.10.19.13.0 3 Ajaw 8 Yaxk'in, 260 days after 9.10.19.0.0. On that day, K'ahk' U Ti' Witz' K'awiil conducted rituals involving (Figure 3.2a):

> the images of the eight thousand heavenly gods, the eight thousand earthly gods (*u baah jun pik chanal k'uh, jun pik kabal k'uh*) in the Copan sky and cave, at Uxwitik … at the Edge of the Underworld, at the Shining[2] Pool Place, in the Copan sky and cave (*?xukup chan ch'e'n, uxwitik … ti' way, ?lem nahbnal, ?xukup chan ch'e'n*).

Uxwitik is the ancient name of Copan, or even of the Main Group; *chan ch'e'n*, "sky and cave" or "sky and rocky outcropping," is a poetic expression referring to the city or to a specific location within it (Stuart 1992; Stuart and Houston 1994: 12–13; Stephen D. Houston, personal communication 2009). The reading of the glyphic compound rendered here as *xukup* is problematic (Looper 1991; Lopes and Davletshin 2004; Schele and Mathews 1998: 133; Stuart 1987: 11–13), and the title likely refers to the ruling dynasty instead of, or in addition to, naming Copan as a city (Stuart and Houston 1994: 3–7). All three stelae conclude with accounts of the eleventh *k'atun* ending itself. Stela 12 records period-ending rituals involving a host of gods, and one deified ancestor, at a place identified as *naah kab* ("Great Earth" or

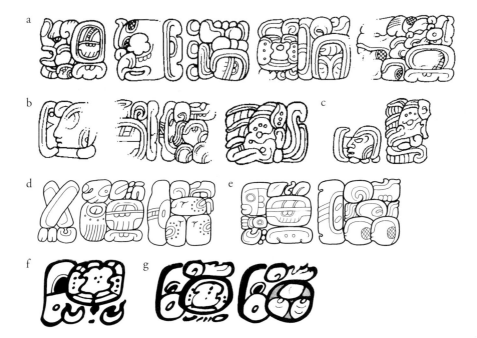

Figure 3.2. a. Passage from Copan Stela 10 alluding to events "at the 'Copan' sky and cave/outcropping at Uxwitik ... the Edge of the Underworld, the Shining Pool, at the 'Copan' sky and cave/outcropping" (?xukup chan ch'e'n uxwitik ... ti' way, ?lem nahbnal, ?xukuup chan ch'e'n); b. Passage from Copan Stela 12 naming "Great Earth, the Edge of the Sky, the First Hearth Place cave/outcropping" (naah kab, ti' chan, yax ? nal ch'e'n); c. Passage from Copan Stela 2 naming "Great Earth" (naah kab); d. Passage from the Main Panel of the Temple of the Cross, Palenque: "The hearth is changed at the Edge of the Sky, at the First Hearth Place" (tz'ahkaj k'oob ti' chan, yax ? nal); e. Passage from Quirigua Stela C reading "It happened at the Edge of the Sky, at the First Hearth Place," in reference to the planting of a mythological stone; f. Ik' waynal mythological toponym from a Late Classic polychrome vessel; g. Mythological toponyms ik' waynal and ik' nahbnal from a Late Classic codex-style vessel. All drawings by the author after (a–c) field sketches by David Stuart; (d) Maudslay (1889b: Plate 73); (e) Maudslay (1889a: figure 19); (f) a photograph by Justin Kerr (K1440 in Kerr's photographic database of Maya ceramics, 2013); (g) Schele and Miller (1986: figure 122).

"First Earth"), ti' chan ("the Edge of the Sky"), and yax ? nal ch'en ("the First 'Hearth' Place cave/outcropping") (Figure 3.2b). Stela 2 describes the same rites, but uses only naah kab ch'en (Figure 3.2c) for the site where K'ahk' U Ti' Witz' K'awiil celebrated the k'atun ending.

What is striking about the places named in these three texts is that only some of them can have been real places. These include Uxwitik and the "sky and cave" of the Copan dynasty. *Naah kab*, which is attested only at Copan, and which also takes the *ch'e'n* topographical designation, also seems to be a physical place. By contrast, *ti' chan* and *yax ? nal* name a mythological location associated in other texts with creation, the establishment of cosmic order, and the inception of new *piktun* cycles of more than 5,000 years. The main panel from the Temple of the Cross at Palenque records that, at the beginning of the present *piktun* on August 14, 3114 B.C., "the hearth was changed at the Edge of the Sky, at the First Hearth Place" (Figure 3.2d). Quirigua Stela C describes the "planting" (*tz'ap*) of three monuments, conceived of as the three stones of the solar hearth, on that day by a triad of gods (Schele and Villela 1996: 15). Each stone is planted at a different supernatural location, the last of which is *ti' chan, yax ? nal* (Figure 3.2e). While Copan Stela 10 may bear the only presently known example of *?lem nahbnal, ti' way*, it is strongly reminiscent of another well-attested mythological toponym, *ik' way* ("Black Underworld") or *ik' waynal* ("Black Underworld Place") associated with caves, ritual ballgames, and otherworldly powers (Stuart and Houston 1994: 71–74) (Figure 3.2f). On an unprovenanced plate painted in the "codex style" associated with the Late Classic Mirador Basin, *ik' waynal* is paired with *ik' nahbnal* ("Black Pool Place") (Figure 3.2g), a toponym also mentioned at Copan (Fash et al. 1992: 432–433; Stuart and Houston 1994: 72, 74).

Stelae 10 and 12, then, record ritual visits – pilgrimages – to two supernatural sites identified with real places in or near the Main Group at Copan. The most appealing candidates for these locations are the hills on which those stelae were planted. If the identification is correct, the two monuments would mark an east-west axis, defined by the solar circuit and aligned with the horizontal position of the sun on the equinoxes. With named, liminal places at either end – the hearthstones of creation in the east, the entrance to the Underworld in the west – and the Copan Acropolis in the center, the axis created by these two monuments plus Stela 2 constructed the Maya universe in miniature. The stelae defined the eastern and western edges of a ritual microcosm with the Acropolis at its heart, named specific locations on the physical landscape, and sacralized that landscape by connecting those places with mythological sites. Like Maya kings, who could personify supernatural beings in ritual performances, the sites where those rituals took place could evidently "impersonate" mythological locations, manifesting an ideal cosmology in the physical realm.

"It Happened at Chiik Nahb": The Multiscalar Meanings of Calakmul's North Acropolis

In a 1994 monograph, David Stuart and Stephen Houston (1994) linked two glyphic toponyms – *oxte'tun* and *nabtunich*, now read *uxte'tuun* and *chiik nahb* – to the Classic Maya metropolis of Calakmul and to the Kan ("Snake") dynasty, which exercised hegemony over much of the central Maya Lowlands during the sixth and seventh centuries A.D. (Martin and Grube 1994). Their suggestion bolstered a proposal by Jeffrey Miller (1974) and Joyce Marcus (1976: 51) that Calakmul had been the seat of the "Snake" lords. Present evidence confirms that the Kan kings did rule at Calakmul during part of the Late Classic period, and that Uxte'tuun ("Three Stones") and Chiik Nahb ("Coati Pool") name parts of their domain (Martin 2005). But to what, specifically, did these toponyms refer? How did they fit into the political landscapes imagined by the inhabitants of Calakmul and other sites? An examination of the spatial, temporal, and political contexts in which *chiik nahb* and *uxte'tuun* appear offers some clues.

To date, the earliest known reference to Chiik Nahb is on Calakmul Stela 114, erected to commemorate the 9.0.0.0.0 *k'atun* ending (December 8, A.D. 435) and the accession of a ruler in A.D. 411. While much of the text is unclear, it contains a statement about the parentage of a *ch'ok* – "sprout," or, by extension, "youth" – who bears the title *chiik nahb ajaw*, "Chiik Nahb lord" (Figure 3.3a). At the time the stela was carved, it is unlikely that Calakmul was yet under the control of the Kan dynasty, which was based at Calakmul during the Late Classic period, but ruled from Dzibanche until ca. A.D. 635 (Stuart 2012). Rather, Calakmul appears to have been governed in the fifth century A.D. by kings using a still-undeciphered "Bat" title (Martin 2005). *Chiik nahb* next turns up on an inscribed stairway which Teobert Maler excavated at Naranjo, but which was originally commissioned by the ruler of Caracol to commemorate the 9.10.10.0.0 half-*k'atun* ending (December 1, A.D. 642) and an allied Calakmul-Caracol victory over Naranjo in A.D. 631 (Stone et al. 1985). The carved blocks of the steps were subsequently captured and reset by a resurgent Naranjo (Martin 2000). The relevant passage records the "fall" (*jub*) of Naranjo, an event said to have been overseen by one Yuknoom "Head" (part of whose name remains undeciphered). This king's titles – *Kan ajaw ta uxte'tuun, aj chiik nahb*, "the Kan lord at Uxte'tuun, he of Chiik Nahb" (Figure 3.3b) – indicate a shift from Dzibanche to Calakmul as the seat of Kan power.

William J. Folan et al. (2001: 223) suggest that *uxte'tuun* – "three stones" – may have referred originally to Structure II at Calakmul, a complex of three temple buildings atop an elevated platform constructed in the Late Preclassic

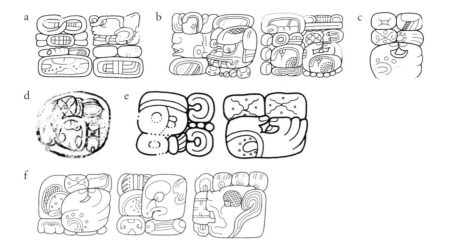

Figure 3.3. a. Passage from Calakmul Stela 114 referring to a "youth, the Chiik Nahb lord" (*ch'ok, chiik nahb ajaw*); b. Passage from Naranjo Hieroglyphic Stairway 1 (originally from Caracol) naming Yuknoom "Head" as "the Kan lord at Uxte'tuun, he of Chiik Nahb" (*Kan ajaw ta uxte'tuun, aj chiik nahb*); c. "Chiik Nahb lord" (*chiik nahb ajaw*), on Calakmul Monument 6; d. "Chiik Nahb wall" (*chiik nahb kot*), from the southern façade of Calakmul's North Acropolis; e. Passage from an unprovenanced panel from the region of Cancuen reading "It happened at Chiik Nahb" (*uhtiiy chiik nahb*); f. Passage from La Corona Panel 1A reading "Traveled to Chiik Nahb the elder brother person, the youth, K'ihnich Je' ?Yookil" (*bixan chiik nahb sakun winik, ch'ok, kihnich je' yookil*[?]). All drawings by the author: a. after Martin (2005: figure 8a) and Pincemin et al. (1998: figure 7); b. after Martin and Grube (2008: 106); c. after Martin (2005: figure 8c); d. after a photograph by Jorge Pérez de Lara in Carrasco Vargas and Colón González (2005); e. after a photograph of the Peabody Essex Museum; f. after a photogrpah by David Stuart.

period. Structure II continued to be overbuilt by subsequent generations of Calakmul kings until, by Late Classic times, it had become a massive pyramid, 45 m high and 120 m wide at the base, with its characteristic triple-shrine layout preserved at each stage of construction. Complicating this possibility is the appearance of *uxte'tuun* in inscriptions at the site of Oxpemul, 22 km north of Calakmul. Oxpemul appears to have been subject to the Kan dynasty throughout much of the Late Classic period, yet on Oxpemul Stela 7, dedicated in the late eighth century A.D., a ruler using the old "holy 'Bat' lord" title claims the title of *uxte'tuun kaloomte'*, "Uxte'tuun overlord" (Martin and Grube 2008: 115). Another "holy 'Bat' lord" is mentioned on Calakmul Stela 62, erected in A.D. 751, the same year that a carved hieroglyphic block (Calakmul Monument 6; see Figure 3.3c) calls a certain Bolon K'awiil a

"Chiik Nahb lord" (*chiik nahb ajaw*) (Martin 2008: 6–7). It thus remains unclear whether the "Bat" kings mentioned at Oxpemul ruled a regional state from Calakmul or claimed descent from a royal house once based there – in which case Uxte'tuun could refer to Calakmul specifically – or whether Uxte'tuun is a regional toponym including both cities, as Alexandre Tokovinine proposes (Martin 2008: 5; Tokovinine 2008: 103–104).

We are on firmer ground in connecting Chiik Nahb to Calakmul as a city, and perhaps even to a specific architectural feature of its urban core. Excavations in 2001 at Calakmul's North Acropolis, an architectural complex about 2.5 ha in area, uncovered a three-tiered, pyramidal platform (Structure 1) remodeled in seven successive stages between as early as A.D. 420 and as late as 1020 (Carrasco Vargas et al. 2009; Carrasco Vargas and Cordeiro Banqueiro 2012). The platform walls of the third phase, constructed sometime between A.D. 620 and 700, were painted with murals showing individuals carrying burdens or proffering or consuming products including *atol*, tamales, salt, and ceramic vessels. Accompanying hieroglyphic captions identify the persons offering goods according to their apparent occupation specialties, e.g., *aj tz'aam*, "he of the salt," or *aj jaay*, "she of the clay vessels" (Martin 2012). The absence of proper names, as much as the presence of these titles, suggests that the figures represent archetypical merchants and producers engaged in crafting and trade (Carrasco Vargas et al. 2009: 19248). Indeed, the 67 smaller buildings comprising the rest of the North Acropolis define alleys and small plazas reminiscent of contemporary Maya marketplaces (Dahlin et al. 2010). The southern border of the North Acropolis is separated from the rest of the urban center by a walkway running along the edge of the elevated platform, accessible by means of stairways placed at intervals. In its Late Classic form, the southern face of the platform was painted with aquatic motifs – birds, supernatural water serpents, and water lilies – interspersed with glyphic cartouches reading *chiik nahb kot*, "the Chiik Nahb wall" (Figure 3.3d) (Carrasco Vargas and Colón Gonzalez 2005: 44; Garcia Moreno et al. 2008). Chiik Nahb, then, was the ancient name of urban Calakmul, and perhaps even referred specifically to the North Acropolis as a focus of civic and economic life.

Chiik Nahb also occupied a prominent place in the broader Classic Maya political landscape, standing synecdochically for the Calakmul polity and its "Bat" or Kan rulers. An admittedly impressionistic distributional consideration of the Late Classic glyphic corpus reveals that foreign references to Chiik Nahb are largely confined to the inscriptions of Calakmul's allies and dependents during the kingdom's political apogee in the seventh century under the Kan ruler Yuknoom Ch'e'n and his successor, Yuknoom Yich'aak K'ahk'. Texts from rival polities, by contrast, tend to refer to individual Kan lords and their subordinates rather than the physical geography of Calakmul. The exception is Tonina Monument 153, of uncertain date, which records the capture of an individual called *aj chiik nahb*, "he of Chiik Nahb," by a Tonina king sometime between A.D. 708 and 723. Nevertheless, if genuine, this pattern of emphasis, not just on Calakmul as a physical place but on named parts of the urban landscape, could correspond to political strategies whereby the Kan kings required the presence of subordinate nobles in the capital, and those lords in turn used their association with the charisma of Chiik Nahb and Uxte'tuun to emphasize their own prestige.

At Dos Pilas, a key ally in the Kan lords' struggle against Tikal for hegemony in the central Lowlands, an inscribed monument records the ruler Bajlaj Chan K'awiil's attendance at the accession of Yuknoom Yich'aak K'ahk', in A.D. 686. The text specifies that "it happened at Chiik Nahb" (Martin 1997: 851–852). When, in A.D. 738, the Quirigua ruler K'ahk' Tiliw Chan Yopaat rebelled against his overlord, Waxaklajuun U Baah K'awiil of Copan, Quirigua Stela I records that he did so with the support of a holy lord from Chiik Nahb named Wamaaw K'awiil (Looper 1999; Tunesi 2007). Yet perhaps the most intriguing clues to the meaning of Chiik Nahb for Calakmul's network of client polities comes from a number of hieroglyphic inscriptions from the site of La Corona, whose ruling house intermarried with the Kan lineage (Martin 2008). According to these texts, the 19-year-old heir apparent to the local lordship, K'ihnich Je' Yookil, traveled to Chiik Nahb in A.D. 664 (Figure 3.3e). His reception at the capital involved a formal audience with Yuknoom Ch'e'n, followed, 12 days later, by a ritual adornment "by the hands of the seven youths, the sons of the Kan lord" (*t-u k'ab wuk-tikil ch'ok-taak, y-unen kan ajaw*). K'ihnich Je' Yookil spent three years at the Kan court before returning, after the deaths of both his parents, to take the throne (Houston and Stuart 2001: 67; Martin 2001: 183).

The significance of Chiik Nahb seems to have outlasted the height of Kan influence in the Lowlands. For example, an inscribed panel from the vicinity of one of the Kan dynasty's vassal kingdoms, Cancuen, mentions the death of a certain K'ihnich Pak' Nehn Ahk Bolon Otoot – likely a local dignitary – in A.D. 653, "at Chiik Nahb" (Figure 3.3f). The context is unclear, and the circumstances of his death equivocal: there is no overt mention of violence in the text. The panel itself, looted prior to 1981, is probably the second of a pair, and the background story would have been recorded on the missing first panel. At present, it is unclear whether K'ihnich Pak' Nehn Ahk Bolon Otoot was a lord of Cancuen (if he was, the inscription omits his title) and whether he was executed or died of natural causes during a diplomatic visit. In any case, the Kan lord Yuknoom Ch'e'n – here called *uxte'tuun kaloomte'*, "the Uxte'tuun overlord" – oversaw the accession of a new ruler of Cancuen in A.D. 656, perhaps at Calakmul as well (Martin 2001: 181), and of that ruler's successor in 677. The panel itself was commissioned in A.D. 799, when Calakmul's power was in steep decline (Braswell et al. 2004; Martin and Grube 2008: 114–115).

Whatever region of space the name designates, Chiik Nahb was, in Smith's (2003) terms, a place: a site used, remodeled, and endowed with shifting meanings by generations of Calakmul's inhabitants. As the North Acropolis and the other buildings of central Calakmul were modified over time, the ways in which humans interacted daily with the built environment – the kinds of movement through it that were possible or appropriate, the kinds of activities carried out there, the phenomenological and aesthetic experiences it produced – also changed. Public texts played an important role in constructing Chiik Nahb as a component of Calakmul's sociopolitical and linguistic landscapes. The *chiik nahb kot* emblems painted on the North Acropolis's southern façade were a public display of culturally prestigious calligraphic technique and may even have defined which part of downtown Calakmul was the actual "Coati Pool." The glyphic labels on the murals of Structure 1 are especially interesting from a linguistic landscape perspective, since they, almost alone in the whole corpus of Maya inscriptions, refer to commoners, even if by occupation rather than by personal name. Also, the captions, unlike most public inscriptions, make heavy use of consonant-vowel syllabic signs instead of logograms, spelling out linguistically specific word-forms at the same time that they hint at some degree of literacy among the murals' expected audience, whether commoners or elites.

On a larger scale, Chiik Nahb held a different sort of meaning for the potentates, merchants, and emissaries who traveled there when Calakmul was the seat of the Kan dynasty. Their impressions of Chiik Nahb as the bustling center of a hegemonic state, a concentration of political, economic, and cultural capital (Bourdieu 1979) able to "make inequality enchant" (cf. Geertz 1980), made it a meaningful place in the larger landscape. If the elder sons of subordinate lineages fostered at the Kan court were something like hostages, they must also have been students and then emissaries of courtly culture as practiced at what was, under Yuknoom Ch'e'n, the pre-eminent Lowland Maya court (Houston and Stuart 2001: 67; Martin 2001: 183). But Chiik Nahb did not begin accumulating cultural charisma with the arrival of the Kan dynasts, who arrived as strangers and stayed for only a few generations: its already accumulated meanings, among other strategic considerations, surely played a role in the Snake kings' choice to make Calakmul their capital. The fame of the city and the phenomenological experiences of the allies and enemies (e.g., Guenter 2003: 18–20) who visited it were indispensible components of Kan political power in a society where authority was the performance of authority (Demarest 1992) and political ties were personal ones.

Distributional Analysis and Classic Maya Linguistic Landscapes

Examinations of variable linguistic and orthographic forms attested in the hieroglyphic record in their spatial and temporal contexts can contribute to an understanding of the Classic Maya linguistic landscape in a sense like that used by, for example, Labov and Boberg (1997): a diachronic picture of a changing linguistic situation. Valuable work along these lines has been carried out by Alfonso Lacadena and Søren Wichmann, who have argued from the hieroglyphic data for the influence of local Yucatecan and Tzeltalan substrates on the Ch'olan prestige language and for a dialectal division between eastern and western forms of Classic Mayan (Lacadena 2000; Lacadena and Wichmann 2005; Wichmann 2002, 2006). Yet an archaeological, anthropological epigraphy must treat Maya inscriptions as items of material culture, produced strategically in specific social – not just spatiotemporal – contexts, not as straightforward reflections of the spoken word. Just as the languages of political and intellectual elites have historically differed from those of the common people (Houston et al. 2000: 336), it may be useful to think of a written prestige language as standing in a similar relation to the spoken form as spoken acrolects have to vernacular speech.

Allowing for considerable disjunction between the written and spoken word at Classic Maya centers, such an alternative perspective would see the distributional patterns of orthographic and grammatical alternatives in the hieroglyphic record as corresponding to networks of political and cultural influence more than to relatively homogeneous dialect zones. Further, it would treat the linguistic landscape revealed by the epigraphic record as a landscape of *texts*, that is, of semiotically polyvalent objects produced by interested agents, intended for particular audiences, embedded in local literate cultures, and contributing to the construction of places. A classic example of this approach is a model proposed by Hruby and Child (2004), in which the positional verbal suffix *-wan* or *-wan-i*, used in the Chontal Mayan language, entered the written languages of Late Classic Maya courts in the northwestern Lowlands (where ancient forms of Chontal would have been the vernacular languages) as a deliberate index of a local Chontal identity. It subsequently spread to sites to the south and east where Chontal was not spoken, partially or completely replacing an older Ch'olti'an suffix *-l-aj* in some local scribal traditions, although the two affixes coexisted for the rest of the script's Classic history. Hruby and Child (2004: 24) see this process of replacement as potentially resulting from, or contributing to, political and economic ties between those sites and centers in the northwest.

Considered in the light of Classic Maya political history, the distributional data for other types of linguistic and orthographic variation may bear out Hruby and Child's (2004) suggestion that ties among royal courts could have contributed to changes in written and spoken dialects of Classic Mayan. For example, the Classic prestige language used two general-purpose prepositions – *ta* and *ti* – with exactly equivalent meanings ("to," "in," "on," "at," "from," etc.) (Law 2006: 55–56; cf. Macri 1991: 268–271). While *ti* is attested at a few sites in the Early Classic period, sometimes in the same inscriptions as *ta*, *ta* was by far the more common of the two prepositions until the beginning of the eleventh *k'atun*, around A.D. 652. *Ti* achieved sudden, widespread distribution over the next few decades, appearing first in texts at Yaxchilan, Piedras Negras, and La Corona, then virtually replacing *ta* on dateable, provenanced monuments in the central and eastern Lowlands until the cessation of monumental inscriptions in the Terminal Classic period. *Ta* appears at least once at Tikal, in an inscription from the fifteenth *k'atun*; sites along the Usumacinta River continued to use both prepositions interchangeably, although *ti* is the more abundant of the two at Piedras Negras, Yaxchilan, and their dependent polities (Carter 2010: 18). The major exceptions to the pattern are the western sites of Palenque and Tonina, whose scribes overwhelmingly preferred *ta* during the entire Late Classic period; for Tonina, at least, a vernacular Tzeltalan substrate could explain the apparent conservatism of the local written language, since Tzeltal uses *ta* and not *ti* as a preposition.

Although it may be coincidental, the shift to *ti* began in earnest during the rule of Yuknoom Ch'e'n of Calakmul, who came to the throne in A.D. 636. Yuknoom Ch'e'n's rule corresponded to a period of significant monumental construction at Calakmul and political and military domination abroad, during or shortly after which *ti* predominated in the inscriptions at sites known to have been under Kan political influence (Carter 2010: 20; Martin and Grube 2008: 108–109, 125–126, 144). If *ti* was the preferred form at Calakmul in the seventh century, its strong representation in the Late Classic corpus may have resulted from the cultural prestige attached to the courtly language of Chiik Nahb. Yet given the poor state of monumental preservation at Calakmul, it is not yet possible to say whether the preposition shift originated at that site. It is also important to note that *ti* appears in both Early and Late Classic texts at the Kan rulers' longtime nemesis, Tikal.

Perhaps a better case can be made for the role of scribes at another highly prestigious court, that of Late Classic Copan, in promulgating two orthographic changes in the Maya script: the conflation of two formerly distinct sets of spirant-initial syllabograms and the abandonment of certain vowel-disharmonic syllabic spellings. Neither change took hold at every Maya site, but they were adopted most consistently at sites in the southeastern Lowlands having political ties to the Copan court.

Nikolai Grube (2004) demonstrated the existence of a contrast between a series of signs for consonant-vowel syllables beginning with a glottal spirant (*h* in contemporary epigraphic orthography) and a velar spirant (*j*, pronounced as in Spanish), which did not substitute for one another until the Late Classic period. According to Grube (2004: 79), the distinction between the two sets first began to collapse in the early eighth century, with the substitution of **ji** for **hi** in the spelling of an *u baah* ("it is his image") expression at Naranjo in A.D. 706, and it disappeared in the eastern Lowlands over the next 50 years. He remarks that *j*- and *h*-initial syllabograms began to substitute for one another at Copan and in the Usumacinta River Valley – especially at Yaxchilan – between A.D. 731 and 751, but that the distinction persisted at Palenque for the duration of that site's known glyphic record (Grube 2004: 79).

A general consensus exists among epigraphers that spoken Classic Mayan, at least early in its history, featured both short and complex – that is, long, aspirated, or glottalized – vowels, and that the quality of the central vowels in consonant-vowel-consonant roots could be indicated in the script through fully phonetic spellings or optional phonetic complementation of logograms with consonant-vowel syllabograms. Such spellings could either be synharmonic, with the unpronounced vowel of the final syllabic sign the same as the vowel of the root, or disharmonic, with a different silent vowel. While there has been considerable controversy over the precise rules governing syllabic vowel harmony (e.g., Houston et al. 2004; Lacadena and Wichmann 2004, 2005; Robertson et al. 2007; Wichmann 2006), it is broadly accepted that synharmonic spellings cue simple root vowels, while disharmony indicates vowel complexity of some kind. Like the distinction between *j* and *h*, disharmonic spellings began to be replaced in the Late and Terminal Classic inscriptions of Copan, the Maya Mountains of southern Belize, and the area of the Pasión River (Houston et al. 2004: 97).

Presumably, innovatively synharmonic spellings were adopted at sites where the spoken language of the literate elite no longer featured vowel complexity. Houston et al. (2004: 97) propose two possible models for the relationship between synharmony and the loss of vowel complexity, which could be applied equally well to the collapse of the *j*/*h* distinction. In the first, changes in spelling were roughly contemporaneous with changes in the pronunciation of Classic Mayan, and the areas where orthographic changes are attested correspond to dialect zones. In the second model, orthographic

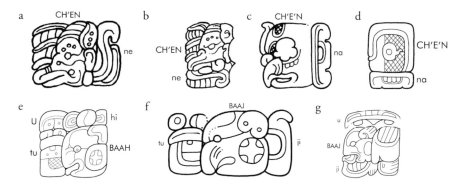

Figure 3.4. Early, innovative synharmonic spellings of the word for "cave, outcropping" at Copan: a. **CH'EN-ne**, from Copan Stela 12; b. **CH'EN-ne**, from Copan Stela 2. Standard, disharmonic spellings of the same word: c. **CH'E'N-na**, from Copan Stela 10, contemporaneous with Stelae 2 and 12; d. **CH'E'N-na**, from Tikal Stela 5. e. Standard spelling of the word for "image, person, self" as **BAAH-hi**, from the central panel of the Temple of the Inscriptions at Palenque. Early, innovative spellings of the same word substituting **ji** for **hi**: f. **tu-BAAJ-ji** for *t-u baaj*, "to his image," from Copan Stela E; g. **u-BAAJ-ji**, "his image," from Copan Stela P. All drawings by the author; a.–c. after unpublished field sketches by David Stuart; d. and f. from photographs of the monuments; e. after Maudslay 1989b: plate 59.

innovations represent deliberate reform of the script, intended to make it correspond more closely to a spoken language which may have long since ceased to distinguish between *j* and *h* or between simple and complex vowels (Grube 2004: 80–81; Houston et al. 2004: 97).

At present, the earliest instances of innovative synharmony known to me are the **CH'EN-ne** (instead of **CH'E'N-na**) spellings for "cave/outcropping" on Copan Stelae 2 and 12 (see Figure 3.4a–d), from A.D. 652. Interestingly, Stela 10, the third component of their monumental program, bears one of the earliest examples of **BAAJ-ji** (*baaj*) in place of the standard **BAAH-hi** (*baah*) (Figure 3.4e) as the word for "image." The same spelling appears on Stela E (Figure 3.4f), also dedicated by K'ahk' U Ti' Witz' K'awiil, as well as on Stela P (Figure 3.4g), dedicated in A.D. 623 by his predecessor (Carter 2010: 28), pushing the beginnings of the spirant collapse back by close to a century (cf. Grube 2004: 79). Synharmonic spellings of previously disharmonically spelled words continued at Copan through the rest of the Late Classic, although the replacement of older spellings was never complete. Outside of Copan, the new spellings appear at Nim Li Punit after A.D. 711, Machaquila after 731, Quirigua after 771, Caracol and Naranjo after 790, and Seibal after 849 (Carter 2010: 32). Additional such spellings are attested in the late Late Classic painted inscriptions at the cave of Naj Tunich, a pilgrimage destination for elites from sites (including Caracol) throughout the Maya Mountains (Stone 1995).

The distributional overlap between innovatively synharmonic spellings and attestations of the spirant collapse is remarkable, suggesting that the distinction of Copan's literary tradition – made possible by the power and influence of its ruling dynasty – made both innovations attractive, prestigious practices for scribes throughout the southern and eastern Lowlands, at sites both with and without strong historical and political connections to Copan. At the same time, the inconsistency with which the new spellings occur even at Copan implies that many scribes continued to regard the older rules as more prestigious. A further implication is that the innovations did not result from consistent rules being used to record language change in "real time." While the shift away from vowel complexity and a spirant contrast must have already occurred, at least at Copan, by the time the new spellings had been innovated, the absence of such spellings in a given time or place does not prove the persistence of the older phonological system in the spoken, courtly language. What the glyphic record shows, then, looks less like a dialect region than a zone of Copanec cultural influence.

Yet to speak of zones of influence is itself potentially misleading, and misses the point at which a landscape-oriented approach to ancient scribal choices aims. If variations in the monumental corpus do not transparently reflect the linguistic situation at a given point in time, neither were they chosen without reference to that situation. The available data on Classic Maya linguistic landscapes are largely confined to inscriptions intended for display: from monuments intended for public exhibition (as with the stelae of Copan's Main Plaza or the murals of the Chiik Nahb Acropolis), to panels and lintels viewed in restricted spaces by small groups of elites, to texts on painted vessels that could only be read by one person at a time. If the Classic Maya used hieroglyphs to keep accounts, to record contracts, or to write letters, no examples of such utilitarian texts have survived to the present day. Consequently, all extant Classic texts reflect their creators' engagement with aesthetic canons about the written word, including thematic and poetic conventions, calligraphic techniques, and the kinds of orthographic and grammatical choices considered above. Whether or not we define them to include texts on small, portable objects, Classic Maya linguistic landscapes are made up of artists' statements about what constitutes prestigious, distinctive, or correct scribal practice in a given time and place. Linguistic landscapes, in other words, are both reflections of linguistic situations and active attempts to shape those situations through the production, display, and circulation of texts which privilege some linguistic and graphic alternatives over others.

By considering them in this light, we come to see the monumental corpus as recording not just the linguistic, historical, and conceptual messages of those texts, but long-silenced conversations about the values and meanings of their other semiotic features.

Conclusions

Maya texts offer archaeologists and epigraphers insights of a type unparalleled in the New World – that is, insights into the meanings that features of the natural and built environments had for at least the elite segment of the societies that produced them. The examples discussed above represent only a fraction of the available data, but their implications are clear enough: a full understanding of Classic Maya inscriptions requires attention both to what the texts have to say about space and places and to those inscriptions' placements on local landscapes. Not just the historical and political content, but the religious ideas discussed in those texts were inseparable from physical landscapes invested with ritual and political meanings over the long term. On a larger scale, the distribution of features within texts, including toponyms and grammatical and orthographic alternatives, provide clues to the nature and construction of Classic Maya political landscapes, which should themselves be conceived as constituted through relationships among socially situated individuals and among the places they understood as significant. While incomplete, the extant hieroglyphic corpus is, among other things, a record of the cultural and intellectual influences scribes exerted on one another across space and time, and identifying the networks within which those influences operated contributes to a fuller picture of ancient Maya political relationships.

The concept of the linguistic landscape is an especially promising tool with which to address such issues. Currently underutilized in the archaeology of texts, linguistic landscape studies are a natural fit for epigraphic and iconographic considerations of public monuments in ancient societies. Scholarly discussions of Classic Maya linguistic landscapes will bear on and overlap with reconstructions of shifting linguistic situations in the ancient Lowlands, but the linguistic landscape is at once a broader concept (in that, from a Peircean perspective, it can include nonlinguistic signs) and a more specific one (in that linguistic landscape studies have hitherto tended to focus on textual and other visual signs encountered in the phenomenological experience of landscapes). By engaging with a body of theory which is, at present, mainly limited to contemporary linguistic-anthropological issues, epigraphers working with texts from the Maya region, other parts of Mesoamerica, and the Old World can reinvigorate multi-disciplinary, anthropological archaeology and bring new perspectives to bear on old problems.

Acknowledgements

I wish to thank the Department of Egyptology and Assyriology, the Joukowsky Institute for Archaeology and the Ancient World, and especially the editors of this volume, Morag Kersel and Matthew Rutz, for their kind invitation to participate in the Archaeologies of Text symposium from which this paper derives. I would also like to gratefully acknowledge the encouragement, support, and advice of my advisors and professors at the University of Texas and Brown University – David Stuart, Stephen Houston, Susan Alcock, John Cherry, Thomas Garrison, and Paja Faudree – with whom it has been a privilege to talk over most of the ideas in this chapter. Many thanks are also due to Simon Martin of the University of Pennsylvania Museum of Archaeology and Anthropology, as well as to Kate Blankenship, Daniel Law, Jenn Newman, and, for maps and proofreading, Katharine Lukach.

Notes

1   Because of the mathematical properties of the Maya Calendar Round – composed of a 260-day *tzolk'in* year and a 365-day *ha'b*, both of which operate simultaneously – any given day name in the *tzolk'in* can normally only fall on one of four numbered days in the 20-day "months" (plus one "month" of five days) in the *ha'b* calendar. For the day-name Ajaw, these are the fourth, eighth, fourteenth, and eighteenth days of the month. The ninth of Mol is thus one day ahead of what we would expect to find given the standard correlation between the two calendars. Yet such "impossible" dates are not uncommon in Classic texts, and may reflect different starting times for the days in each calendar (Martin and Skidmore 2012).

2   See Stuart (2010: 293) for the reading ?LEM, "shiny," "a shining thing," for the so-called "mirror" logogram T24.

References

Aguilar-Moreno, Manuel
    2009 Malinalco: A Place between Heaven and Earth. In *Landscapes of Origin in the Americas: Creation Narratives Linking Ancient Places and Present Communities*, edited by Jessica Joyce Christie, pp. 57–76. University of Alabama Press, Tuscaloosa.

Andrews, E. Wyllys, and Cassandra R. Bill
    2005 A Late Classic Royal Residence at Copán. In *Copán: The History of an Ancient Maya Kingdom*, edited by E. Wyllys Andrews and William R. Fash, pp. 239–314. School of American Research Press, Santa Fé.

Ashmore, Wendy, and Chelsea Blackmore
    2008   Landscape Archaeology. In *Encyclopedia of Archaeology*, edited by Deborah Pearsall, pp. 1569–1578. Elsevier, Oxford.

Bourdieu, Pierre
    1979   *La distinction: une critique social du jugement.* Les Éditions de Minuit, Paris.

Bourhis, Richard Y., and Rodrigue Landry
    2002   La loi 101 et l'aménagement du paysage linguistique du Québec. In *L'aménagement linguistique au Québec: 25 ans d'application de la Charte de la langue française*, edited by Pierre Bouchard and Richard Y. Bourhis, pp. 107–132. Publications du Québec, Quebec.

Brady, James E.
    2003   In My Hill, In My Valley: The Importance of Place in Ancient Maya Ritual. In *Mesas and Cosmologies in Mesoamerica*, edited by Douglas Sharon, pp. 83–91. San Diego Museum Papers 42. San Diego Museum of Man, San Diego.

Braswell, Geoffrey E., Joel D. Gunn, María del R. Domínguez Carrasco, William J. Folan, Laraine Fletcher, Abel Morales, and Michael D. Glascock
    2004   Defining the Terminal Classic at Calakmul, Campeche. In *The Terminal Classic in the Maya Lowlands: Collapse, Transition, and Transformation*, edited by Arthur A. Demarest, Prudence M. Rice, and Don S. Rice, pp. 162–194. University of Colorado Press, Boulder.

Carrasco, David
    1991   *To Change Place: Aztec Ceremonial Landscapes.* University Press of Colorado, Niwot, Colorado.

    1999   *City of Sacrifice: The Aztec Empire and the Role of Violence in Civilization.* Beacon Press, Boston.

Carrasco Vargas, Ramón, and Marinés Colón González
    2005   El Reino de Kaan y la Antigua Ciudad Maya de Calakmul. *Arqueología Mexicana* 13(75): 40–47.

Carrasco Vargas, Ramón, and María Cordeiro Banqueiro
    2012   The Murals of Chiik Nahb Structure Sub 1–4, Calakmul, Mexico. In *Maya Archaeology 2*, edited by Charles Golden, Stephen Houston, and Joel Skidmore, pp. 8–59. Precolumbia Mesoweb Press, San Francisco.

Carrasco Vargas, Ramón, Verónica A. Vázquez López, and Simon Martin
    2009   Daily Life of the Ancient Maya Recorded on Murals at Calakmul, Mexico. *Proceedings of the National Academy of Science* 106(46): 19245–19249.

Carter, Nicholas P.
    2010   Paleographic Trends and Linguistic Processes in Classic Ch'olti'an. Unpublished A.M. thesis, Department of Anthropology, Brown University, Providence, Rhode Island.

Dahlin, Bruce, Daniel Blair, Tim Beach, Matthew Moriarty, and Richard Terry
    2010   The Dirt on Food: Ancient Feasts and Markets Among the Lowland Maya. In *Pre-Columbian Foodways: Interdisciplinary Approaches to Food, Culture, and Markets in Ancient Mesoamerica*, edited by John Edward Staller and Michael Carrasco, pp. 191–232. Springer, New York.

Demarest, Arthur A.

    1992   Ideology in Ancient Maya Cultural Evolution: The Dynamics of Galactic Polities. In *Ideology and Pre-Columbian Civilization*, edited by Arthur A. Demarest and Geoffrey W. Conrad, pp. 135–158. School of American Research Press, Santa Fe.

Fash, Barbara

    2004   Early Classic Sculptural Development at Copan. In *Understanding Early Classic Copan: A Classic Maya Center and Its Investigation*, edited by Marcello A. Canuto, Ellen E. Bell, and Robert J. Sharer, pp. 249–264. University of Philadelphia Museum of Archaeology and Anthropology, Philadelphia.

    2005   Iconographic Evidence for Water Management and Social Organization at Copán. In *Copán: The History of an Ancient Maya Kingdom*, edited by E. Wyllys Andrews and William R. Fash, pp. 103–138. School of American Research Press, Santa Fe.

Fash, William R.

    2001   *Scribes, Warriors, and Kings*. Revised edition. Thames and Hudson, London.

    2005   Toward a Social History of the Copán Valley. In *Copán: The History of an Ancient Maya Kingdom*, edited by E. Wyllys Andrews and William R. Fash, pp. 73–102. School of American Research Press, Santa Fe.

Fash, Barbara, William Fash, Sheree Lane, Rudy Larios, Linda Schele, Jeffrey Stomper, and David Stuart

    1992   Investigations of a Classic Maya Council House at Copan, Honduras. *Journal of Field Archaeology* 19(4): 419–442.

Folan, William J., Joel D. Gunn, and María del Rosario Domínguez Carrasco

    2001   Triadic Temples, Central Plazas, and Dynastic Palaces: A Diachronic Analysis of the Royal Court Complex, Calakmul, Campeche, Mexico. In *Royal Courts of the Ancient Maya, Vol. 2: Data and Case Studies*, edited by Takeshi Inomata and Stephen D. Houston, pp. 223–265. Westview Press, Boulder, Colorado.

Garcia Moreno, Renata, David Strivay, and Bernard Gilbert

    2008   Maya Blue-Green Pigments Found in Calakmul, Mexico: A Study by Raman and UV-Visible Spectroscopy. *Journal of Raman Spectroscopy* 39: 1050–1056.

Geertz, Clifford

    1980   *Negara: The Theatre State in Nineteenth-Century Bali*. Princeton University Press, Princeton.

Gorter, Durk

    2006a Further Possibilities for Linguistic Landscape Research. In *Linguistic Landscape: A New Approach to Multilingualism*, edited by Durk Gorter, pp. 81–89. Multilingual Matters, Clevedon, England.

    2006b Introduction. In *Linguistic Landscape: A New Approach to Multilingualism*, edited by Durk Gorter, pp. 1–6. Multilingual Matters, Clevedon, England.

Gorter, Durk (editor)

    2006   *Linguistic Landscape: A New Approach to Multilingualism*. Multilingual Matters, Clevedon, England.

Grube, Nikolai

    2004   The Orthographic Distinction between Velar and Glottal Spirants in Maya Hieroglyphic Writing. In *The Linguistics of Maya Writing*, edited by Søren Wichmann, pp. 61–81. University of Utah Press, Salt Lake City.

Guenter, Stanley P.
  2003 The Inscriptions of Dos Pilas Associated with B'ajlaj Chan K'awiil. Electronic document, *Mesoweb*: mesoweb.com/features/guenter/DosPilas.pdf, accessed January 6, 2011.

Guernsey Kappelman, Julia
  2001 Sacred Geography at Izapa and the Performance of Rulership. In *Landscape and Power in Ancient Mesoamerica*, edited by Rex Koontz, Kathryn Reese-Taylor, and Annabeth Headrick, pp. 81–111. Westview Press, Boulder.

Hicks, Davyth
  2002 Scotland's Linguistic Landscape: The Lack of Policy and Planning with Scotland's Place-Names and Signage. Paper presented at the World Congress on Language Policies, Barcelona.

Houston, Stephen D.
  2010 Panel Describing a King's Pilgrimage to the Sea. In *The Fiery Pool: The Maya and the Mythic Sea*, edited by Daniel Finamore and Stephen D. Houston, p. 201. Yale University Press, New Haven.

Houston, Stephen D., Héctor Escobedo, Donald ve   , Perry Hardin, David Webster, and Lori Wright
  1998 On the River of Ruins: Explorations at Piedras Negras, Guatemala, 1997. *Mexicon* 20(1): 16–22.

Houston, Stephen D., John S. Robertson, and David Stuart
  2004 Disharmony in Maya Hieroglyphic Writing: Linguistic Change and Continuity in Classic Society. In *The Linguistics of Maya Writing*, edited by Søren Wichman, pp. 83–101. University of Utah Press, Salt Lake City.

Houston, Stephen D., and David Stuart
  2001 Peopling the Classic Maya Court. In *Royal Courts of the Ancient Maya, Vol. 1: Theory, Comparison, and Synthesis*, edited by Takeshi Inomata and Stephen D. Houston, pp. 54–84. Westview Press, Boulder.

Houston, Stephen D., David Stuart, and John S. Robertson
  2000 The Language of Classic Maya Inscriptions. *Current Anthropology* 41(3): 321–356.

Houston, Stephen D., David Stuart, and Karl Taube
  1989 Folk Classification of Classic Maya Pottery. *American Anthropologist* 91: 720–726.

Hruby, Zachary X., and Mark B. Child
  2004 Chontal Linguistic Influence in Ancient Maya Writing: Intransitive Positional Verbal Affixation. In *The Linguistics of Maya Writing*, edited by Søren Wichman, pp. 13–26. University of Utah Press, Salt Lake City.

Kerr, Justin
  2013 *Maya Vase Database: An Archive of Rollout Photographs Created by Justin Kerr*. Electronic document, www.mayavase.com, accessed September 20, 2013.

Kreslins, Janis
  2003 Linguistic Landscapes in the Baltic. *Scandinavian Journal of History* 28: 165–174.

Kubler, George
  1985 Pre-Columbian Pilgrimages in Mesoamerica. In *Fourth Palenque Round Table, 1980*,

edited by Elizabeth P. Benson, pp. 313–316. Pre-Columbian Art Research Institute, San Francisco.

Labov, William, Sharon Ash, and Charles Boberg
  1997 *A National Map of the Regional Dialects of American English*. Electronic document, www.ling.upenn.edu/phono_atlas/NationalMap/NationalMap.html, accessed September 20, 2013.

Lacadena, Alfonso
  2000 Nominal Syntax and the Linguistic Affiliation of Classic Maya Texts. In *The Sacred and the Profane: Architecture and History in the Maya Lowlands*, edited by Pierre R. Colas, Kai Delvendahl, Marcus Kuhnert, and Annette Schubart, pp. 119–128. Acta Mesoamericana Vol. 10. Anton Sauerwein, Markt Schwaben, Germany.

Lacadena, Alfonso, and Søren Wichmann
  2004 On the Representation of the Glottal Stop in Maya Writing. In *The Linguistics of Maya Writing*, edited by Søren Wichmann, pp. 83–99. University of Utah Press, Salt Lake City.
  2005 The Dynamics of Language in the Western Lowland Maya Region. In *Art for Archaeology's Sake: Material Culture and Style Across the Disciplines*, edited by Andrea Waters-Rist, Christine Cluney, Calla McNamee, and Larry Steinbrenner, pp. 32–48. University of Calgary Archaeological Association, Calgary.

Landry, Rodrigue, and Richard Y. Bourhis
  1997 Linguistic Landscape and Ethnolinguistic Vitality: An Empirical Study. *Journal of Language and Social Psychology* 16: 23–49.

Law, Daniel A.
  2006 A Grammatical Description of the Early Classic Maya Hieroglyphic Inscriptions. Unpublished Master's thesis, Department of Linguistics and English Language, Brigham Young University, Provo, Utah.

Looper, Matthew G.
  1991 The Name of Copan and of a Dance at Yaxchilan. *Copán Notes* No. 95. Copán Mosaics Project, Austin.
  1999 New Perspectives on the Late Classic Political History of Quirigua, Guatemala. *Ancient Mesoamerica* 10: 263–280.

Lopes, Luís, and Albert Davletshin
  2004 The Glyph for Antler in the Mayan Script. *Wayeb Notes* No. 11. Electronic document, www.wayeb.org/notes/wayeb_notes0011.pdf, accessed August 29, 2014

Macri, Martha J.
  1991 Prepositions and Complementizers in the Classic Period Inscriptions. In *Sixth Palenque Round Table, 1986*, edited by Merle Greene Robertson and Virginia Fields, pp. 266–272. University of Oklahoma Press, Norman.

Marcus, Joyce
  1976 *Emblem and State in the Classic Maya Lowlands: An Epigraphic Approach to Territorial Organization*. Dumbarton Oaks Research Library and Collection, Washington, D.C.

Martin, Simon
  1997 The Painted King List: A Commentary on Codex-Style Dynastic Vases. In *The Maya*

Vase Book, Volume 5: A Corpus of Roll-Out Photographs, edited by Justin Kerr, pp. 846–863. Kerr Associates, New York.

2000   At the Periphery: The Movement, Modification and Re-use of Early Monuments in the Environs of Tikal. In *The Sacred and the Profane: Architecture and Identity in the Southern Maya Lowlands*, edited by Pierre R. Colas, Kai Delvendahl, Marcus Kuhnert, and Annette Schubart, pp. 51–62. Acta Mesoamericana Vol. 10, Anton Sauerwein, Markt Schwaben, Germany.

2001   Court and Realm: Architectural Signatures in the Classic Maya Southern Lowlands. In *Royal Courts of the Ancient Maya, Vol. 1: Theory, Comparison, and Synthesis*, edited by Takeshi Inomata and Stephen D. Houston, pp. 168–194. Westview Press, Boulder.

2005   Of Snakes and Bats: Shifting Identities at Calakmul. *The PARI Journal* 6(2): 5–15.

2008   Wives and Daughters on the Dallas Altar. Electronic document, *Mesoweb*: www. mesoweb.com/articles/martin/Wives&Daughters.pdf, accessed September 20, 2013.

2012   Hieroglyphs from the Painted Pyramid: The Epigraphy of Chiik Nahb Structure Sub 1–4, Calakmul, Mexico. In *Maya Archaeology 2*, edited by Charles Golden, Stephen Houston, and Joel Skidmore, pp. 60–81. Precolumbia Mesoweb Press, San Francisco.

Martin, Simon, and Nikolai Grube

1994   Evidence for Macro-Political Organization Amongst Classic Maya Lowland States. Electronic document, *Mesoweb*: www.mesoweb.com/articles/martin/Macro-Politics. pdf, accessed September 20, 2013.

1995   Maya Superstates. *Archaeology* 48(6): 41–43.

2008   *Chronicle of the Maya Kings and Queens*. 2nd edition. Thames and Hudson, New York.

Martin, Simon, and Joel Skidmore

2012   Exploring the 584286 Correlation between the Maya and European Calendars. *The PARI Journal* 13(2): 3–16.

Mathews, Peter

1985   Maya Early Classic Monuments and Inscriptions. In *A Consideration of the Early Classic Period in the Maya Lowlands*, edited by Gordon R. Willey and Peter Mathews, pp. 5–54. Institute for Mesoamerican Studies, State University of New York at Albany, Albany.

Mathews, Peter, and John Justeson

1984   Patterns of Sign Substitution in Mayan Hieroglyphic Writing: "The Affix Cluster." In *Phoneticism in Mayan Hieroglyphic Writing*, edited by John S. Justeson and Lyle Campbell, pp. 212–213. Institute for Mesoamerican Studies, State University of New York at Albany, Albany.

Maudslay, Alfred Percival

1889a *Biologia Centrali-Americana, or, Contributions to the Knowledge of the Fauna and Flora of Mexico and Central America, Vol. 1: Copan.* R.H. Porter and Dulau and Co., London.

1889b *Biologia Centrali-Americana, or, Contributions to the Knowledge of the Fauna and*

Flora of Mexico and Central America, Vol. 4: Palenque. R.H. Porter and Dulau and Co., London.

Miller, Jeffrey H.

1974   Notes on a Stelae Pair Probably from Calakmul, Campeche, Mexico. In *First Palenque Round Table, 1973: Part 1*, edited by Merle Green Robertson, pp. 149–161. The Robert Louis Stevenson School, Pebble Beach, California.

Morley, Sylvanus Griswold

1920   *The Inscriptions at Copán, Honduras.* Carnegie Institution of Washington, Washington, D.C.

Pincemin, Sophia, Joyce Marcus, Lynda Florey Folan, William J. Folan, Maria del Rosario Dominguez Carrasco, and Abel Morales Lopez

1998   Extending the Calakmul Dynasty Back in Time: A New Stela from a Maya Capital in Campeche, Mexico. *Latin American Antiquity* 9(4): 310–327.

Proskouriakoff, Tatiana

1973   The Hand-Grasping-Fish and Associated Glyphs on Classic Maya Monuments. In *Mesoamerican Writing Systems*, edited by Elizabeth P. Benson, pp. 165–178. Dumbarton Oaks Research Library and Collection, Washington, D.C.

Rapoport, Amos

1990   *History and Precedence in Environmental Design.* Plenum Press, New York.

Reese-Taylor, Kathryn, and Rex Koontz

2001   The Cultural Poetics of Power and Space in Ancient Mesoamerica. In *Landscape and Power in Ancient Mesoamerica*, edited by Rex Koontz, Kathryn Reese-Taylor, and Annabeth Headrick, pp. 1–27. Westview Press, Boulder.

Robertson, John S., Stephen D. Houston, Marc U. Zender, and David Stuart

2007   Universals and the Logic of the Material Implication: A Case Study from Maya Hieroglyphic Writing. *Research Reports on Ancient Maya Writing* No. 62. The Mesoamerica Center, University of Texas at Austin. Electronic document, www.utmesoamerica.org/pdf_meso/RRAMW62.pdf, accessed January 1, 2011.

Schele, Linda, and Julia Guernsey Kappelman

2001   What the Heck's Coatepec? The Formative Roots of an Enduring Mythology. In *Landscape and Power in Ancient Mesoamerica*, edited by Rex Koontz, Kathryn Reese-Taylor, and Annabeth Headrick, pp. 29–53. Westview Press, Boulder.

Schele, Linda, and Matthew Looper

2005   Seats of Power at Copán. In *Copán: The History of an Ancient Maya Kingdom*, edited by E. Wyllys Andrews and William R. Fash, pp. 345–372. School of American Research Press, Santa Fe.

Schele, Linda, and Peter Mathews

1998   *The Code of Kings: The Language of Seven Sacred Maya Temples and Tombs.* Simon and Schuster, New York.

Schele, Linda, and Mary Ellen Miller

1986   *The Blood of Kings: Dynasty and Ritual in Maya Art.* George Braziller, New York.

Schele, Linda, and Khristaan Villela

1996   Creation, Cosmos, and the Imagery of Palenque and Copan. In *Eighth Palenque*

Round Table, 1993, edited by Martha J. Macri and Jan McHargue, pp. 15–30. Pre-Columbian Art Research Institute, San Francisco.

Sharer, Robert J., David W. Sedat, Loa P. Traxler, Julia C. Miller, and Ellen E. Bell

2005   Early Royal Classic Power in Copán: The Origins and Development of the Acropolis (ca. A.D. 250–600). In *Copán: The History of an Ancient Maya Kingdom*, edited by E. Wyllys Andrews and William R. Fash, pp. 139–200. School of American Research Press, Santa Fe.

Shohamy, Elana, and Shoshi Waksman

2009   Linguistic Landscape as an Ecological Arena: Modalities, Meanings, Negotiations, Education. In *Linguistic Landscape: Expanding the Scenery*, edited by Elana Shohamy and Durk Gorter, pp. 313–331. Routledge, New York.

Smith, Adam T.

2003   *The Political Landscape: Constellations of Authority in Early Complex Polities.* University of California Press, Berkeley.

Spinden, Herbert J.

1913   *A Study of Maya Art: Its Subject Matter and Historical Development.* Memoirs of the Peabody Museum of American Archaeology and Ethnology, Vol. 6. Harvard University, Cambridge.

Stone, Andrea

1995   *Images from the Underworld: Naj Tunich and the Tradition of Maya Cave Painting.* University of Texas Press, Austin.

Stone, Andrea, Dori Reents, and R. Coffman

1985   Genealogical Documentation of the Middle Classic Dynasty of Caracol, El Cayo, Belize. In *Fourth Palenque Round Table, 1980*, edited by Elizabeth P. Benson, pp. 267–276. Pre-Columbian Art Research Institute, San Francisco.

Stuart, David

1987   Ten Phonetic Syllables. *Research Reports on Ancient Maya Writing* No. 14. Center for Maya Research, Washington, D.C.

1989   Hieroglyphs on Maya Vessels. In *The Maya Vase Book, Vol. 1*, edited by Justin Kerr, pp. 149–160. Kerr Associates, New York.

1992   Hieroglyphs and Archaeology at Copan. *Ancient Mesoamerica* 3(1): 169–184.

1997   The Hills are Alive: Sacred Mountains in the Maya Cosmos. *Symbols* (Spring): 13–17.

1998   The Fire Enters His House: Architecture and Ritual in Classic Maya Texts. In *Function and Meaning in Classic Maya Architecture*, edited by Stephen D. Houston, pp. 373–426. Dumbarton Oaks Research Library and Collection, Washington, D.C.

2004   The Beginnings of the Copan Dynasty: A Review of the Hieroglyphic and Historical Evidence. In *Understanding Early Classic Copan: A Classic Maya Center and Its Investigation*, edited by Marcello A. Canuto, Ellen E. Bell, and Robert J. Sharer, pp. 215–248. University of Philadelphia Museum of Archaeology and Anthropology, Philadelphia.

2005a   *The Inscriptions from Temple XIX at Palenque: A Commentary.* The Pre-Columbian Art Research Institute, San Francisco.

2005b A Foreign Past: The Writing and Representation of History on a Royal Ancestral Shrine at Copán. In *Copán: The History of an Ancient Maya Kingdom*, edited by E. Wyllys Andrews and William R. Fash, pp. 373–394. School of American Research Press, Santa Fe.

2010 Shining Stones: Observations on the Ritual Meaning of Early Maya Stelae. In *The Place of Stone Monuments: Context, Use, and Meaning in Mesoamerica's Preclassic Tradition*, edited by Julia Guernsey, John E. Clark, and Barbara Arroyo, pp. 283–298. Dumbarton Oaks Research Library and Collection, Washington, D.C.

2012 Notes on a New Text from La Corona. *Maya Decipherment: A Weblog on the Ancient Maya Script.* Electronic document, decipherment.wordpress.com/2012/06/30/notes-on-a-new-text-from-la-corona, accessed September 18, 2013.

Stuart, David, and Stephen D. Houston

1994 *Classic Maya Place Names*. Studies in Pre-Columbian Art and Archaeology No. 33. Dumbarton Oaks Research Library and Collection, Washington, D.C.

Stuart, David, and George Stuart

2008 *Palenque: Eternal City of the Maya*. Thames and Hudson, New York.

Taube, Karl

2004 Structure 10L-16 and its Early Classic Antecedents: Fire and the Evocation and Resurrection of K'inich Yax K'uk' Mo'. In *Understanding Early Classic Copan: A Classic Maya Center and Its Investigation*, edited by Marcello A. Canuto, Ellen E. Bell, and Robert J. Sharer, pp. 265–296. University of Philadelphia Museum of Archaeology and Anthropology, Philadelphia.

Tokovinine, Alexandre

2008 The Power of Place: Political Landscape and Identity in Classic Maya Inscriptions, Imagery, and Architecture. Unpublished Ph.D. dissertation, Department of Anthropology, Harvard University, Cambridge.

Tunesi, Raphael

2007 A New Monument Mentioning Wamaaw K'awiil of Calakmul. *The PARI Journal* 8(2): 13–19.

Webster, David

1994 Classic Maya Architecture: Implications and Comparisons. In *Function and Meaning in Classic Maya Architecture*, edited by Stephen D. Houston, pp. 5–48. Dumbarton Oaks Research Library and Collection, Washington, D.C.

Wichmann, Søren

2002 *Hieroglyphic Evidence for the Historical Configuration of Eastern Ch'olan*. Research Reports on Ancient Maya Writing No. 51. Center for Maya Research, Washington, D.C.

2006 Mayan Historical Linguistics and Epigraphy: A New Synthesis. *Annual Review of Anthropology* 35: 279–294

Now You See It, Now You Don't:
The Dynamics of Archaeological and Epigraphic
Landscapes from Coptic Egypt

Scott Bucking

In 1893, when Edouard Naville began his clearance of the New Kingdom mortuary temple of Queen Hatshepsut at Deir el-Bahri, he removed without formal documentation all of the architecture of the Coptic Christian monastery that had been built on the upper terrace of the temple (Davies 1982: 57–60; Godlewski 1986: 18–19; Naville 1894, 1895). One year later, following his clearance of the upper range of Middle Kingdom tombs at Beni Hasan, Percy Newberry published a list of Coptic graffiti that he recorded inside these tombs (Newberry 1893: 65–68). Among those documented is a graffito from Tomb 22, which consisted of the Coptic word ⲀⲠⲀ (*Apa*)–a reverential title used in Christian monastic circles–written ten times (Newberry 1893: 67, no. 69); in 2009, when I re-surveyed the graffiti at Beni Hasan, this ⲀⲠⲀ graffito had disappeared. Both sites illustrate the human and natural agencies that contribute to the dynamic aspects of archaeological and epigraphic landscapes. This chapter offers some reflections on the complex relationship between these two landscapes, with an eye towards problematizing the kinds of contextual frameworks that may be used to interpret non-portable inscriptions of the type referred to as graffiti, typically found on walls or other architectural elements. Some results of my 2009 survey of three graffiti-intensive sites will serve as case studies: two are the aforementioned sites of the Hatshepsut temple and Beni Hasan, and the third is the New Kingdom temple of Seti I at Abydos (Figure 4.1). All three have yielded Coptic graffiti produced by Christian communities present at these sites beginning around the sixth century A.D.

Before proceeding, however, some critical disciplinary and terminological issues must be addressed. As recent research has pointed out, the term graffiti as applied to ancient writing is problematical and carries a great deal of baggage,

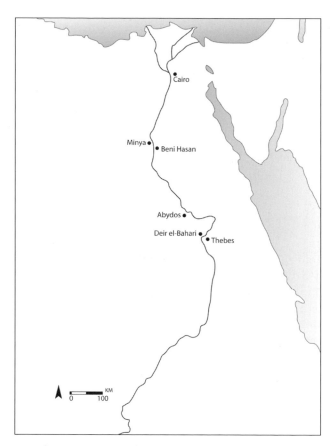

Figure 4.1. Map of Egypt, showing sites mentioned in this chapter.

especially in light of its modern-day associations with illicit or subversive activities and vandalism (on the various issues, see especially Baird and Taylor 2011a; Navrátilová 2007: 15–24; Westerfeld 2010: 115–121). Adding to the problem is the tendency among scholars to see such writing as the work of less-educated individuals at the lower end of the social spectrum who are producing texts or pictures in places where one would not ordinarily expect to find them. Thus, we are confronted by a host of biases and assumptions, which only in the past decade or so have begun to be examined. Going hand-in-hand with this examination is the recognition of the wide range of texts and images that occur as graffiti, as well as the various kinds of tools used to produce them: although the etymology of the term graffiti is the Italian word, *graffio*, meaning "a scratch," they could also be painted onto a surface, for which the technical term dipinti is often used (see, for example, Baird and Taylor 2011b: 3; Dilley

2008: 112; Łajtar 2006: 87; Stern 2013: 138). However, the more generic term graffiti will be retained in this chapter, with the understanding that it embraces all modes of production.

The study of graffiti from Greco-Roman Egypt can be said to straddle the disciplines of epigraphy and papyrology, even though the latter is more concerned with the study of portable texts (written chiefly on papyrus, parchment, wood, and ostracon) than non-portable ones (Bagnall 2009; Bülow-Jacobsen 2009). Indeed, graffiti and other types of epigraphic material are sometimes edited and published with papyrological texts (see, for example, P. Mon. Epiph.; P. Rain. Unterricht Kopt.; O. Mon. Phoib.; Bagnall and Sheridan 1994).[1] Methodologically, the two disciplines share a philological focus, but this has been broadening over the past two decades to address the fundamental issue of context. One historically neglected aspect of context concerns situating these texts within their archaeological settings, and it is this aspect that frames my discussion of the graffiti at Beni Hasan, Deir el-Bahri, and Abydos. Such an approach builds on an emerging body of epigraphic and papyrological research that views inscriptions and papyri through the considerably wider lens of archaeology (Bagnall 1988; Baird and Taylor 2011b; Bingen 1996; Bucking 2006, 2007, 2012; Darnell 2002; Gagos et al. 2005; MacCoull 1998; van Minnen 1994; Morrison and Lycett 1997; O'Connell 2007; Römer 2004; Russell 1999; Rutherford 2003; Talbot 1999).

Landscape archaeology provides an especially useful way in which to re-integrate graffiti back into their physical settings and to see archaeological context as a dynamic concept shaped by both human and natural agencies. Much attention has been given to this branch of archaeology and within it are schools of thought corresponding to the cultural-historical, processual, and post-processual approaches of the larger discipline (useful overviews in Anschuetz et al. 2001; David and Thomas 2010; Fleming 2006; Knapp and Ashmore 1999; Wilkinson 2003: 3–14). For the purpose of obtaining a general working definition of landscape archaeology, one may look to the following recent formulation:

> Landscape archaeology is concerned with the analysis of the cultural landscape through time. This entails the recording and dating of cultural factors that remain as well as their interpretation in terms of social, economic, and environmental factors. It is assumed that the "natural landscape" has been reorganized either consciously or subconsciously for a variety of religious, economic, social, political, environmental, or symbolic purposes [Wilkinson 2003: 3–4].

The complex nature of these cultural landscapes cannot be overstated and is particularly evident in my three case studies, given the pattern of use and re-use of the sites at which the graffiti are found. Such a pattern captures very well the idea of superimposed cultural landscapes, a palimpsest effect that is indeed a cornerstone principle of landscape archaeology. It is the dynamism of these landscapes that will be profiled in the present chapter, using an integrative approach to their epigraphic and archaeological components (hence my use of the terms epigraphic and archaeological landscapes). Because of the ways in which these landscapes have changed over time and in particular, the frequent lack of adequate records documenting the changes arising from modern excavation, such profiles tend to draw more attention to the problems of contextualizing the graffiti than to the construction of stable narratives to explain them. To illustrate, I will consider three aspects of context – spatial, structural, and relational – with the understanding that these three aspects do not function independently of one another.

Spatial Context

Spatial analysis has gained much momentum in the field of archaeology, especially with the development of Geographical Information Systems (GIS) over the past ten years or so (see, for example, Conolly and Lake 2006; Hietala 1984; Hodder and Orton 1976; Robertson et al. 2006), and its potential applications to the study of inscriptions at archaeological sites are enormous. Indeed, an accurate mapping of graffiti in three-dimensional space provides an integrated view of the previously mentioned aspects of archaeological context (on the use of such mapping techniques in art history and epigraphy, see, for example, Dorman 2008; Esser and Mayer 2007; de Santis 2009). Thus, the texts can be located precisely on architectural elements, while at the same time can be viewed within the larger structural context of the ancient buildings in which they were originally produced and seen in relation to other graffiti (textual and figural) or archaeological features that may be present. Although epigraphic studies have traditionally paid little attention to these aspects of context, focusing more on the reading of the text itself, there has been some recent movement towards developing a broader perspective. This may be seen, for example, in Adam Łajtar's 2006 study of Greco-Roman period graffiti at the Hatshepsut temple (predating the time of the Christian monastery), which plots the relevant texts on their architectural features, albeit two-dimensionally (Łajtar 2006: plans 3–8.)

The importance of plotting graffiti in three-dimensional space is evident when considering the relationship between the specific location of a text on its architectural element and the possible function(s) of the text. An especially interesting set of issues arises from graffiti that have been written out of human reach from ground level. All three case-study sites offer examples of such graffiti. At the Hatshepsut temple, a Greek abecedary, most likely from

Figure 4.2. Northeastern corner of central court, upper terrace, Hatshepsut temple, Deir
    el-Bahri.

the time of the Coptic monastery, was written 2.3 m from ground level on
the eastern jamb of a door in the northeastern corner of the upper terrace's
central court (Figure 4.2; initially recorded in Bataille 1951: 131–132, no.
185; most recently analyzed in Bucking 2012: 235–243). The abecedary is
arranged vertically in four columns and takes up a space of approximately
14 × 12 cm. Beyond the door is a corridor, which, based on the presence of
other graffiti, was also re-used in the Coptic period (Bucking 2012: 238–243;
Godlewski 1986: 101–102, nos. 36–38); this corridor originally connected the
central court to the so-called Chapel of the Night Sun, but had been blocked
off prior to the Coptic period (Godlewski 1986: 28, 32–33).

Even higher off the ground are some of the graffiti documented at Beni
Hasan and the Seti I temple at Abydos. Significant concentrations of Coptic
graffiti are located in the southern wing of the Seti I temple in the so-called
Butcher's Court and in one of the rooms just off this court (Figure 4.3;
Coquin and Martin 1991; Grossmann 1991; Ikram 1995: 98–102 [for the
original function of this wing as an abattoir]; Kemp 1975: 39–40). Walter
Ewing Crum (1904) published a number of these graffiti, based upon the
transcriptions made by Urbain Bouriant in 1884–1885 and by Margaret
Murray in 1901–1902 during their archaeological work at the temple (see now

Figure 4.3. Butcher's Court looking southwest towards Room Z, Seti I temple, Abydos.

Figure 4.4. Architrave with Coptic religious texts, Butcher's Court, Seti I temple, Abydos.

Delattre 2003: nos. 1–10; SB Kopt. III.1514–1536; Westerfeld 2010: 135–151 and appendix A). On the architrave in the western part of the court are two extensive (albeit somewhat faded) religious texts in red paint, written side by side, approximately 3.5 m from ground level (Figure 4.4; designated as

B11 and B12 in Crum 1904: 41–42, and most recently published as SB Kopt. III.1534–1535; see Westerfeld 2010: 201, nos. 27–28). They are separated by a roughly drawn, curved line, also in red paint. The left-hand text calls for the prayerful assistance of the "God of Michael" on behalf of a particular monk, while the right-hand text begins with a rather formulaic invocation that mentions an Apa Moses, who is probably the same individual credited in Coptic literature with the direction of a female monastic community (Bagnall 2008 [for the limitations of the literary sources]; Coquin 1991; Grossmann 1999; Westerfeld 2010: 46–61). This may also be the community responsible for much of the Coptic graffiti here in the southern wing of the temple (Coquin and Martin 1991; Crum 1904: 38–39; Westerfeld 2010: 146–151).

Similarly, a room off the Butcher's Court contains textual and figural graffiti that have been written at a significant height from ground level; this room has been variously labeled by early investigators of the temple as Room B´, Z, and 17 (Figure 4.3; Calverley et al. 1933: plate 1A; Mariette 1869: plate 3; Murray 1904: 36; Westerfeld 2010: 136, no. 70; following Westerfeld, the Room Z designation has been retained in this chapter). The northern wall of Room Z features a 16-line Coptic text that is over 3 m off the ground (Crum 1904: 39, Number 26; SB Kopt. III.1528; Westerfeld 2010: 205, no. 73). It invokes the names of women from the town of Pertes (modern-day Bardis, north of Abydos), who are most likely affiliated with the previously mentioned monastic community.

Among the Middle Kingdom tombs at Beni Hasan re-used for habitation by Christian monks are graffiti that have been written over 3 m above floor level of the tombs: some names with a Christian symbol appear on the protruding panel of the northern wall of Tomb 15, and an elaborately decorated cross and a separate religious text (probably names) in a *tabula ansata* design are on the northern wall of Tomb 18. Unlike the previously mentioned Greek abecedary graffito on the door jamb at the Hatshepsut temple, which could have been produced at a raised ground level due to the accumulation of debris, the higher-placed graffiti at Beni Hasan and the Seti temple cannot be explained in the same way since a greater accumulation of debris in these spaces would have rendered them inaccessible. At such a significant height, these graffiti were apparently intended for display purposes.

Structural Context

The structural or architectural context of inscriptions is well illustrated by Naville's clearance of the upper terrace of the Hatshepsut temple in 1893 as part of his archaeological investigations at the site. One sees in the surviving photographic archive the remains of Coptic-period buildings in the central court of the upper terrace–buildings which Naville disengaged with virtually no documentation, save for these photographs of the clearance work in progress and a few passing comments in his published excavation reports (James 2007; Naville 1894, 1895, 1896). Naville's comments reveal not only his lack of concern for this later architecture, but also his disdain for it in light of the Copts' recycling of building materials from the original New Kingdom temple (see especially Naville 1894: 6). Although unintentional, Naville's photographs constitute a partial record of the Coptic monastery, one which Włodemierz Godlewski (1986) made good use of in his reconstruction of the monastic structures on the upper terrace. However, in spite of these efforts, there is no escaping the reality that the surviving graffiti from the Coptic monastery in the central court are completely devoid of their contemporary structural context. This is illustrated by a cluster of Coptic graffiti on the third course of blocks near the northeastern corner of the central court, just west of the door leading into the Chapel of the Night Sun (Figure 4.2). The cluster was not produced in the open area of the court, as its current situation at the site would suggest, but rather it was inside a monastic structure in this corner, referred to in Godlewski's reconstruction as Building G (Godlewski 1986: 32–33) – a building that is visible in the photographs of Naville's clearance work of the upper terrace (Bucking 2012: 240, figure 10.5 for the key photograph).

Although the Middle Kingdom rock-cut tombs at Beni Hasan provide the overall structural context for the graffiti produced by the later Christian inhabitants of these tombs, there are indications that at least some of the interior spaces had been significantly modified as part of their adaptive re-use. Any remains of interior architecture from the time of Coptic habitation would have presumably been removed during Newberry's clearance work in 1890–1891. However, in Tomb 23, one of the most graffiti-intensive tombs at the site, various cuts in the floor (noted as evidence of quarrying activities in Newberry 1893: 77) and numerous holes in the northern and eastern walls provide evidence of substantial interior redesign. It is also along these same walls that the Coptic graffiti are concentrated and therefore the production of the graffiti cannot be assumed to have taken place in the now open floor space of the tomb. The extensive nature of interior modifications may be seen in other tombs at Beni Hasan containing built-ins, which could not be removed in the course of any kind of clearance work. Of particular note are those in Tomb 29, which contain two niches cut into the eastern and southern walls. The niche in the eastern wall has three large Christian symbols painted in red ink above it, and rectangular slots carved into the upper and lower front edges of the niche suggest that either a single or double door had been fitted to create a proper cupboard (Figure 4.5; for comparable built-ins in other

Figure 4.5. Coptic period niche in eastern wall of Tomb 29, Beni Hasan.

Egyptian tombs adapted by Christians for habitation, see, for example, Jones 1991). By contrast, the niche in the southern wall was cut at floor level and actually qualifies as a small room, with its entryway measuring about 150 cm in height and 90 cm in width.

A similar pattern of interior modifications is seen in Room Z, the graffiti-intensive room off the Butcher's Court in the Seti I temple at Abydos. This room has various holes and slots occurring on both the upper and lower portions of all four walls, suggesting that the room had undergone some major alterations during its use, most likely by the previously mentioned female monastic community (Figure 4.6 for examples on eastern wall). In the court itself, a rectangular plastered installation survives that probably belongs to the period of Christian habitation (Figure 4.7). It has gone virtually unnoticed in the recent scholarly literature (save for a brief mention in Ikram 1995: 98), reflecting an almost exclusive reliance on the graffiti to establish the presence of a Christian community at the site. The brick installation, measuring around 325 cm in length, 195 cm in width, and 90 cm in height (at its maximum towards the back) is located in the northeastern corner of the court. It contains three large built-in storage vessels, each of which is approximately 55 cm wide at the mouth and has an inside depth of 75 cm. Large storage vessels of this kind are well attested in Coptic-period assemblages (Ballet 1991: 490) and one finds comparable installations at other monastic sites, including that of Kellia (Daumas and Gillaumont 1969: plate 21d). Around the exposed rim of one of the vessels

Figure 4.6. Coptic period graffiti and holes, northeastern corner of Room Z, Seti I temple, Abydos.

Figure 4.7. Plastered installation in northeastern corner of Butcher's Court, Seti I temple, Abydos.

is a "piecrust" design that is consistent with pottery styles of late antique Egypt (see, for example, Egloff 1977: plate 54, nos. 3–5; Wilson et al. 2003: 5); some very faded painted decorations are also present on the shoulder (on which, see Ballet 1991: 490). The vessels' shape informs ideas about function, which were most likely intended for the storage of dry goods, such as grain or other foodstuffs. Given their large capacity, it may be inferred that these vessels were supporting a small permanent population based at the site. This makes an important contribution to the current debate concerning whether the female monastic community actually resided there (see most recently Westerfeld 2010: 146–151). Using ceramic assemblages thus also has precedent, as can be seen in the analysis of pottery recovered at Coptos to document changes in patterns of use at that site from the Pharaonic to Roman periods (Herbert and Berlin 2003: 22–24).

Relational Context

The final aspect of context to be addressed concerns the relationships among graffiti in the same location and the relationships between graffiti and nearby archaeological features. This relational aspect has historically received little attention in the course of assessing the production and function of the graffiti, as well as in their actual documentation. The documentation issue is particularly noticeable with regard to the relationships between textual and figural graffiti at a given location. For example, even in the relatively recent catalogues of Coptic-period graffiti at the Hatshepsut temple, the textual graffiti are separated from the figural ones, in spite of the fact that both types may occur together in the same location (Godlewski 1986: 91–107, 141–152). In the case of the much earlier catalogue of the Coptic graffiti at Beni Hasan, only the texts are documented, effectively rendering the figural graffiti "invisible," even if they bear some direct relationship to the texts (Newberry 1893: 65–68). A good illustration of the nature of this relationship is afforded by a graffito on the eastern wall of Tomb 23, which I documented for the first time in 2009 (Figure 4.8). It depicts a male *orant* flanked by two beasts. The male figure is thought to be Daniel (written to the right of the male figure's waist), from the biblical book of the same name, and therefore the two beasts are most likely lions; and emerging from the left side of Daniel is a figure that may be interpreted as an angel. The biblical story to which this graffito alludes (Daniel 6: 1–28) and the arrangement of the figures in the graffito are well attested in Christian iconography and more specifically in Coptic contexts (du Bourguet 1991; Jensen 2000: 174–178; Schlosser 1968; Seasoltz 2005: 115).

The eastern wall of Tomb 23 not only provides an excellent example of the integral relationship between textual and figural graffiti, but it also demonstrates the importance of identifying archaeological features that may bear on the assessment of graffiti. Two relevant features on this wall are small niches, which could have been used to hold lamps that served, among other things, as a light source for either producing or interacting with the texts and figures painted on the wall; however, very few traces of soot deposits were noticeable in these niches during my 2009 investigation. Actual lamps may

Figure 4.8. Daniel in the lion's den graffito on eastern wall of Tomb 23, Beni Hasan.

have been among the debris that Newberry cleared from the tomb, although no published report on the Coptic-period portable finds from any of the tombs was ever made, save for the brief statement that "a good deal of Coptic pottery was found, most of it broken" (Naville et al. 1891: 19–20).

Niches similar to those in Tomb 23 at Beni Hasan were cut into the walls and pillars in Room Z off the Butcher's Court of the Seti I temple. One of them, cut into the eastern column, shows considerable soot deposits, presumably from the burning lamps themselves. Room Z also shows how the relationship between certain graffiti can be defined archaeologically through an examination of the remaining areas of plaster applied to the room by its Christian inhabitants. For example, the *orans* figure and associated name of Martha, the little, was painted directly on the original surface of the western wall and therefore represents an earlier phase than the Coptic New Testament quotation (Matthew 28: 20) written below the figure on a layer of plaster that was subsequently applied to the wall by its inhabitants (Crum 1904: 39, no. 2; Westerfeld 2010: 203, no. 49). Since portions of the plaster surface have deteriorated over time, the quote itself has significant lacunae.

The Physical and Psychological Dynamics of Epigraphic Landscapes

As the state of this graffito from the Gospels suggests, the dynamism of epigraphic landscapes may be defined in terms of the physical changes that may occur to inscriptions over time. Indeed, the present chapter began with the mention of a graffito in Tomb 22 at Beni Hasan that was documented in the late nineteenth century, but no longer extant in 2009 when I conducted my epigraphic survey. The surface degradation on the walls of the tombs at this site has been explored with specific reference to the original Middle Kingdom paintings (Wilson-Yang and Burns 1982; 1987), and the contributing environmental and climatic factors have had a similar effect on the Coptic graffiti that have been painted in red ochre on top of the Middle Kingdom wall paintings.

A similar problem arises at the Hatshepsut temple for two copies of a pangram, the first of which is smudged and faded and the second of which is faded after the initial line (Bataille 1951: 132–134, nos. 187–188; Bucking 2012: 238–243). Since it is a well-known verse that exhausts the letters of the Greek alphabet, the lost portions can be restored with a fair degree of certainty, although in the case of the first, there seems to have been another text following the pangram. Notably, both pangrams are located in the corridor that connects the central court on the upper terrace to the original Chapel of the Night Sun. As mentioned above, this corridor is accessed through a door in the northeastern corner of the central court (Figure 4.2), and the entrance into the chapel from the corridor had been blocked off prior to the Coptic period, effectively turning the corridor into a large niche. However, because Naville removed the wall that blocked off the corridor, we cannot know whether it contained additional graffiti; the same may be said of any of the monastic constructions removed by Naville in the central court. Thus, we are reminded of the limitations associated with analyzing the distribution patterns of surviving graffiti, since the patterns themselves can be easily altered over time through both human and natural agencies.

Ideology also plays an important role in the physical changes to graffiti. The previously mentioned graffito in Tomb 23 at Beni Hasan relating to the biblical figure of Daniel provides a suitable illustration. One notes what appears to be the intentional hacking out of Daniel's eyes, as well as most of his face, his hands, his feet, and part of his name (Figure 4.8). Such actions are most likely the result of iconoclasm in the Islamic period, and there are other Christian graffiti in this tomb that have been altered in a similar manner: for example, on the eastern wall, a large cross in red paint measuring approximately 60 cm high was hacked out, leaving only an outline of it in sunken relief (on iconoclasm, see especially King 1985, which specifically addresses Muslim attitudes towards Christian crosses). Some Arabic graffiti scratched into the northern wall of Tomb 23 towards the northeastern corner reinforce the idea that the tomb was indeed accessed during the Islamic period. None of these graffiti were recorded during the initial clearance of the tomb. On the whole, they are not very legible, save for a large etched *Bism Allah* (بسم الله) at a height of approximately 140 tomb floor. This graffito, a standard Muslim invocatio meaning "in the name of God"), was actually written over the top portion of a Coptic alphabet table that was created presumably by one of the monks who had inhabited the tomb (see Bucking 2012: 256–262; Newberry 1893: plate XXV); the act of writing the *bismillah* over it was in all likelihood another expression of iconoclasm that "neutralized" the table as a perceived symbol of Christian ritual power (on the various uses of the *bismillah*, see Piamenta 1979: 32–39).

Aside from the physical changes to graffiti that occur over time, graffiti can "disappear" as part of the imagined landscape that is constructed for cultural heritage. This is especially evident in archaeological guide books, which present the tombs at Beni Hasan only as part of the pharaonic past. For example, the following description of Tomb 15 (Tomb of Baqet) completely ignores the extensive number of Coptic graffiti in this tomb:

> Baqet was an 11th-dynasty governor of the Oryx nome (district). His rectangular tomb chapel has seven tomb shafts and some well-preserved wall paintings. They include Baqet and his wife on the left wall watching weavers and acrobats – mostly women in diaphanous dresses in flexible poses. Further along, animals, presumably possessions of Baqet, are being counted. A hunting scene in the desert shows mythical creatures among the gazelles. The back wall shows a sequence of wrestling moves that are still used today. The right (south) wall is decorated with scenes from the nomarch's daily life, with potters, metalworkers and a flax harvest, among others [Firestone et al. 2008: 223].

The left or northern wall contains the highest concentrations of Coptic graffiti (both textual and figural) in red paint, and from this description it would seem that they do not exist. Even in the original archaeological report on the tomb, the drawings follow the standard practice of documenting only the pharaonic scenes depicted on each wall. This is well illustrated by comparing the original drawing of the northern wall of Tomb 15 (Newberry 1893: plate IV) with a photograph of one of the more significant graffiti clusters on this wall, which I documented in 2009 (Bucking 2012: 262, figure 10.14). Thus, the dynamics of epigraphic landscapes are shaped by the way in which modern societies (re)construct the ancient past, whether for scientific study or touristic purposes.

Putting It All Together: Towards an Integrated Cultural Landscape

The interplay of the various factors discussed in this chapter (i.e., the physical, spatial, structural, and relational contexts) helps to situate graffiti within integrated cultural landscapes and at the same time aids in the understanding of the dynamism associated with these landscapes. As a concluding example, let us return to Room Z, the graffiti-intensive room off of the Butcher's Court in the Seti I temple, bearing in mind the ultimate goal of problematizing how this particular space was re-used and transformed by a monastic community in late antiquity. One of the significant activity areas that can be identified is in the northeastern corner of the room (see Figure 4.6). The northern wall at this location was discussed earlier in connection with a graffito painted high up, invoking some religious women from Pertes. On the eastern wall are a number of painted graffiti, six of which have texts written within frames. Three of these are located on the third course of blocks, approximately 1.5 m from ground level (Crum 1904: 39, no. 23; 40, no. 11; 41, no. 36; Westerfeld 2010: 202–203, nos. 40, 41, 46). The other three texts are about 25 cm higher, painted on the fourth course of blocks: two of them are published by Crum only in facsimile reproduction with other graffiti (Crum 1904: plate XXV, no. 1), while the third is recorded in both catalogue and facsimile formats (Crum 1904: 40, no. 31; plate XXXIII, no. 31; see also Westerfeld 2010: 203, no. 44). The texts have faded considerably over time, but based on earlier transcriptions and what could be ascertained during my 2009 survey, the contents seem to have been invocations and prayers, which when assessed in light of the frames surrounding them, were probably meant to serve a liturgical function. One of the better preserved examples invokes God, several angels, and the Apostles. The frames themselves appear to represent tablets of the kind used as liturgical diptychs in Coptic Christian settings (see, for example, McCormick 1981).

Even higher up on the eastern wall, towards the ceiling, are additional religious texts, one of which is painted in large red letters and arranged around a significant longitudinal cut into the wall between the fourth and fifth course of blocks that extends from the corner made with the northern wall (on the text, see Crum 1904: 40, no. 31; Westerfeld 2010: 203, no. 43). Although the exact nature of the architectural modification associated with this cut is difficult to ascertain, it most certainly predated the production of the text. Additional evidence of architectural modifications is provided by a number of holes both on the eastern and northern portions of the wall in this corner of the room (Figure 4.6). These features, when considered together with the concentration of texts at various heights on the wall, speak to the kind of dedicated efforts being made not by some transient population, but rather by more permanent inhabitants at the site, probably a community of female monks; such an idea is certainly reinforced by the previously discussed installation in the Butcher's Court. However, the complex dynamics of the site from ancient through modern times makes it impossible to understand completely how the community re-used this space in late antiquity. Nonetheless, as this chapter has demonstrated, an awareness of the various factors that shape these dynamics allows for more rigorous and robust definitions of context through a better integration of archaeological and epigraphic data.

Acknowledgments

This survey was conducted under the auspices of the Egyptian Supreme Council of Antiquities (SCA), and I wish to thank Zahi Hawass, former Minister of State for Antiquities, and the members of the Permanent Committee of the SCA for facilitating my research. The project was also supported by a fellowship from the National Endowment for the Humanities held through the American Research Center in Egypt (ARCE), and I am grateful to ARCE, especially Deputy Director, Mme. Amira Khattab, for all the logistical support. I wish to thank Andrea Berlin, Professor of Archaeology at Boston University, for her input regarding the assessment of the plastered installation and its three storage vessels. I am grateful to Warren Schultz, Professor of Middle Eastern History at DePaul University, for his identification of this graffito from the photographic record produced during my 2009 survey. Finally, my work could not have been accomplished without the flexible scheduling arrangement granted to me by my university, De Paul University, and I wish to express my gratitude to both the Dean of the College of Liberal Arts and Sciences, Charles Suchar, and Associate Dean and former Chair of the Department of History, Warren Schultz.

Notes

1. References to editions of papyrological texts follow the standard abbreviations given in Sosin et al. 2008.

References

Anschuetz, Kurt F., Richard H. Wilshusen, and Cherie L. Scheick

    2001   An Archaeology of Landscapes: Perspectives and Directions. *Journal of Archaeological Research* 9: 157–211.

Bagnall, Roger S.

    1988   Archaeology and Papyrology. *Journal of Roman Archaeology* 1: 197–202.

    2008   Models and Evidence in the Study of Religion in Late Roman Egypt. In *From Temple to Church: Destruction and Renewal of Local Cultic Topography in Late Antiquity*, edited by Johannes Hahn, Stephen Emmel, and Ulrich Gotter, pp. 23–41. Brill, Leiden.

    2009   Introduction. In *The Oxford Handbook of Papyrology*, edited by Roger S. Bagnall, pp. xvii–xxi. Oxford University Press, Oxford.

Bagnall, Roger S., and Jennifer A. Sheridan
  1994   Greek and Latin Documents from 'Abu Sha'ar, 1992–1993. *Bulletin of the American Society of Papyrologists* 31: 109–120.

Baird, Jennifer, and Claire Taylor (editors)
  2011a   *Ancient Graffiti in Context*. Routledge, New York.

Baird, Jennifer, and Claire Taylor
  2011b   Ancient Graffiti in Context: Introduction. In *Ancient Graffiti in Context*, edited by Jennifer Baird and Claire Taylor, pp. 1–19. Routledge, New York.

Ballet, Pascale
  1991   Coptic Ceramics. In *The Coptic Encyclopedia*, Vol. 2, edited by Aziz S. Atiya, 480–504. Macmillan, New York.

Bataille, André
  1951   *Les inscriptions grecques du temple de Hatshepsout à Deir el-Bahari*. Institut Français d'Archéologie Orientale, Cairo.

Bingen, Jean
  1996   Dumping and the Ostraca at Mons Claudianus. In *Archaeological Research in Roman Egypt*, edited by Donald M. Bailey, pp. 29–38. *Journal of Roman Archaeology* Supplement 19. Journal of Roman Archaeology, Portsmouth, Rhode Island.

Bourguet, Pierre du
  1991   Biblical Subjects in Coptic Art: Daniel in the Lion's Den. In *The Coptic Encyclopedia*, Vol. 2, edited by Aziz S. Atiya, pp. 384–385. Macmillan, New York.

Bucking, Scott
  2006   Recovery and Loss: Archaeological Perspectives on the Papyri from Hellenistic, Roman, and Byzantine Egypt. *Public Archaeology* 5: 151–166.
  2007   Scribes and Schoolmasters? On Contextualizing Ostraca Excavated from the Monastery of Epiphanius. *Journal of Coptic Studies* 9: 21–47.
  2012   Towards an Archaeology of Bilingualism: On the Study of Greek-Coptic Education in Late Antique Egypt. In *Multilingualism in the Graeco-Roman Worlds*, edited by Alex Mullen and Patrick James, pp. 225–264. Cambridge University Press, Cambridge.

Bülow-Jacobsen, Adam
  2009   Writing Materials in the Ancient World. In *The Oxford Handbook of Papyrology*, edited by Roger S. Bagnall, pp. 3–29. Oxford University Press, Oxford.

Calverley, Amice M., Myrtle F. Broome, and Alan H. Gardiner
  1933   *The Temple of King Sethos I at Abydos*, Vol. 1. Egypt Exploration Society, London.

Conolly, James, and Mark Lake
  2006   *Geographical Information Systems in Archaeology*. Cambridge University Press, Cambridge.

Coquin, René-Georges
  1991   Moses of Abydos. In *The Coptic Encyclopedia*, Vol. 6, edited by Aziz S. Atiya, pp. 1679–1681. Macmillan, New York.

Coquin, René-Georges, and Maurice Martin
  1991   Abydos: Archaeological and Literary Evidence. In *The Coptic Encyclopedia*, Vol. 1, edited by Aziz S. Atiya, pp. 39–41. Macmillan, New York.

Crum, Walter Ewing
    1904   Coptic Graffiti, Etc. In *The Osireion at Abydos*, by Margaret A. Murray, pp. 38–43.
           Bernard Quaritch, London.

Darnell, James
    2002   *Theban Desert Road Survey in the Egyptian Western Desert, Volume 1: Gebel Tjauti
           Rock Inscriptions 1–45 and Wadi el-Hôl Rock Inscriptions 1–45*. Oriental Institute of
           the University of Chicago, Chicago.

Daumas, François, and Antoine Guillaumont
    1969   *Kellia I: Kôm 219*. Institut Français d'Archéologie Orientale, Cairo.

David, Bruno, and Julian Thomas

    2010   Landscape Archaeology: Introduction. In *Handbook of Landscape Archaeology*, edited
           by Bruno David and Julian Thomas, pp. 27–43. Left Coast Press, Walnut Creek,
           California.

Davies, W. Vivian
    1982   Thebes. In *Excavating in Egypt: The Egypt Exploration Society 1882–1982*, edited by
           Thomas G.H. James, pp. 51–70. University of Chicago Press, Chicago.

Delattre, Alain
    2003   Les graffitis coptes d'Abydos et la crue du Nil. In *Études coptes VIII, Dixième journée
           d'études Lille, 14–16 juin 2001*, edited by Christian Cannuyer, pp. 133–146. De
           Boccard, Paris.

Dilley, Paul
    2008   Dipinti in Late Antiquity and Shenoute's Monastic Federation: Text and Image in
           the Paintings of the Red Monastery. *Zeitschrift für Papyrologie und Epigraphik* 165:
           111–128.

Dorman, Peter F.
    2008   Epigraphy and Recording. In *Egyptology Today*, edited by Richard H. Wilkinson,
           pp. 77–97. Cambridge University Press, Cambridge.

Egloff, Michel
    1977   *Kellia: La poterie copte. Quatre siècles d'artisanat et d'échanges en Basse Égypte*. Georg,
           Geneva.

Esser, Gerold, and Irmengard Mayer
    2007   3-D Geometry and 3-D Texture: Documenting Early-Christian Wall Paintings at
           the Domitilla Catacomb in Rome. *12th International Congress on Cultural Heritage
           and New Technologies, Archaeology and Computer Workshop, Vienna, 5–7 Nov. 2007.*
           Electronic document, http://www.oeaw.ac.at/antike/fileadmin/user_upload/bilder/
           Domitilla/Eßer_Mayer_Vienna_2007.pdf, accessed September 5, 2014.

Firestone, Matthew D., Zora O'Neill, Anthony Sattin, and Rafael Wlodarski
    2008   *Lonely Planet Egypt*. Lonely Planet Publications, Victoria, Australia.

Fleming, Andrew
    2006   Post-processual Landscape Archaeology: A Critique. *Cambridge Archaeological
           Journal* 16: 267–280.

Gagos, Trianos, Jennifer Gates, and Andrew Wilburn
    2005   Material Culture and Texts of Graeco-Roman Egypt: Creating Context, Debating
           Meaning. *Bulletin of the American Society of Papyrologists* 42: 171–188.

Godlewski, Włodzimierz
    1986   *Deir el-Bahari V: Le monastère de St. Phoibammon.* PWN-Éditions scientifiques de
            Pologne, Warsaw.

Grossmann, Peter
    1991   Abydos: Buildings. In *The Coptic Encyclopedia*, Vol. 1, edited by Aziz S. Atiya, pp.
            41–42. Macmillan, New York.
    1999   Zu Moses von Abydos und die Bischöfe seiner Zeit. *Bulletin de la Société
            d'Archéologie Copte* 38: 51–64

Herbert, Sharon C., and Andrea Berlin
    2003   The Excavation: Occupation History and Ceramic Assemblages. In *Excavations at
            Coptos (Qift) in Upper Egypt, 1987–1992*, edited by Sharon C. Herbert and Andrea
            Berlin, pp. 12–156. *Journal of Roman Archaeology* Supplement 53. Journal of Roman
            Archaeology, Portsmouth, Rhode Island.

Hietala, Harold (editor)
    1984   *Intrasite Spatial Analysis in Archaeology.* Cambridge University Press, Cambridge.

Hodder, Ian, and Clive Orton
    1976   *Spatial Analysis in Archaeology.* Cambridge University Press, Cambridge.

Ikram, Salima
    1995   *Choice Cuts: Meat Production in Ancient Egypt.* Peeters, Leuven.

James, Thomas G.H.
    2007   Deir el Bahari. In *The Egypt Exploration Society: The Early Years*, edited by Patricia
            Spencer, pp. 95–126. Egypt Exploration Society, London.

Jensen, Robin M.
    2000   *Understanding Early Christian Art.* Routledge, London.

Jones, Michael
    1991   The Early Christian Sites at Tell el-Amarna and Sheikh Said. *Journal of Egyptian
            Archaeology* 77: 129–144.

Kemp, Barry J.
    1975   Abydos. In *Lexikon der Ägyptologie*, Vol. 1, edited by Wolfgang Helck and Eberhard
            Otto, pp. 28–41. Harrassowitz, Wiesbaden, Germany.

King, Geoffrey
    1985   Islam, Iconoclasm, and the Declaration of Doctrine. *Bulletin of the School of Oriental
            and African Studies* 48: 267–277.

Knapp, A. Bernard, and Wendy Ashmore
    1999   Archaeological Landscapes: Constructed, Conceptualized, Ideational. In *Archaeologies
            of Landscape: Contemporary Perspectives*, edited by Wendy Ashmore and A. Bernard
            Knapp, pp. 1–32. Blackwell, Oxford.

Łajtar, Adam
    2006   *Deir el-Bahari in the Hellenistic and Roman Periods: A Study of an Egyptian Temple
            Based on Greek Sources.* Warsaw Institute of Archaeology, Warsaw.

McCormick, Michael
    1981   A Liturgical Diptych from Coptic Egypt in the Museum of Fine Arts. *Le Muséon:
            Revue d'études orientales* 4: 47–54.

MacCoull, Leslie S.B.
   1998   Prophethood, Texts, and Artifacts: The Monastery of Epiphanius. *Greek, Roman and Byzantine Studies* 39: 307–324.

Marriette, Auguste
   1869   *Abydos: Description des fouilles exécutées sur l'emplacement de cette ville*, Vol. 1. Imprimerie nationale, Paris.

van Minnen, Peter
   1994   House-to-House Enquiries: An Interdisciplinary Approach to Roman Karanis. *Zeitschrift für Papyrologie und Epigraphik* 100: 227–251.

Morrison, Katherine D., and Mark T. Lycett
   1997   Inscriptions as Artifacts: Precolonial South India and the Analysis of Texts. *Journal of Archaeological Method and Theory* 4: 215–237.

Murray, Margaret A.
   1904   *The Osireion at Abydos*. Bernard Quaritch, London.

Naville, Edouard
   1894   *The Temple of Deir el Bahari: Its Plan, Its Founders, and Its First Explorers, Introductory Memoir*. Egypt Exploration Fund, London.
   1895   *The Temple of Deir el Bahari, Part I*. Egypt Exploration Fund, London.
   1896   *The Temple of Deir el Bahari, Part II*. Egypt Exploration Fund, London.

Naville, Edouard, Percy E. Newberry, and G. Willoughby Fraser
   1891   *The Season's Work at Ahnas and Beni Hasan, 1890–1891*. Gilbert and Rivington, London.

Navrátilová, Hana
   2007   *The Visitors' Graffiti of Dynasties XVIII and XIX in Abusir and North Saqqara*. Czech Institute of Egyptology, Prague.

Newberry, Percy E.
   1893   *Beni Hasan, Part II*. Kegan Paul, Trench, Trübner, London.

O'Connell, Elisabeth R.
   2007   Transforming Monumental Landscapes in Late Antique Egypt: Monastic Dwellings in Legal Documents from Western Thebes. *Journal of Early Christian Studies* 15: 239–273.

Piamenta, Moshe
   1979   *Islam in Everyday Arabic Speech*. Brill, Leiden.

Robertson, Elizabeth C., Jeffrey D. Seibert, Deepika C. Fernandez, and Marc U. Zender (editors)
   2006   *Space and Spatial Analysis in Archaeology*. University of Calgary Press, Calgary.

Römer, Cornelia
   2004   Philoteris in the Themistou Meris: Report on the Archaeological Survey Carried Out as Part of the Fayum Survey Project. *Zeitschrift für Papyrologie und Epigraphik* 147: 281–305.

Russell, John Malcolm
   1999   *The Writing on the Wall: Studies in the Architectural Context of Late Assyrian Palace Inscriptions*. Eisenbrauns, Winona Lake, Indiana.

Rutherford, Ian
  2003   Pilgrimage in Greco-Roman Egypt: New Perspectives on Graffiti from the
         Memnonion at Abydos. In *Ancient Perspectives on Egypt*, edited by Roger Matthews
         and Cornelia Römer, pp. 171–189. UCL Press, London.

Santis, Ludovica Bucci de
  2009   On the Reconstruction of the Spatial Representations in Certain Roman Wall
         Paintings. In *The Splendor of Roman Wall Painting*, by Umberto Pappalardo, pp.
         222–231. J. Paul Getty Museum, Los Angeles.

Schlosser, Hanspeter
  1968   Daniel. In *Lexikon der christlichen Ikonographie*, Vol. 1, edited by Engelbert
         Kirschbaum, pp. 469–473. Herder, Rome.

Seasoltz, R. Kevin
  2005   *A Sense of the Sacred: Theological Foundations of Christian Architecture and Art.*
         Continuum, New York.

Sosin, Joshua D., Roger S. Bagnall, James Cowey, Mark Depauw, Terry G. Wilfong, and
Klaas A. Worp (editors)
  2008   *Checklist of Editions of Greek, Latin, Demotic and Coptic Papyri, Ostraca and Tablets.*
         Electronic document, http://scriptorium.lib.duke.edu/papyrus/texts/clist.html,
         accessed March 22, 2011.

Stern, Karen B.
  2013   Graffiti as Gift: Mortuary and Devotional Graffiti in the Late Antique Levant. In
         The Gift in Antiquity, edited by Michael L. Satlow, pp. 137–157. Wiley-Blackwell,
         Malden, Massachusetts.

Talbot, Alice-Mary
  1999   Epigrams in Context: Inscriptions on Art and Architecture of the Palaiologan Era.
         Dumbarton Oaks Papers 53: 75–90.

Westerfeld, Jennifer T.
  2010   *Landscapes of Memory: Pharaonic Sacred Space in the Coptic Imagination.* Ph.D.
         dissertation, Department of Near Eastern Languages and Civilizations, University
         of Chicago. ProQuest, UMI Dissertations Publishing, 3432782.

Wilkinson, Tony J.
  2003   *Archaeological Landscapes of the Near East.* University of Arizona Press, Tuscon.

Wilson, Penelope, David Jeffreys, Barry Kemp, and Pamela Rosa
  2003   Fieldwork 2002–3: Delta Survey, Memphis, Tell el-Amarna, Qasr Ibrim. *Journal of
         Egyptian Archaeology* 89: 1–25.

Wilson-Yang, Kristine M., and George Burns
  1982   Chemical and Physical Aspects of the Beni Hasan Tombs. *Journal of the American
         Research Center in Egypt* 19: 115–117.
  1987   The X-ray Photoelectron Spectroscopy of Ancient Murals in the Tombs at Beni
         Hasan, Egypt. *Canadian Journal of Chemistry* 65: 1058–1064.

Articulating Neo-Assyrian Imperialism at Tell Tayinat

Timothy P. Harrison

The interplay of ancient textual sources and material culture, and their propensity to produce contradictory or contested histories of the past, is well-worn intellectual ground in the study of ancient Near Eastern history. The list of examples is long and the battle lines well-defined, indeed in too many cases entrenched to the point of intransigence, and it is not uncommon to hear the view that examining them in tandem is an unproductive, even misguided, intellectual exercise. In this paper, I will attempt to counter this claim with an example that illustrates how texts and material culture, when examined together in context, can produce unexpected insight, and indeed need to be studied together, if we are to achieve more than a superficial understanding of the complex social and historical experiences of the cultures we study. In so doing, I hope to demonstrate that archaeological and epigraphic research can be complementary and can lead to more richly textured understandings of the past than the fragmented, often skewed, knowledge that typically results when they are conducted as independent scholarly enterprises.

Excavations at Tell Tayinat, located in the North Orontes Valley in southeast Turkey, have uncovered the remains of a Late Assyrian settlement, including an Assyrian governor's residence and, most recently, a temple and cache, or "collection", of cuneiform tablets dating to the late eighth–seventh centuries B.C. Historical sources attest that Tayinat (ancient Kunulua) was destroyed by the Neo-Assyrian empire-builder Tiglath-pileser III in 738 B.C. and then transformed into an Assyrian provincial capital equipped with its own governor and administration. The Tayinat excavations thus offer an opportunity to examine archaeological and epigraphic evidence from a cultural and historical context that coincided with the rise and fall of the Assyrian Empire, a pivotal period in the political history of the ancient Near East. They reveal a carefully crafted ritual landscape that both manifested and reinforced the ideology of the Assyrian imperial project.

Neo-Assyrian Imperialism

Studies of the Late Assyrian Period (ca. 911–612 B.C.) have begun to explore the material dimensions of Neo-Assyrian imperialism, particularly the physical and visual expressions of Neo-Assyrian imperial power, and to trace its articulation in the archaeological record (see Parker 2001, 2003). The genius of Assyrian imperial ideology is reflected in its manipulation of the material form, ranging from the standardization of architectural styles to the production of large-scale representational art forms such as wall reliefs and sculpture, and elite craft industries such as ceramic fineware production. Art historical studies in particular have emphasized the programmatic nature of Neo-Assyrian royal art and the remarkably sophisticated use of the written word to construct composite visual narratives that communicated ideological messages carefully tailored to each targeted audience, often representing very different constituencies (see, for example, Lumsden 2004; Porter 2000, 2001; Russell 1998, 1999; Winter 1981, 1997). The result was a visual symbolic landscape that projected the ideology of the imperial program in which the Assyrian king was portrayed as supreme ruler of the civilized world, imbued with divinely sanctioned authority as the earthly representative of the god Ashur.

The Assyrian empire achieved its mature form and organization in the latter decades of the eighth century B.C. (Postgate 1979, 1992). Over the course of the eighth century, Assyria's political institutions gradually were consolidated into more professionalized bureaucracies controlled directly by the king, marginalizing the traditional influence of the leading political families of Assyria. In 744 B.C., Tiglath-pileser III exploited this shifting power balance and seized control of an Assyria weakened by internal turmoil, precipitated in part by the growing independence of powerful provincial governors. Upon securing the throne, Tiglath-pileser resumed Assyrian territorial expansion to the west. In contrast to the practice of his predecessors, however, which had involved a combination of periodic military campaigns, the extraction of tribute, and the formation of local pro-Assyrian alliances, Tiglath-pileser embarked on a strategy of total conquest. The rulers of subjugated regions were deposed, their populations subjected to mass deportations, and their conquered lands reorganized as provinces administered directly by Assyria (Grayson 1991a; Hawkins 1982: 409).

Each province within the growing empire was administered by a governor (*bēl pīḫāti*), who was responsible for its civil administration, and in some instances also by a military officer (*šaknu*), who handled its military affairs. The governor's primary duties included the maintenance of the province's road networks and public infrastructure, the levying and collection of taxes, the distribution of land, and the preservation of law and order. He was also responsible for maintaining local supply bases to support the movement and campaigning of the Assyrian imperial army. Village inspectors (*rab ālāni*) formed a secondary administrative tier, monitoring the various districts (*qannu*) that made up the provincial hinterland and reporting on their activities to the governor. To ensure that the provincial administration functioned efficiently, and in keeping with the dictates of the central government, provincial governors were expected to submit regular reports to the king, and their administrations were audited by officials who answered directly to the royal court. The governor's residence or palace thus formed the operational hub of each province's administration, functionally replicating the role of the royal palace at the regional level (for further description of the Assyrian provincial system and administration, see Forrer 1920; Harrison 2005; Pečírková 1977, 1987; Radner 2006).

The Late Assyrian Settlement at Tell Tayinat

Tiglath-pileser III launched his assault on the Syro-Hittite states of northwest Syria in 743 B.C. (for a detailed account of the campaign, see Grayson 1991a: 74–76; Hawkins 1982: 410–411; Weippert 1982: 395–396). This was followed, in 738 B.C., by a second western campaign. As a pretext, Tiglath-pileser accused Tutammu, king of Unqi (^{kur}*un-qi*), of breaking his loyalty oath with Assyria. The consequences of this breach, we are told, were that Tutammu "disregarded his life," Kinalia (^{uru}*Ki-na-li-a*), his royal city, was captured, and many of its citizens deported (Tadmor 1994: Ann. 25: 3–12, Summ. Insc. 6: 20–21, 9: 26–27; Tadmor and Yamada 2011: 39–40 [Tiglath-pileser III 12], 115 [Tiglath-pileser III 46], 131 [Tiglath-pileser III 49]; see also Kessler 1975). Tiglath-pileser then reconstituted Kinalia as the capital of a new Assyrian province by the same name and installed a eunuch (*ša rēši*) as governor (*bēl pīḫāti*). Kinalia remained an Assyrian province until at least the mid-seventh century B.C. (Hawkins 1982: 425, 1983; Millard 1994: 51).

The earliest Assyrian references to the North Orontes Valley region date to the reign of Ashurnasirpal II (883–859 B.C.) and include a description of a campaign conducted ca. 870 B.C. to subdue a series of kingdoms in northwest Syria, including the Kingdom of Patina (^{kur}*pa-ti-na-a-a*) and its capital Kunulua (^{uru}*ku-nu-lu-a*) (see Grayson 1991b: 216–219, A.0.101.1 iii 55–92a; Harrison 2001). The account provides a detailed itinerary of the campaign route that clearly situates Patina in the Amuq Plain and its capital on the southern edge of the plain, just north of the Orontes River, leaving little doubt that Kunulua should be associated with the large Iron Age mound of Tell Tayinat (Figure 5.1). Later Assyrian sources, culminating with

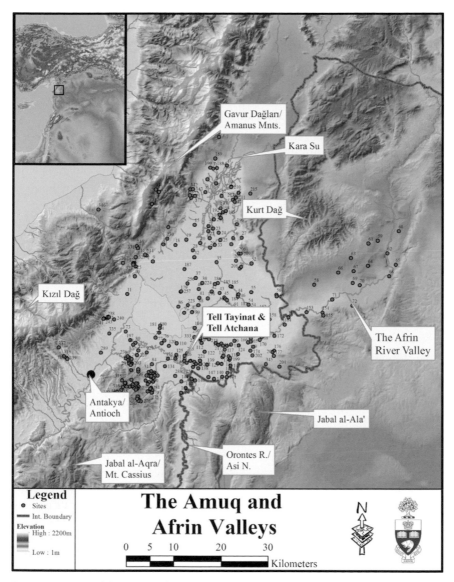

Figure 5.1. Map of the Amuq Plain showing the location of Tell Tayinat and other principal settlements (created by S. Batiuk).

Tiglath-pileser's conquest and annexation in 738 B.C., confirm the existence of a small kingdom, alternatively referred to as Patina or Unqi, its royal city, Kunulua, and its control of the North Orontes Valley and the surrounding region in the ninth and eighth centuries B.C.

The Syrian-Hittite Expedition Excavations

Large-scale excavations were conducted at Tell Tayinat by the University of Chicago over four field seasons between 1935 and 1938 as part of the Syrian-Hittite Expedition. Since the results of these excavations have been described in detail elsewhere (Batiuk et al. 2005; Haines 1971; Harrison 2001, 2005), I will only summarize them briefly here. The excavations focused primarily on the West Central Area of the upper mound (Figure 5.2), although excavation areas were also opened on the eastern and southern edges of the upper mound and in the lower settlement. In all, the Chicago excavations achieved large horizontal exposures of five distinct architectural phases, or Building Periods, dating to the Iron II and III periods (Amuq Phase O, ca. 950–550 B.C.), with the Third through Fifth Building Periods corresponding to the Late Assyrian settlement (Haines 1971: 64–66).

Renovations to a series of large palatial buildings in the West Central Area, part of the citadel of the Syro-Hittite capital, accounted for most of the activity assigned to the Third Building Period, which the excavators dated to the late eighth–early seventh century (ca. 720–680 B.C.; Haines 1971: 65–66). These renovations included the construction of an elevated rectangular structure (Platform XV) along the east side of the West Central Area complex (Haines 1971: 43–44). The Fourth Building Period witnessed further renovations to the buildings in this area but also significant new construction activity, in particular the construction of a sprawling palatial complex, Building IX, which was erected within a large raised enclosure, identified as Building X by the Chicago team (Haines 1971: 61, plates 88 and 110), in the southeast quadrant of the upper mound (Figure 5.2). Together, this enclosure and the buildings of the adjacent West Central Area formed what must have been a visually imposing citadel. To further enhance its grandeur and reinforce the message of Assyrian military strength, the citadel was approached from the east through a monumental gateway (Gateway VII; Haines 1971: 60, plates 87 and 110), flanked by carved stone orthostats depicting Assyrian assault troops carrying decapitated heads and treading on vanquished foes (see Harrison 2005: 26, figure 1). The Fifth Building Period comprised a series of isolated features confined to the highest parts of the upper mound and marked the terminal Iron Age occupational phase at Tayinat (Haines 1971: 66).

Despite its poor preservation, the design and layout of Building IX identify it as an Assyrian governor's palace (Haines 1971: 61–63, plates 84–85, 109; Harrison 2005: 26–29). Interestingly, and perhaps not surprisingly, the Chicago excavations running concurrently at the contemporary Assyrian capital of Khorsabad (ancient Dūr-Sharrukin) prompted their excavator,

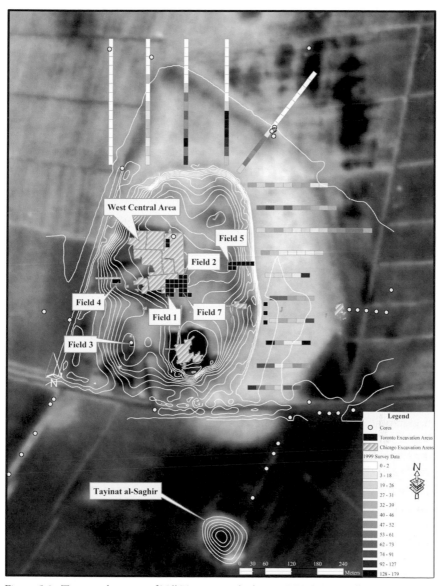

Figure 5.2. Topographic map of Tell Tayinat overlaid on a CORONA satellite image of the site, showing the principal excavation areas and a density distribution (number of sherds per 40m²) of surface pottery in the lower settlement (created by S.

Gordon Loud (1936), to generalize about the formulaic nature of Assyrian architectural planning during this period. Loud's preliminary observations were amplified in a subsequent typological study (Turner 1970), which also emphasized the highly standardized character of Late Assyrian palatial construction. In typical Mesopotamian fashion, the general layout of these palaces consisted of a series of central courtyards which neatly segregated the various functional units of the complex, including their administrative and residential areas. The Late Assyrian palace, however, was further distinguished by the liberal application of the "reception suite," which was used to delineate the principal audience hall or throne room, additional ceremonial areas, and the residential apartments of the palace. The modular replication of the reception suite is perhaps best exemplified in the royal palace and administrative buildings at Khorsabad. However, the pattern is repeated throughout the royal cities of Assyria and also occurs at numerous other Late Assyrian provincial centers (see further in Harrison 2005: 28–29).

The Syrian-Hittite Expedition also recovered a number of isolated finds, unfortunately almost all from poorly preserved contexts, which further hint at the Neo-Assyrian presence at Tell Tayinat. These included several Late Assyrian cuneiform inscriptions, both inscribed stone monument fragments and clay tablets, a number of cylinder seals, a variety of metal objects, including a composite metal roundel inscribed with the royal name of Tiglath-pileser III, and small quantities of the distinctive Assyrian Glazed and Palace Wares.

The Tayinat Archaeological Project Excavations

Targeted excavations were resumed at Tell Tayinat in 2004, following topographic and surface surveys of the site (see Batiuk et al. 2005), as part of the University of Toronto's Tayinat Archaeological Project (TAP), and they have since continued on an annual basis (for yearly reports, see Harrison 2006, 2007, 2008, 2009, 2010, 2011). The Late Assyrian settlement has been encountered in virtually every excavation area investigated to date. For the purposes of this paper, however, I will focus primarily on the results of the investigations in Field 2, located in the center of the upper mound, bordering the southeast corner of the Syrian-Hittite Expedition's West Central Area (Figure 5.2).

Excavations were initiated in Field 2 in 2005. The primary objective was to determine whether anything remained of Building I, the principal palatial building of the Syro-Hittite citadel (part of the Second Building Period complex), and then to excavate earlier levels associated with a large structure identified by the Syrian-Hittite Expedition as Building XIV, which they had assigned to their First Building Period, and thereby better establish the stratigraphic relationships between these two cultural phases. Excavations proceeded to uncover the foundations of a large monumental structure, very probably the southeast corner of Building XIV, but unfortunately no floors or occupational surfaces survived. Consequently, in 2008 the excavations were extended laterally to the east in the hopes that disturbance would be minimal in this area and the stratigraphic sequence therefore more intact. Subsequent excavation in 2008 and 2009 quite unexpectedly revealed the well-preserved remains of an Iron Age temple (Figure 5.3), which has been designated Building (or Temple) XVI (for a more thorough description, see Harrison and Osborne 2012).

The building was approached from the south by means of a wide stone staircase. The staircase led to a porch, which supported an ornately carved basalt column base set deeply into its floor. The column base is virtually identical in size, shape and design to column bases found in the entrance of the nearby Building I. However, its lowest carved register was largely hidden from view, obscured by a ceramic tile-paved surface, suggesting that an earlier floor, or phase, to the building still lies unexcavated below. The porch was separated from the central room of the building by two brick piers. A thick deposit of burnt brick, apparently collapse, covered much of the floor between the two piers. This material, in turn, sealed three heavily charred wooden beams, at least one of which appeared to have been set directly into the floor, and therefore probably served as a threshold for a doorway.

The floor of the central room, though badly burned, appeared to have been plastered. The room was largely devoid of pottery or organic remains, but it did produce a substantial quantity of bronze metal, including riveted pieces and several fragments of carved ivory inlay. Though heavily burned and damaged, these remains suggest the central room had been equipped with furniture or fixtures, perhaps for a door. The room also produced fragments of gold and silver foil, and the carved eye inlay from a human figure. A thick layer of collapsed burnt brick sealed the entire room, and in some places had fused with the brickwork of the temple's outer walls, vivid evidence of the intense conflagration that had consumed the structure.

A second set of piers separated the central room from a small back room, the inner sanctum or cella of the temple. This northern-most room contained an elevated, rectangular platform, or podium, that filled almost the entire room, and clearly represented a renovation to the original design and intended function of the room. The surface of the podium was paved with ceramic tiles, and accessed by steps in its two southern corners. A rectangular, free-standing structure, possibly an altar, stood on the eastern side of the platform. The room had also been burned intensely by fire, preserving a wealth of cultic paraphernalia found strewn across the podium and around its base, including gold, bronze and iron implements, libation vessels, and other ornately decorated ritual objects.

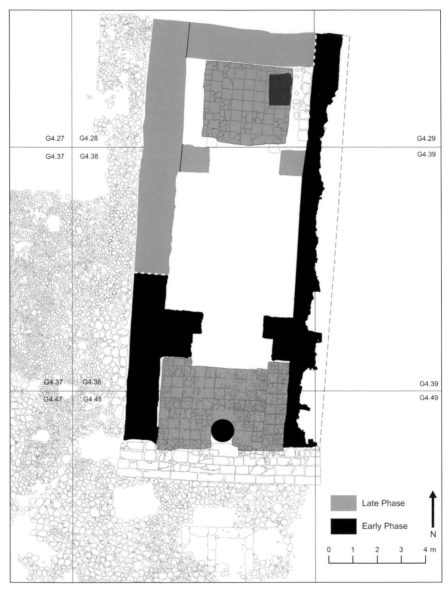

Figure 5.3. Plan of Building XVI (created by S. Batiuk and J. Osborne).

The surface debris also contained a concentration of fragmented cuneiform tablets written in Late Assyrian script. The analysis completed to date by the project epigrapher has identified 11 discrete tablets (Lauinger 2011). All except one (a docket impressed with a stamp seal) are literary or historical documents. The majority (seven, or possibly eight, out of the 10) appear to be *iqqur īpuš* texts, a Mesopotamian hemerological scholarly series that lists the favorable months for undertaking various activities, such as agricultural activities, the construction or demolition of a house, family events such as birth or marriage, medical procedures, and religious ceremonies (Labat 1965). The Tayinat *iqqur īpuš* tablets are arranged in tabular format, the least common of the various attested organizational schemes, with the x-axis listing a sequence of months, and the y-axis the relevant activities.

Of the two remaining tablets, one is a bilingual Sumerian-Akkadian lexical text (T-1921), and the other (T-1801), by far the largest tablet found in the room at 28 × 43 cm, records an oath imposed by the Assyrian king Esarhaddon on the governor of the province of Kinalia, most likely on the 18th day of the second month of the year 672 B.C., binding the governor in loyalty to Esarhaddon's chosen successor, Ashurbanipal (for a full transliteration, see Lauinger 2012). The text of the Tayinat "Oath Tablet" closely parallels the 674 lines of the so-called Vassal Treaties of Esarhaddon, eight copies of which were found in the throne room of a building adjacent to the Temple of Nabu in the Assyrian royal city of Nimrud (ancient Kalhu) during British excavations at the site in 1955 (Wiseman 1958).

The Building XVI discovery context fits well with evidence from the Assyrian heartland. At Nimrud, in addition to the vassal treaties, a collection of tablets was discovered in the Ezida (or Temple of Nabu) itself, in a room directly opposite Nabu's shrine (Postgate and Reade 1980: 309, figure 2). The Nabu Temple at Khorsabad, located adjacent to the Ziggurat Temple complex, contained a room with pigeonholes very likely for storing texts, which probably had been removed when the city was abandoned (Loud and Altman 1938: 46, 60–62, plates 19C, 24D). Tablets were also kept in the vicinity of the Temple of Nabu at Nineveh (Fincke 2004: 55). As the patron god of scribes and writing, the association of these tablet collections with Nabu is not surprising.

More intriguing, however, is the possibility that the vassal, or oath, treaties were deliberately kept in places which their oath-takers were expected to visit on a regular basis (Steymans 2006: 343). As Lauinger (2011: 10–12) has noted, the other tablets found with the Tayinat Oath Tablet help to establish the broader social context for this remarkable collection of cuneiform documents. In particular, two tablets (T-1923 and T-1927) preserve markings that suggest they belonged to a class of amulet-shaped tablets that primarily served a votive function (Reiner 1959). In addition, one of these tablets (T-1923) was pierced horizontally, as was also the Oath Tablet, indicating that both – and possibly the others – were intended to be suspended or mounted. In other words, the tablets recovered from the inner sanctum of Building XVI were intentionally designed for exhibition and display and,

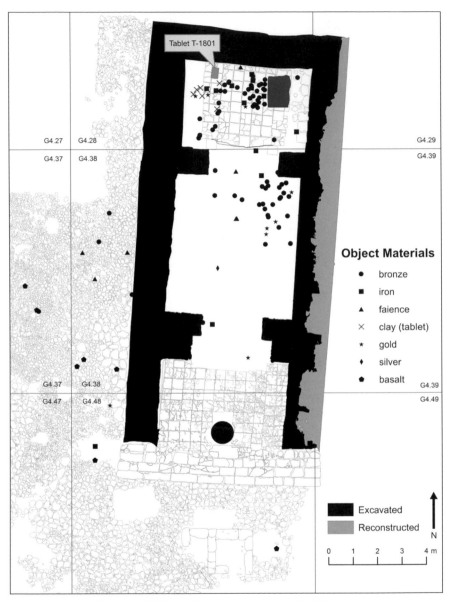

Figure 5.4. Plan of Building XVI showing the distribution of artifacts and tablets in its inner sanctum (created by S. Batiuk and J. Osborne).

therefore, were not part of an archive, a literary collection, or a library as such. Their provenance, distributed across the western part of the elevated podium, facing an altar-like installation positioned on the podium's eastern

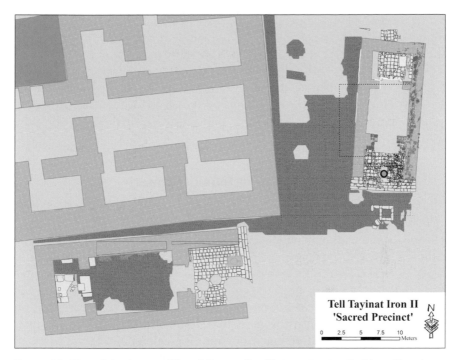

Figure 5.5. Plan of the Assyrian "Sacred Precinct" at Tayinat, showing Buildings II and
          XVI (created by S. Batiuk).

side (Figure 5.4), provides further evidence of their cultic function. Moreover,
the position and condition of the Oath Tablet, which exhibits a break pattern
that radiates out from an initial contact point along its base, suggests that
the tablet was found precisely where it fell when the temple was destroyed.
The tablet was uncovered lying face down on the podium, with its back (or
reverse) facing up, and had clearly fallen forward during the conflagration
that engulfed the building.

Thus far, the excavations of Building XVI have only uncovered its
terminal phase; its earlier construction history and dating therefore remain
unclear. Nevertheless, the distinctive architectural style and design it shares
with the nearby Building II, excavated by the Syrian-Hittite Expedition
(see Haines 1971: 53–55, plates 80–81, 100B, 103), including the evidence
of similar renovations and associated material culture, indicate that both
temples likely formed part of a larger Assyrian religious complex or "sacred
precinct" (Figure 5.5), possibly dedicated to the cult of Nabu and his female
partner, Tašmetu, and the scene of loyalty oath rituals as part of an annual
akitu ceremony (Lauinger 2013: 111–113). Their perpendicular arrangement,

facing a shared central courtyard, replicates a well-established Assyrian double temple tradition best exemplified by the similarly aligned twin temples in the Ziggurat complex on the citadel at Khorsabad. In light of this similarity, it is tempting to speculate that Platform XV, assigned by the Syrian-Hittite Expedition to this period, might have served as an elevated platform for an Assyrian cultic monument, perhaps even a small ziggurat-like structure, situated immediately to the north of Building XVI, further mirroring the layout at Khorsabad.

Landscapes of Imperial Power

The construction of royal citadels, equipped with sprawling palaces lined with elaborately carved orthostats and colossal stone figures, ornately decorated religious monuments and buildings, and vast administrative complexes, was a defining characteristic of the Late Assyrian period. As visual manifestations of Assyrian royal authority, these imposing regal centers represented "landscapes" of power that facilitated both the consolidation of royal authority and the expansion of the Assyrian Empire during this period. The standardization of Assyrian palatial construction in the eighth century, and its modular replication at provincial centers throughout the empire during the reigns of Tiglath-pileser III and his successors, should, therefore, be seen not only as evidence of Assyrian bureaucratic ingenuity and efficiency but also as the physical embodiment of Assyrian imperial ideology.

In this context, the archaeological remains preserved at Tell Tayinat offer a revealing glimpse into the imperial administrative apparatus Tiglath-pileser and his successors installed. As we have seen, this included the construction of standardized palatial and religious architecture, large-scale representational art forms such as wall reliefs and sculpture, and the consumption of elite craft industries such as ceramic fineware production. Moreover, the utilization of these media was not haphazard, but carefully calibrated to maximize their effect on their intended audiences. As Lauinger (2011) has demonstrated in his analysis of the cuneiform tablets found in Building XVI, this extended to the written form as well, with these remarkable documents clearly intended as display objects within the inner sanctum of the temple. In effect, the double temple complex or sacred precinct at Tayinat functioned as a stage for enacting the rituals and theater of divine sanction, with the Oath Tablet and its associated cultic objects serving as both written and visual reminders of the community's sworn loyalty to the Assyrian king, the divinely appointed ruler of the world.

Building XVI, with its displayed tablets and cultic paraphernalia, also illustrates why context is so important, and why textual and material cultural evidence need to be examined together, rather than as fragmented, disembedded sources of information about the past. Viewed in isolation, the Oath Tablet preserves the largely formulaic language of a document commemorating a previously known and recorded historical event, and as such, likely would have been identified as an archival document. When understood within its intended social context, however, the tablet and its message are transformed, physically articulating Assyrian imperial authority, cloaked in divine sanction and religious ritual.

Acknowledgments

The Tayinat Archaeological Project has received research grants from the Social Sciences and Humanities Research Council of Canada (SSHRCC), the Institute for Aegean Prehistory (INSTAP), the Brennan Foundation, and the University of Toronto, for which we are deeply grateful. I wish also to thank the Directorate of Cultural Heritage and Museums of Turkey, which has graciously awarded the research permits necessary to conduct each of our excavation seasons, the landowners who have generously permitted us to work on their land, and the Reyhanlı Residential School and staff for their warm hospitality throughout our stay. Finally, each season's successful results would not have been possible without the dedicated contribution of all our project staff. This paper is a product of their collective team effort.

References

Batiuk, Stephen, Timothy P. Harrison, and Laurence Pavlish
   2005   The Taʻyinat Survey, 1999–2002. In *The Amuq Valley Regional Projects. Vol. I: Surveys in the Plain of Antioch and Orontes Delta, Turkey, 1995–2002*, edited by K. Aslıhan Yener, pp. 171–192. Oriental Institute Publications Vol. 131. Oriental Institute of the University of Chicago, Chicago.

Fincke, Jeanette C.
   2004   The British Museum's Ashurbanipal Library Project. *Iraq* 66: 55–60.

Forrer, Emilio O.
   1920   *Die Provinzeinteilung des assyrischen Reiches*. J.C. Hinrichs'sche Buchhandlung, Leipzig.

Grayson, A. Kirk
   1991a   Assyria: Tiglath-pileser III to Sargon II (744–705 B.C.). In *The Cambridge Ancient History, Vol. 3/2: The Assyrian and Babylonian Empires and other States of the Near East, from the Eighth to the Sixth Centuries B.C.*, edited by John Boardman, I.E.S. Edwards, N.G.L. Hammond, E. Sollberger, and C.B.F. Walker, pp. 71–102. Cambridge University Press, New York.

1991b *Assyrian Rulers of the Early First Millennium B.C., I (1114–859 B.C.).* The Royal Inscriptions of Mesopotamia, Assyrian Periods, Vol. 2. University of Toronto Press, Toronto.

Haines, Richard C.

1971 *Excavations in the Plain of Antioch II: The Structural Remains of the Later Phases: Chatal Hüyük, Tell al-Judaidah, and Tell Ta'yinat.* Oriental Institute Publications Vol. 92. University of Chicago Press, Chicago.

Harrison, Timothy P.

2001 Tell Ta'yinat and the Kingdom of Unqi. In *The World of the Aramaeans II: Studies in History and Archaeology in Honour of Paul-Eugene Dion,* edited by P.M. Michèle Daviau, John W. Wevers, and Michael Weigl, pp. 115–132. Journal for the Study of the Old Testament Supplement Vol. 325. Sheffield Academic Press, Sheffield.

2005 The Neo-Assyrian Governor's Residence at Tell Ta'yinat. *Bulletin of the Canadian Society for Mesopotamian Studies* 40: 23–33.

2006 2004 Yılı Tayinat Höyük Kazıları. *Kazı Sonuçları Toplantısı* 27: 353–362.

2007 Neo-Hittites in the North Orontes Valley: Recent Investigations at Tell Ta'yinat. *Journal of the Canadian Society for Mesopotamian Studies* 2: 59–68.

2008 Tayinat Höyük Kazıları. *Kazı Sonuçları Toplantısı* 29: 285–298.

2009 Tayinat Höyük Kazıları, 2006–2007. *Kazı Sonuçları Toplantısı* 30(2): 503–520.

2010 Tayinat Höyük Kazıları, 2008. *Kazı Sonuçları Toplantısı* 31(3): 491–504.

2011 Tayinat Höyük Kazıları, 2009. *Kazı Sonuçları Toplantısı* 32(3): 368–384.

Harrison, Timothy P., and James F. Osborne

2012 Building XVI and the Neo-Assyrian Sacred Precinct at Tell Tayinat. *Journal of Cuneiform Studies* 64: 125–143.

Hawkins, J. David

1982 The Neo-Hittite States in Syria and Anatolia. In *The Cambridge Ancient History, Vol. 3(2): The Prehistory of the Balkans, the Middle East and the Aegean World, Tenth to Eighth Centuries B.C.,* edited by John Boardman, I.E.S. Edwards, N.G.L. Hammond, and E. Sollberger, pp. 372–441. Cambridge University Press, New York.

1983 Kullani(a). *Reallexikon der Assyriologie und Vorderasiatischen Archäologie* 6: 305–306.

Kessler, Karlheinz

1975 Die Anzahl der assyrischen Provinzen des Jahres 738 v. Chr. in Nordsyrien. *Die Welt des Orients* 8: 49–63.

Lauinger, Jacob

2011 Some Preliminary Thoughts on the Tablet Collection in Building XVI from Tell Tayinat. *Journal of the Canadian Society for Mesopotamian Studies* 6: 5–14.

2012 Esarhaddon's Succession Treaty at Tell Tayinat: Text and Commentary. *Journal of Cuneiform Studies* 64: 87–123.

2013 The Neo-Assyrian *adê*: Treaty, Oath, or Something Else? *Zeitschrift für Altorientalische und Biblische Rechtsgeschichte* 19: 99–115.

Labat, René

1965   *Un calandrier babylonien des travaux des signes et des mois (séries iqqur îpuš)*. Librairie Honoré Champion, Paris.

Loud, Gordon

1936   An Architectural Formula for Assyrian Planning Based on the Results of Excavations at Khorsabad. *Revue d'assyriologie* 33: 153–160.

Loud, Gordon, and Charles B. Altman

1938   *Khorsabad, Part II: The Citadel and the Town*. Oriental Institute Publications Vol. 40. University of Chicago Press, Chicago.

Lumsden, Stephen

2004   Narrative Art and Empire: The Throneroom of Aššurnasirpal II. In *Assyria and Beyond: Studies Presented to Mogens Trolle Larsen*, edited by Jan G. Dercksen, pp. 359–385. Nederlands Instituut voor het Nabije Oosten, Leiden.

Millard, Alan R.

1994   *The Eponyms of the Assyrian Empire 910–612 B.C.* State Archives of Assyria Studies Vol. 2. Helsinki University Press, Helsinki.

Parker, Bradley J.

2001   *The Mechanics of Empire: The Northern Frontier of Assyria as a Case Study in Imperial Dynamics*. Helsinki University Press, Helsinki.

2003   Archaeological Manifestations of Empire: Assyria's Imprint on Southeastern Anatolia. *American Journal of Archaeology* 107: 525–557.

Pečírková, Jana

1977   The Administrative Organization of the Neo-Assyrian Empire. *Archiv orientální* 45: 211–228.

1987   The Administrative Methods of Assyrian Imperialism. *Archiv orientální* 55: 162–175.

Porter, Barbara N.

2000   Assyrian Propaganda for the West: Esarhaddon's Stelae for Til Barsip and Sam'al. In *Essays on Syria in the Iron Age*, edited by Guy Bunnens, pp. 143–176. Ancient Near Eastern Studies Supplement Vol. 7. Peeters Press, Leuven.

2001   The Importance of Place: Esarhaddon's Stelae at Til Barsip and Sam'al. In *Historiography in the Cuneiform World: Proceedings of the XLVᵉ Rencontre Assyriologique Internationale*, edited by Tzvi Abusch, Paul-Alain Beaulieu, John Huehnergard, Peter Machinist, and Piotr Steinkeller, pp. 373–390. CDL Press, Bethesda, Maryland.

Postgate, J. Nicholas

1979   The Economic Structure of the Assyrian Empire. In *Power and Propaganda: A Symposium on Ancient Empires*, edited by Mogens Trolle Larsen, pp. 193–221. Mesopotamia: Copenhagen Studies in Assyriology Vol. 7. Akademisk Forlag, Copenhagen.

1992   The Land of Assur and the Yoke of Assur. *World Archaeology* 23: 247–263.

Postgate, J. Nicholas, and Julian E. Reade

1980   Kalhu. *Reallexikon der Assyriologie und Vorderasiatischen Archäologie* 5: 303–323.

Radner, Karen

2006   Provinz. C. Assyrien. *Reallexikon der Assyriologie und Vorderasiatischen Archäologie* 11: 42–68.

Reiner, Erica

 1959   Plague Amulets and House Blessings. *Journal of Near Eastern Studies* 19: 148–155.

Russell, John M.

 1998   The Program of the Palace of Assurnasirpal II at Nimrud: Issues in the Research and Presentation of Assyrian Art. *American Journal of Archaeology* 102: 655–715.

 1999   *The Writing on the Wall: Studies in the Architectural Context of Late Assyrian Palace Inscriptions.* Mesopotamian Civilizations Vol. 9. Eisenbrauns, Winona Lake, Indiana.

Steymans, Han Ulrich

 2006   Die literarische und historische Bedeutung der Thronfolgevereidigung Asarhaddons. In *Die deuteronomistischen Geschichtswerke: Redaktions- und religionsgeschichtliche Perspektiven zur "Deuteronomismus" -Diskussion in Tora und Vorderen Propheten,* edited by Markus Witte, Konrad Schmid, Doris Prechel, and Jan Christian Gertz, pp. 331–349. Beihefte zur Zeitschrift für die alttestamentliche Wissenschaft Vol. 365. W. de Gruyter, Berlin.

Tadmor, Hayim

 1994   *The Inscriptions of Tiglath-Pileser III King of Assyria.* Israel Academy of Sciences and Humanities, Jerusalem.

Tadmor, Hayim, and Shigeo Yamada

 2011   *The Royal Inscriptions of Tiglath-pileser III (744–727 B.C.) and Shalmaneser V (726–722 B.C.), Kings of Assyria.* The Royal Inscriptions of the Neo-Assyrian Period Vol. 1. Eisenbrauns, Winona Lake, Indiana.

Turner, Geoffrey

 1970   The State Apartments of Late Assyrian Palaces. *Iraq* 32: 177–213.

Weippert, Manfred

 1982   Zur Syrienpolitik Tiglathpilesers III. In *Mesopotamien und seine Nachbarn,* edited by Hans-Jörg Nissen and Johannes Renger, pp. 395–408. 2 Vols. Dietrich Reimer, Berlin.

Winter, Irene J.

 1981   Royal Rhetoric and the Development of Historical Narrative in Neo-Assyrian Reliefs. *Studies in Visual Communication* 7(2): 2–38.

 1997   Art *in* Empire: The Royal Image and the Visual Dimensions of Assyrian Ideology. In *Assyria 1995: Proceedings of the 10th Anniversary Symposium of the Neo-Assyrian Text Corpus Project,* edited by Simo Parpola and Robert M. Whiting, pp. 359–381. Helsinki University Press, Helsinki.

Wiseman, Donald J.

 1958   The Vassal-Treaties of Esarhaddon. *Iraq* 20: 1–99.

The Archaeology of Mesopotamian Extispicy: Modeling Divination in the Old Babylonian Period

Matthew T. Rutz

Rediscovering Mesopotamia: Divination and Models

Beginning in the eighteenth and nineteenth centuries, European explorers poking around at the eastern margins of the Ottoman Empire gradually uncovered the material remains of Mesopotamia's ancient past (André-Salvini 1999; Kuklick 1996; Larsen 1996; Trümpler 2008). Although ancient Mesopotamian scripts and languages had not been known for more than 1500 years, there was a long living memory of associating divination with the ancient inhabitants of the land between the Tigris and Euphrates Rivers. Ancient texts passed down through the received manuscript traditions of the Bible and classical sources painted vague pictures of Chaldean astrologers looking at the night sky and Babylonian kings examining a sheep's liver for signs to read and interpret (Meyer 1993a; Rochberg-Halton 1988: 2–7). However, with the decipherment of the cuneiform (or wedge-shaped) script just over 150 years ago, it became possible to exploit native Mesopotamian sources to gain insights into a vast number of topics of significance, not least among them the ancient meaning, theory, and practice of divination. What has come to light is a massive reservoir of evidence, thousands of clay tablets bearing cuneiform inscriptions in various languages, primarily the language isolate Sumerian and Semitic Akkadian – though it must be said that only a small but vitally important fraction of this corpus pertains to divination. The field devoted to the study of the ancient Mesopotamian text corpus as a whole, Assyriology, would never have existed but for the antiquarian curiosity that eventually ushered in archaeology as a mode of inquiry about the past. By extension, without the benefit of archaeology, scholars investigating Mesopotamia would still know only what can be gleaned from canonical texts transmitted via various intermediaries to the

religious communities and academies of the Middle East, Europe, and the
Americas. The authors of Biblical, Qur'anic, and classical texts were interested
in ancient Mesopotamia and its people in only a peripheral way. However,
archaeological investigations in the Near East have made it possible to recover
and prioritize ancient evidence in the service of nuanced reconstructions of
ancient Mesopotamia in all its historical and cultural complexity.

Divination was one facet of that complex in Mesopotamia's early
historical periods. This elaborate system of knowledge claimed the ability
to read and interpret the signs putatively encoded by the gods in the fabric
of the phenomenal world: the entrails of a sheep, earthquakes, happenings
in the sky, facets of the urban landscape and city life, the days in the
calendar, medical symptoms, the appearance of the human body as well as
birth defects, human sexual habits, dreams, and myriad other domains of
experience (Annus 2010; Koch 2011; Maul 2003). In the present article I will
look at one type of divination in particular, extispicy, the practice of reading
and interpreting the entrails of a sacrificial animal, known already from the
Bible and identified early on in cuneiform tablets in the 1870s (Jeyes 1989;
Koch-Westenholz 2000, 2002; Koch 2005; Leiderer 1990; Meyer 1987;
Robson 2011; Starr 1990).

The study of divination in ancient Mesopotamia still labors under the
heavy burden of its early efforts in the nineteenth century. I would argue that
this is due in large part to how ancient textual data were first acquired and
interpreted: much of the so-called archaeological activity in the nineteenth
century bore little resemblance to scientific archaeology, even by the emerging
standards of the day (Trigger 2006). For example, in the apologetic chronicle
of his travels in Egypt and Mesopotamia on behalf of the British Museum
from 1886 to 1913, E. Wallis Budge recounts the following anecdote about
his time in Baghdad in 1889:

> During Mr H. Rassam's excavations on that site [= Tell Abu Habbah, ancient
> Sippar-Yaḥrurum] his workmen discovered various chambers filled with sun-dried
> tablets, in number "between forty and fifty thousand." Had these tablets been
> taken out and dried slowly in the sun all might have been brought unbroken
> to England, but the natives baked them in the fire with the terrible result that
> they either cracked in pieces or their inscribed surfaces flaked off. Several natives
> bought large quantities of these fragments at Abû Ḥabbah, and hoped to sell
> them, and were greatly disappointed when they found they could not do so. In
> one house I found a large collection containing many valuable tablets, which
> was offered to me on behalf of a highly-placed Baghdâd official... Besides these
> there was an odd object of baked clay, the like of which I had never seen. Its
> owner attached a high value to it, because he had shown it to a French savant in
> Baghdâd, who told him that it was an instrument used by the ancient Babylonian

Figure 6.1.   Old Babylonian liver model (BM 92668 top, ca. 14.6 × 14.6 cm; Robson and
Horry 2011), early second millennium B.C., allegedly from Sippar (Tell Abu
Habbah) © Trustees of the British Museum.

astronomers in making their calculations and forecasts, and who offered him a
comparatively large sum of money for it. I did not share the opinion of the savant,
although the inscriptions upon the object, which were arranged in squares, looked
like tables of calculations. I feared at first that the object might be a forgery, for
I had seen several forgeries that had been made by the Jews at Kâẓimên and they
were very cleverly made, but after examining it for two days I felt sure that it was
genuine, and as I knew it to be unique I decided to acquire it with the rest of
the collection. Its shape and general appearance seemed strangely familiar to me,
and at length I remembered that it closely resembled the plaster cast of a sheep's
liver ... from a bronze original inscribed in Etruscan, which had been found near
Piacenza in 1877 ... The more I thought about it the more I became convinced
that the object from Abû Ḥabbah was the model of a sheep's liver which had
been used for purposes of divination, and I bought the whole collection and made
arrangements to take it with me to London [Budge 1920: 124–125].

Indeed, the inscribed liver model that Budge correctly identified and
purchased is currently held in the collection of the British Museum in
London (Figure 6.1; Leichty et al. 1988: 177).

Several points of interest are packed into Budge's narrative: the plunder of archaeological sites for objects, including tablets; the competition and cooperation among "natives," local officials, and expatriates over the ownership and interpretation of antiquities; the struggle to find suitable comparanda to assimilate a new and at that time unique datum; the awareness of forgeries in circulation; and, finally, the concern with the significance of provenience, largely though not solely in the service of authentication. Refuting the interpretation of the unnamed "French savant" in Baghdad does double duty. First, Budge shrugs off one learned classical association, namely, that of the Chaldean astronomer, in favor of another, that of the Etruscan *haruspex*, specifically as represented by the bronze liver model found by a farmer in his field near Piacenza, Italy (van der Meer 1987: 5; cf. Meyer 1985). Second, by the time Budge's account was published in 1920 the geopolitical landscape had changed significantly since 1889. The Ottoman Empire had ceased to exist, and Britain and France were actively staking out positions in the newly minted political geography of the post-war Near East, with Britain emerging as the major player in what would soon come to be Iraq (Fromkin 1989). Budge was also keenly aware of, and anxious about, the culture of fakes and forgeries. By one interested reckoning,

> [f]our-fifths of all the antiquities offered for sale in Bagdad are spurious... One would suppose that Bagdad, surrounded as it is by the ruins of the ancient Babylonian cities, would have enough genuine antiquities without producing imitations" [Banks 1904: 60].

It is here that the issue of provenience comes into play for Budge. Particularly worthy of note is the move by which Budge turns "an odd object of baked clay" he had spotted "in a house" into "the object from Abû Ḥabbah." The results of this legerdemain have been far reaching: the clay model he bought is frequently referred to as the "Sippar" model, Sippar being the ancient name of the site Tell Abu Habbah.

Such attributions of provenience are representative of habits of thought that are only gradually being dislodged in the field of Assyriology, and the acquisition of the clay liver model in nineteenth-century Baghdad highlights the problem of "modeling divination" in the title of this chapter. One type of model is simply the corpus of ancient representations made out of clay, physical, two- and three-dimensional models of the internal organs of a sacrificial animal: the liver, lungs, spleen, and coils of the colon. The second type of model is more familiar: modern scholars' interpretive models, in this case, models of the theory, practice, and significance of extispicy in its various ancient contexts. Both the first and second types of models are schemes of representation that are at once descriptive and explanatory, though the descriptive and explanatory aims of each type of model are naturally as different as the ancient and modern modes of inquiry that inform them. Both types of models present specific opportunities and problems that are inextricably connected with the topic of archaeology and the study of the ancient textual record in Mesopotamia in general and Mesopotamian divination in particular.

Mesopotamian Extispicy in the Old Babylonian Period

Several types of evidence are available for the study of ancient Mesopotamian divination, such as the texts, spaces, and material culture that can be associated with the practice and its practitioners. Omen texts themselves have understandably occupied a central place in scholars' discussions of Mesopotamian divination since the nineteenth century, so it is worthwhile touching on what we know about each textual genre, despite the limitations of a purely genre-centered approach. In order to highlight some of those limitations, I would also like to explore how scholars have dealt with or, just as often, side-stepped the issue of situating the textual material in the archaeological record. My discussion will focus primarily on the early second millennium B.C., also known as the Middle Bronze Age, Old Babylonian, or Amorrite period in southern Mesopotamia. This politically fragmented era in Babylonia's history witnessed a dynamic of competition, cooperation, and conflict among various city-states such as Isin, Larsa, Eshnunna, and Babylon. The Old Babylonian period is perhaps most well known for the exploits of Hammurapi, whose famous stele and law collection are practically synonymous with ancient Mesopotamia itself, and the end of the First Dynasty of Babylon in the mid-second millennium is an important (if controversial) terminus in the absolute chronology of ancient Mesopotamia. The Old Babylonian period is particularly significant for the study of extispicy in Mesopotamia because it is during this period that the three major textual genres of divination are all represented for the first time (Richardson 2010). It is no coincidence that during this era major changes were taking place in the cuneiform writing system itself (Veldhuis 2011). Professional diviners also make an appearance on the political scene in the early second millennium, acting as political and military advisors, spies, and diplomats in the king's service (Charpin 2011). Indeed Old Babylonian diviners, Akkadian *bârûm*, literally "seers" or "inspectors," should not be thought of as "priests" or cultic functionaries associated with large urban religious institutions. A letter from the diviner Erib-Sin to the king of Mari illustrates some of the dynamics at work:

The troops are well. I made extispicies for the well-being of the two hundred
[troops] who are going with Meptum [on the route] from Yabliya to Qaṣa for
fifteen days, and my extispicies were sound. The intestines were bloated in my
verification. Dada [made extispicies] for the well-being of two hundred troops
for [...] In his verification the stomach was bruised like a ... on the right. I
baked (aṣrup) those extispicies and sealed them in a box and sent (it) to my lord
[Heimpel 2003: 213–214; cf. Durand 1988: 262–263, no. 98].

The "baking" of the results of extispicy is known from a similar context in
at least one other letter, and opinion is still divided about how to interpret
this practice (Durand 1988: 52–53). One possibility is to see it as an example
of the language used to describe the manufacture of a liver model (Heimpel
2003: 173–174), though another recent view is that this is a description of
the actual organs themselves being soaked in some preservative (Glassner
2005: 277).

There are only oblique indicators of the practice of divination in the third
millennium written record: lists of professions that include diviners; year names
that describe the appointment of cultic officials "by means of a goat"; and
laconic literary accounts (Richardson 2010). The early second millennium B.C.
saw the first clear textual evidence for the theory and practice of extispicy, and
this documentation persisted in various guises down to the end of cuneiform
tradition in the first century A.D. (Koch 2005; Robson 2011). In that time
span, the most significant sources of evidence about ancient Mesopotamian
extispicy are collections or compendia of omens, omen reports and queries,
and models of the organs themselves, though various letters, prayers, rituals,
and literary narratives also contribute to the overall picture.

I now briefly describe some of the principles of extispicy and then look
at each major type of evidence from Mesopotamia in the Old Babylonian
period, i.e., compendia, reports, and models. I conclude with a discussion
of the archaeological distribution of each data set, considering both local
contexts and regional patterns, with an eye toward establishing what an
archaeology of Mesopotamian extispicy might achieve.

Divination by Extispicy: The Textual Sources

Divination by extispicy is predicated on the notion that divine signals are
literally "written" on a sacrificial animal's internal organs. From the second
millennium on, this animal was usually a sheep. The major organs inspected
by Mesopotamian diviners included the lungs, heart, and liver, but the
liver enjoyed a particular prestige in this system, and a detailed procedure
and nomenclature were developed for describing its features (Jeyes 1988;
Koch-Westenholz 2000; Koch 2005). This descriptive technical jargon and

Figure 6.2. Old Babylonian omen compendium (BM 96948 obverse, ca. 19.7 × 12.1 cm;
Jeyes 1989: 156–170, plates 17–18, no. 14), early second millennium B.C.,
allegedly from Sippar (Tell Abu Habbah) © Trustees of the British Museum.

a complementary set of conventions for its visual representation inform all
three major classes of data, compendia, reports, and models.

Written collections of omens, commonly called "compendia," encode
statements about the appearance of various features on the organs, describing
their presence or absence, their color, their shape, and their arrangement
(Durand 1988: 63–68; Kraus 1987; Jeyes 1989: 2–4, 7–8; Oshima 2011).
Compositions of this kind were first written down and organized in the Old
Babylonian period (Glassner 2009). Like other Mesopotamian intellectual

products, omen compendia take the form of lists (Figure 6.2). In this case, lists of propositions are structured "If P: then Q," where the so-called protasis P supplies a description of some feature of the internal organs, and the so-called apodosis Q gives its correlate. In the Old Babylonian period this correlate ("Q") is usually (though not always) some event in the world of state politics or the social world, events that were thought to be somehow signaled by the organs' features (Jeyes 1989; Richardson 2010). While it may be tempting to view omen statements as causal or specifically predictive, recent work on the logical and grammatical structure of the omen collections suggests that these texts are best seen as schemes of association, correlation (i.e., P implies Q), or interpretation (i.e., the meaning of P is Q) in which the production of meaning was not so narrowly construed (Cohen 2010; Rochberg 2010). The recurrence of a past event, textually encoded in a generalized way, is "presented," that is, exhibited but also made relevant to the present, with some positive or negative correlate.

A number of omen compendia highlight the ancient perception of the liver as a tablet on which the gods literally wrote text using cuneiform signs. For example, a text from the early second millennium states: "If (the feature called) the View is like (the cuneiform sign) BAD, the man's wife will have (illicit) sexual intercourse" (Frahm 2010: 100). A similar example from the first millennium reads: "If the coils of the colon are like (the cuneiform sign) AN, the army of the prince will have no rival" (Frahm 2010: 111). Although these texts are descriptive and may leave the impression that they are based on primary observations, they are also thoroughly generalized. Thus, they are at least as theoretical as empirical in character.

In contrast to the general character of the compendia, the texts referred to as omen reports are tied directly to a specific social moment: a mundane query, written or unwritten, followed by the slaughter of an animal and the diviner's examination and listing of the features of the exta he observed, including both normal and abnormal configurations (Koch-Westenholz 2002; Richardson 2007). For example, the following is an excerpt from an omen report dated to Ammi-ṣaduqa's tenth year on the throne of Babylon (month XII/day 21), the penultimate king of the First Dynasty of Babylon:

> One sheep for the performance of extispicy for the god Marduk, performed concerning an undertaking in Addaru (month XII). The extispicy: It has a Presence, it has a Path, it has a Strength, it has a Well-being. ... There are 14 Coils of the colon; they protrude. ... Concerning the query which was made, the extispicies indicate delay [Koch-Westenholz 2002: 133–134].

The text is dated to the same month as the one mentioned in the query, the twelfth and last month of the standard Babylonian calendar. The procedure

Figure 6.3. Old Babylonian omen report (BM 26594 obverse, ca. 4.2 × 4.5 × 2.0 cm; Koch-Westenholz 2002: 132, no. 3; Richardson 2002: 239–241, no. 3), early second millennium B.C., allegedly from Sippar (Tell Abu Habbah) © Trustees of the British Museum.

seems to have been that the diviner would tally up the positive and negative features found on the exta, with the result that the extispicy was either positive, negative, or indeterminate requiring another round (Veldhuis 2006). Interestingly, the tablets on which omen reports were written are generally non-descript (Figure 6.3). Whereas the structural organizing principles of the compendia and the representational likeness of the models stand out as distinctive features, the omen reports could, at first glance, easily be classified as administrative records. Tellingly a handful of omen reports are found embedded within letters, most famously in a number of letters to the last king of Mari on the Euphrates (Koch-Westenholz 2002: 131). Extispicy reports are also known from the latter half of the second millennium as well as, perhaps most famously, in the Neo-Assyrian period, when they attest to the diviners' roles in court life and state politics (Kraus 1985; Robson 2011; Starr 1990).

The last major sources of evidence are the models themselves. Most of the models of the organs are attested in the Near East in the second millennium B.C., though a handful are known from the first millennium as well (Meyer 1987; cf. Koch 2005). The clay models mimic physical things in the world (i.e., sheep and their organs: liver, lungs, spleen, and colon), represented in the round with incised marks as well as applied features. Their precise referent must have been obvious to anyone with even a passing practical acquaintance with a sheep's internal anatomy (Leiderer 1990), and here it is worth recalling Budge's first puzzled remarks quoted above. From the beginning of the second millennium, these models were both inscribed (first only in Akkadian, later on also in Hittite in Anatolia and Ugaritic in coastal Syria) and uninscribed, which implies at least two distinct crafts at work in the objects' production: the craft of fabricating the model and the craft of inscribing it, both of which would have been concerned with the proper or normative representation and "reading" of the features. Some inscriptions refer to the physical features represented on the model, pointing to a physical moment in a ritualized social context that was isolated and frozen, perhaps as an idealized case, for example, the perforations on the "Sippar" liver model (Figure 6.1; Jeyes 1989: 84; Robson and Horry 2011). Other inscriptions also point away from the model, invoking historical episodes from the past as they were imagined centuries later. For example, an early liver model from Mari reads "Omen (lit. liver) of the city of Kish, concerning Sargon (I)," – that is, Sargon the Great of Akkad, a southern Mesopotamian king whose mid-third millennium empire became something of a template for later petty dynasts with larger political ambitions (Meyer 1987: 190–191; Rutten 1938). Such inscriptions help to embed an anatomical feature or constellation of features on the liver within a nexus of cultural meanings and thereby answer the question of why a mark or configuration of the liver was good or bad, that is, positive or negative in the system as it operated in the omen reports.

In some cases the physical form of the model and text of the inscription are not related in such obvious ways. For example, in a house at the site of Tell es-Sib in the Diyala River valley, salvage excavations uncovered a model that mentions Dadusha, king of Eshnunna, a contemporary of Hammurapi of Babylon (Meyer 2003). The text is broken, but what can be deciphered reads as follows:

> The belly was dark on the left. The heart was dark on the left. There were fourteen loops of the colon. "(If) the breastbone is ... on the right, from/at the left (of the) ...: victory is mine." By the hands of (?) ..., the diviner, son of... . Dadusha in [...] and the (extispicy) ritual. The entrails [...] ... [...] The day of the new moon that Dadusha [ascended] the throne [...] Šimurrum (and) Batir [...] The omens [were favorable(?)]. At the (assumption of) kingship by Dadusha, this was (the state of) the entrails [Al-Rawi 1994: 39].

Interestingly, the text makes no mention of the liver, probably because its configuration was represented visually on the object's other side. An unprovenienced clay tablet similarly has an omen report on its obverse and represents the coils of the colon on its reverse (Koch-Westenholz 2002: 132, no. 13; http://www.cdli.ucla.edu/P414653).

It is worth noting that these models constitute a relatively minor class of objects, even a small fraction of the total set of epigraphic data devoted to divination. So why focus on the models at all? The models visually illustrate the various zones of the liver mentioned in other textual genres, and Meyer (1987) has rightly insisted that the models themselves are "readable" and should be understood as representing the same kinds of information that are communicated textually in the omen compendia and reports. For instance, the early model that Budge attributed to Sippar is inscribed not with "tables of calculations," as he had thought, but rather with omens on the model of "If P: then Q," for example: "If the top of the View [a.k.a. Presence] is pierced right through: the *en*-priestess will repeatedly steal sacred property. They shall seize her and burn her. Or: the *šangû*-priest will repeatedly have sex with the *en*-priestess" (Robson and Horry 2011). Other passages are more laconic: "If the right side." Followed by: "The king's personal attendant will repeatedly divulge secrets." The inscribed and physical features of the models are deeply interconnected and embrace elements of both the compendia and the reports. However, to fully assess the significance of the liver models in the early second millennium, we must look at the archaeological distribution of each of the Old Babylonian sources of evidence.

Contexts of Divination: Archaeology and/of Models

The topic of the origins and practice of liver divination has long supplied ammunition in the contentious debates about cultural practice and identity in Bronze Age Mesopotamia. Some scholars see distinct, identifiable, and suspiciously static ethnic groups, such as the Amorrites, playing a pivotal role in shaping Mesopotamian culture, and in so doing scholars accept, often tacitly and uncritically, various notions of invasion, diffusion, and identity formation as mechanisms for change over time. According to some scholars, liver divination was a local practice (e.g., in Bronze Age Syria, see Durand and Marti 2004: 1–5), while other scholars view hepatoscopy as a distinctly Babylonian technique that was exported from southern Mesopotamia to the north and west, Syria, the Levant, Anatolia, and Mediterranean, where it would have been foreign, exotic, and esoteric (e.g., Bottéro 2004: 176). Perhaps it is because the omen compendia are structured to be generic and therefore broadly capable of quite general signification that these documents have come to be treated as decontextualized texts floating in a space of ideas. Such texts can then come to represent the mentality or worse mind of the inhabitants of ancient Mesopotamia, reified as Mesopotamians or Babylonians or Amorrites and their cultural practices. One question that has not been addressed in this debate pertains to the assimilation of difference: that is, how long does it take for a community to view an imported practice as a local one? At what point, if ever, was divination perceived as an Amorrite or Babylonian practice outside of its alleged community or locale of origin? If there ever was such a perception, how long did it take to fade? A generation? Less? Answers to questions like these will be difficult to find in the texts themselves. Rather, it will be necessary to look at textual information as part of a broader context of objects and spaces, perhaps also having recourse to ethnographic analogy.

Down at the level of the contexts in which divination was practiced – contexts that are neither obvious nor self-evident to reconstruct in each and every instance – I am also willing to hazard that there must have been communities who could neither read nor write (or did so at a low level) but who would have been able to identify the models of the exta and participate in their meanings. Perhaps such an audience could not "read" the features of the exta or the texts that described and interpreted the organs, but they may well have recognized the referent and its powerful cultural role. The bodies of sheep and goats as vehicles for divine communication may lead us to speculate about how socio-economic factors condition and constrain the practice of divination, though we will never be able to answer even the seemingly basic question "why sheep?" In order to gauge the quality and quantity of any such social interactions among variously literate elements of a given population, we need to be able to infer something about the objects' functions and circulation. For such information we can look both to the objects themselves and, most profitably, to the contexts in which they were found.

The patterns of distribution are revealing and highlight the problem of archaeological context when dealing with the omen compendia, reports, and models from the early second millennium. Even by a generous reckoning of the 115 omen compendia from the early second millennium, only about 11 to 14 (or 10 to 12%) were excavated at places like Mari on the Euphrates, sites in the Diyala River basin like Tell Yelkhi, and at Ur in Babylonia

Site	Number of Sources	Bibliography
Mari	2	Durand 1988: 63–68; Heimpel 2003: 175–176
Tell Yelkhi	8	Saporetti 1984; Rouault and Saporetti 1985
Ur	1	Woolley and Mallowan 1976: 113 n. 11; Jeyes 1989: 3; Shaffer 2006: 25–26, 32
Ishchali (?)	1	Greengus 1979: 1–3, 57, pls. XCII–XCIII
Khafaje (?)	1	Goetze 1947: 1
Nippur (?)	1	Kraus 1987: 194–196, no. 1
Unprovenienced		Jeyes 1989: 2–8; Oshima 2011; George 2013: 27–48, 110–111, 294–313; Khait 2012
Sippar?	20	
Larsa?	40	
Unknown	41	
TOTAL	115 (10–12% excavated, 3–6 sites)	

Table 6.1. Provenience and number of omen compendia, early second millennium B.C.

Site	Number of Sources	Bibliography
Mari	18	Koch-Westenholz 2002: 131
Babylon	7	Koch-Westenholz 2002: 133; Pedersén 2005: A1:386, A2:7, 8, 24, 25, 55, 194
Sippar-Amnanum	11	De Meyer 1982: 271 n. 8; Tanret 2011: 283
Unprovenienced		Koch-Westenholz 2002; Richardson 2007; George 2013: 13–25, 287; van Dijk 1976: pl. LXVI
Sippar?	40	
TOTAL	76 (48% excavated, 3 sites)	

Table 6.2. Provenience and number of omen reports, early second millennium B.C.

(Table 6.1). The secondary literature is full of discussions of the textual traditions from "Sippar" and "Larsa," but in actuality these place names are merely optimistic code for tablets bought on the antiquities market. The tablets were either acquired together or are thought to share certain traits in how they were written (e.g., Jeyes 1989: 4–5). For the omen compendia, the differentiation between "Sippar" in the north and "Larsa" in the south essentially devolves to a distinction between unprovenienced tablets held in London (British Museum) and New Haven (Yale Babylonian Collection), respectively (Dyckhoff 1998, 2002; Kalla 1999; Michalowski 2006: 254–255). However, I hasten to point out that in his ground-breaking study Goetze (1945) showed a cautious awareness of the limitation of inferring provenience from orthography. Archaeologically provenienced tablets from Mari, Hattusha, Susa, Ugarit, Emar, Ashur, Nineveh, and Uruk all suggest relationships among place, period, script, and orthography that are complex and multilayered. Archaeology teaches us that inferring provenience from such internal features alone is problematic at the very least.

The situation with the early omen reports is scarcely better: of the 76 omen reports known, only 36 (or 48%) were excavated. The excavated tablets come from only three sites: Mari, Babylon (where most remain unpublished), and Sippar-Amnanum (where all remain unpublished), in monumental (i.e., palatial) and domestic contexts (Table 6.2).

However, when we look at the clay models, the situation improves significantly: of the approximately 93 models presently known, 75 (or 81%) were excavated at sites in the Diyala River basin as well as in Syria and the Levant (Table 6.3). Although we still await the full publication of the contexts in which some of these models were found, some preliminary reports indicate that models were found in contexts associated with domestic (Tell as-Sib, Tell Haddad), palatial (Mari, Tuttul), and sacred (Ebla, Halawa,

Site	Number of Sources	Bibliography
Tell as-Sib	1	Al-Rawi 1994: 38–40
Tell Haddad	1	Al-Rawi 1994: 41
Mari	33	Rutten 1938; Meyer 1993b
Tuttul	5	Strommenger and Miglus 2010: 103–105
Ebla	26	Marchetti 2009
Halawa	1	Meyer 1994: 196–198, 203
Hazor	6	Meyer 1987: 24–29; Horowitz and Oshima 2006: 66–68; Horowitz et al. 2010
Megiddo	2	Meyer 1987: 29–32
Unprovenienced		George 2013: 273–279
Sippar?	3	see Figure 6.1; www.cdli.ucla.edu/P365126
Larsa?	7	Goetze 1947: pls. CXXXIII–CXXXIV
Nippur?	2	
Unknown	6	Meyer 1987: 273, pl. 27; www.cdli.ucla.edu/P258913
TOTAL	93 (81% excavated, 8 sites)	

Table 6.3. Provenience and number of clay models, early second millennium B.C.

Hazor, and Megiddo) architecture. If we are looking to ground the analysis of extispicy in the archaeological record, the models appear to be the most promising place to start.

Discussion: The Contexts of Extispicy

The following observations touch on what we know and what we would like to know about the sources for extispicy, their regional distribution, and their local contexts. First, the palace of Zimri-Lim at Mari contained compendia, reports (embedded in letters), and models, along with the single richest archive of correspondence pertaining to diviners and divination before the Neo-Assyrian period, about a thousand years later (Charpin 2011). However, this rich array of data does not by itself suggest that extispicy was a western or Amorrite practice.

The other two sites (really two buildings) in which omen compendia were found require comment as well. Originally referred to simply as an Old Babylonian building at Tell Yelkhi, the discovery of a small room with a podium prompted excavators to refer to it later on as a temple, though one that they had to concede was not a "great temple" (Bergamini 1984: 231–233; Invernizzi 1980: 34–37). The discovery of omen compendia in the building's other rooms was thought to lend credence to this revised interpretation (Rouault and Saporetti 1985: 25, 28–33), but the presence of liver omen compendia cannot bear such a burden: an omen compendium does not itself point to a building or room's sacred or cultic function.

The other surprise comes from the domestic quarter at Ur in the south. During the fifth campaign at Ur in 1926–1927, C. Leonard Woolley's team worked in Area EM where they were surprised to uncover one of two important domestic quarters at Ur that date to the Old Babylonian period. Area EM is situated right next to Ekishnugal, the sacred complex of Ur most famous for its ziggurat (or temple tower). The house known as No. 7 Quiet St. fits neatly into the urban plan of Old Babylonian Ur and cannot be mistaken for a cultic structure (Charpin 1986: 26–93). Based on some of the dates found in the tablets from this building, it seems to have been destroyed around year 11 in the reign of Samsu-iluna, Hammurapi of Babylon's son and immediate successor. Although Woolley identified room 5 in the house as a "chapel," there is no way that the building as a whole could be identified as a temple. The tablets from this house contain two dossiers that are not easily related to one another: five letters are to one Ur-Nanna, a *šandabakkum* or temple administrator; and several legal tablets and administrative records related to the cult can be associated with the family of one Ku-Ningal (Charpin 1986). Ku-Ningal was a cultic functionary, called an *abriqqum*, who was associated with the nearby temple complex, and Ku-Ningal's son, Enamtisud, also functioned as an *abriqqum* of the god Enki, probably after his father's death, which is noted in the text corpus. While it may be tempting to see a connection between the families of Ur-Nanna and Ku-Ningal, none is evident in the texts. What is significant is that neither the *šandabakkum* nor the *abriqqum* is a diviner per se. The broken tablets from two rooms in the house (rooms 5 and 6) included administrative records, legal documents, and letters along with textual genres associated with scribal education, such as lexical, mathematical, and literary texts, and copies of earlier royal inscriptions (Charpin 1986: 35–42). The outliers in the bunch are the Akkadian dialogue referred to as "At the Cleaners" (Charpin 1986: 431–432; George 1993: 73–74; Wasserman 2013) and the single solitary omen compendium (in Akkadian) that deals with a feature referred to as the *ṣibtum* or "Increment" (Jeyes 1989: 137–143, plates 10–11, no. 10). This omen compendium has only recently been associated with the building and its assemblage, and the meaning of its presence in the text corpus has never been discussed. Whatever this family's official capacities, I know of no study of this text corpus that even tries to account for what an omen compendium is doing in their house.

Turning to the omen reports, with the exception of the reports from Mari, the excavated text corpus remains largely unpublished (Babylon, Sippar-Amnanum). The omen reports from Babylon were found in two private houses in the so-called Merkes area of the site. One report comes from a partially excavated house in which excavators uncovered some 452 tablets, including letters, legal and administrative documents, and literary texts associated with scribal education (Pedersén 2005: 19–37, A1). The proprietor of the house is unknown, but one Marduk-naṣir, UGULA DUMU.MEŠ E₂.DUB.BA.A, "overseer of the students," figures prominently in a number of documents found in the building. Interestingly, the report found in this building is rather unusual in that it contains quotations from the extispicy compendia (Pedersén 2005: 35, A1:386; cf. Veldhuis 2006: 488). The other six omen reports from Babylon (mostly unpublished) were all found in a nearby house that contained about 240 tablets in all and is commonly referred to as the archive of a merchant (*tamkārum*) named Kurû (Pedersén 2005: 37–53, A2). However, the actual owner of the house is unclear. North of Babylon, the so-called house of Ur-Utu in Sippar-Amnanum contained some 2,500 tablets, and various documents round out the picture of the roles divination played in the lives of its occupants (Tanret 2011). Letters concerning diviners and divination, extispicy prayers, and presumably the unpublished omen reports from the house of Ur-Utu confirm what we should have already expected: the likely and logical disposition of the omen report itself was with the client. Once the omen reports from the archives in Babylon and Sippar-Amnanum have been properly published, it may be possible to situate their contents within the context of the various families' economic ups and downs as well as the final abandonment of the houses themselves.

Finally, the wide regional distribution of models prompts a number of questions, including: Does reading the liver require text? Some studies of the inscribed models make little or no mention of uninscribed models from the same period, region, or site. For example, uninscribed models found at Megiddo are not even mentioned by Horowitz and Oshima (2006: 66–68, 102–108), though to be fair their focus is expressly on the presence of the cuneiform script in the southern Levant. Even so, such an omission could skew an interpretive approach to the models from the Levant by focusing only on the inscribed specimens. The ability to source the clay may shed light on questions about whether these objects were locally produced or imported from elsewhere, an approach that could also be used to analyze the compendia and reports. Even without sources of clays, certain local styles can be observed, including rounded liver models in Syria and Anatolia, significantly more square forms in Palestine, and larger models in general from the Hittite capital (Meyer 1987).

The liver and spleen models from Zimri-Lim's palace in Mari provide an example of the connections made among the compendia, reports, and models. This is the one building where all three are found together (e.g.,

Malamat 1986: 162–165; Parrot 1958: 102). The inscribed models use archaizing script and spelling, and their contents betray an interest in the distant (and not-so-distant) past: rulers of Akkad (Sargon, Rimush, and Manishtushu), the Third Dynasty of Ur (Ibbi-Suen), and the first king of Isin (Meyer 1987, 1993; Rutten 1938). There is also a sense of experimentation with the system as a whole: for instance, in the apparent switching of the protasis ("if P") and apodosis ("then Q") (e.g., Meyer 1987: 202, M 19). The omen compendia, reports, and archaizing models must all be fit into the sets of practices created and adapted in the service of legitimating kingship. But the contextual analysis of the sources points away from this as the sole purpose of Old Babylonian extispicy, with compendia, reports, and models appearing in domestic contexts as well.

Turning from the richest context to the most perplexing, the clay liver model (rounded in typical Syrian style) from Halawa A is probably the earliest uninscribed model identified thus far (Meyer 1994). It was found in an unusual feature just north of a house: in the street excavators identified a small (1 × 1.5 m) enclosure with a standard fieldstone foundation, but it is unclear whether there was then a corresponding mud-brick superstructure. The floor of the feature corresponds with the level of the street, and Meyer (1994: 197) has tentatively proposed that the feature may have been an offering podium where a diviner practiced his craft. Another possibility is to see the liver model as a foundation deposit in the structure, whose meaning is ultimately unclear.

Finally, an important group of models of the liver and the entrails was excavated at the site of Ebla in the mid-1970s and 1980s (Marchetti 2009). They were found in and around a building near what appears to be a small sacred structure (based on architectural layout), not far from a large Middle Bronze Age temple. Unknown until quite recently is that these models of the liver (some painted red) and colon were found along with various animal models that connect with other types of divination practiced in greater Mesopotamia, especially the observation of animals with various birth defects (Leichty 1970). Surprisingly, also present were models that attest to a divinatory practice that is altogether missing from the extensive textual record: divination using turtle shells. Such connections and gaps in the divinatory systems of Mesopotamia are expected but seldom explicitly documented, especially in the absence of any of the relevant textual genres at the site (i.e., neither compendia nor reports are attested at Ebla).

As each of these brief examples suggests, the archaeology of extispicy pushes the study of divination toward more complex scenarios afforded by contextual analysis, and similar problems in the archaeology of extispicy persist as divinatory traditions were transmitted and adapted in the international context of the Late Bronze Age, as well as later on in Neo-Assyrian and Late Babylonian times. The compendia, reports, models, and other sources of evidence are all different facets of the same embedded cultural practice whereby divination was literally objectified, i.e., made into an object that could endure beyond the moment in which divination was a lived practice. Such objects externalize divination, making it both concrete and decontextualized. Such decontextualized objects can in turn point away from any one specific moment and represent more generic social truths. The clay models in particular are portable, non-perishable representations of the bloody mess first encountered by the diviner.

As important as it is to analyze the minutiae of each category of object that serves as evidence for extispicy in ancient Mesopotamia, it is equally important to appreciate that internal features and archaeological context are independent axes of knowledge: one can in no way be inferred, recovered, or reconstructed from the other. The best analyses will reconstruct context through archaeological inference rather than manufacture or fabricate it from a reading or interpretation of content or, as in the case of Budge and the "Sippar" model, a dealer's anecdote.

Acknowledgments

I am grateful to Richard Zettler, Jon Taylor, and Christopher Walker for their helpful comments and suggestions about the tablets from Ur. I presented aspects of this work in a few other venues beyond the Archaeologies of Text symposium, including the Culture and Religion in the Ancient Mediterranean (CRAM) seminar at Brown University, The Memory and Identity Working Group of the Department of Near Eastern Studies, University of California, Berkeley, and the Louis J. Kolb Foundation Fellows' Colloquium at the University of Pennsylvania Museum of Archaeology and Anthropology. I am grateful for the critical comments I received in each of these settings. The photographs of tablets in Figures 6.1–3 are reproduced here thanks to the enlightened policies of the Trustees of the British Museum regarding the scholarly use of images of objects in their collections.

References

Al-Rawi, Farouk N.H.
   1994   Texts from Tell Haddad and Elsewhere. *Iraq* 56: 35–43.
André-Salvini, Béatrice
   1999   Les débuts de la recherche française en Assyriologie: Milieu et atmosphère du déchriffement. *Journal asiatique* 287: 331–355.

Annus, Amar (editor)
    2010   *Divination and the Interpretation of Signs in the Ancient World.* Oriental Institute Seminars Vol. 6. The Oriental Institute of the University of Chicago, Chicago.

Banks, Edgar James
    1904   Spurious Antiquities in Bagdad. *American Journal of Semitic Languages and Literatures* 21: 60–62.

Bergamini, Giovanni
    1984   The Excavations in Tell Yelkhi. *Sumer* 40: 224–244.

Bottéro, Jean
    2004   *Religion in Ancient Mesopotamia.* Translated by Teresa Lavender Fagan. University of Chicago Press, Chicago.

Budge, Ernest A.T. Wallis
    1920   *By Nile and Tigris: A Narrative of Journeys in Egypt and Mesopotamia on behalf of the British Museum between the Years 1886 and 1913*, Vol. 2. John Murray, London.

Charpin, Dominique
    1986   *Le clergé d'Ur au siècle d'Hammurabi (XIXᵉ–XVIIIᵉ siècles av. J.-C.).* Hautes études orientales Vol. 22. Librairie Droz, Geneva.
    2011   Patron and Client: Zimri-Lim and Asqudum the Diviner. In *The Oxford Handbook of Cuneiform Culture*, edited by Karen Radner and Eleanor Robson, pp. 248–269. Oxford University Press, Oxford.

Cohen, Eran
    2010   Conditional Structures in the Old Babylonian Omens. In *Language in the Ancient Near East. Proceedings of the 53ᵉ Rencontre Assyriologique Internationale*, Vol. 1, Part 2, edited by L. Kogan, N. Koslova, S. Loesov, and S. Tischenko, pp. 709–727. Babel und Bibel Vol. 4(2). Orientalia et Classica Vol. XXX(2). Eisenbrauns, Winona Lake, Indiana.

De Meyer, Léon
    1982   Deux prières *ikribu* du temps d'Ammī-ṣaduqa. In *Zikir Šumim: Assyriological Studies Presented to F.R. Kraus on the Occasion of His Seventieth Birthday*, edited by G. Van Driel, Th. J.H. Krispijn, M. Stol, and K.R. Veenhof, pp. 271–278. E.J. Brill, Leiden.

Durand, Jean-Marie
    1988   *Archives épistolaires de Mari I(1).* Archives Royales de Mari Vol. 26(1). Éditions Recherche sur les Civilisations, Paris.

Durand, Jean-Marie, and Lionel Marti
    2004   Les textes hépatoscopiques d'Émar (I). *Journal asiatique* 292: 1–61.

Dyckhoff, Christian
    1998   Balamunamhe von Larsa – eine altbabylonische Existenz zwischen Ökonomie, Kultus und Wissenschaft. In *Intellectual Life of the Ancient Near East. Papers Presented at the 43rd Rencontre Assyriologique Internationale, Prague, July 1–6, 1996*, edited by Jiři Prosecký, pp. 117–124. Academy of Sciences of the Czech Republic, Oriental Institute, Prague.
    2002   Priester und Priesterinnen im altbabylonischen Larsa: Das Amtsarchiv als Grundlage für prosopographische Forschung. In *Sex and Gender in the Ancient Near East:*

Proceedings of the 47th Rencontre Assyriologique Internationale, Helsinki, July 2–6, 2001, edited by Simo Parpola and Robert M. Whiting, pp. 123–128. The Neo-Assyrian Text Corpus Project, Helsinki.

Frahm, Eckart
    2010   Reading the Tablet, the Exta, and the Body: The Hermeneutics of Cuneiform Signs in Babylonian and Assyrian Text Commentaries and Divinatory Texts. In *Divination and the Interpretation of Signs in the Ancient World*, edited by Amar Annus, pp. 93–141. Oriental Institute Seminars Vol. 6. The Oriental Institute of the University of Chicago, Chicago.

Fromkin, David
    1989   *A Peace to End All Peace: The Fall of the Ottoman Empire and the Creation of the Modern Middle East*. Avon Books, New York.

George, Andrew R.
    1993   Ninurta-Pāqidāt's Dog Bite, and Notes on Other Comic Tales. *Iraq* 55: 63–75.
    2013   *Babylonian Divinatory Texts Chiefly in the Schøyen Collection*. Cornell University Studies in Assyriology and Sumerology Vol. 18. CDL Press, Bethesda, Maryland.

Glassner, Jean-Jacques
    2005   L'aruspicine paléo-babylonienne et le témoignage des sources de Mari. *Zeitschrift für Assyriologie und Vorderasiatische Archäologie* 95: 276–300.
    2009   Écrire des livres à l'époque paléo-babylonienne: le traité d'extispicine. *Zeitschrift für Assyriologie und Vorderasiatische Archäologie* 99: 1–81.

Goetze, Albrecht
    1945   The Akkadian Dialects of the Old-Babylonian Mathematical Texts. In *Mathematical Cuneiform Texts*, edited by Otto Neugebauer and Abraham Sachs, pp. 146–151. American Oriental Series Vol. 29. American Oriental Society and American Schools of Oriental Research, New Haven, Connecticut.
    1947   *Old Babylonian Omen Texts*. Yale Oriental Series, Babylonian Texts Vol. X. Yale University Press, New Haven, Connecticut.

Greengus, Samuel
    1979   *Old Babylonian Tablets from Ishchali and Vicinity*. Uitgaven van het Nederlands Historisch-Archaeologisch Instituut te Istanbul Vol. 44. Nederlands Historisch-Archaeologisch Instituut, Istanbul.

Heimpel, Wolfgang
    2003   *Letters to the King of Mari*. Mesopotamian Civilizations Vol. 12. Eisenbrauns, Winona Lake, Indiana.

Horowitz, Wayne, and Takayoshi Oshima
    2006   *Cuneiform in Canaan: Cuneiform Sources from the Land of Israel in Ancient Times*. Israel Exploration Society and The Hebrew University of Jerusalem, Jerusalem.

Horowitz, Wayne, Takayoshi Oshima, and Abraham Winitzer
    2010   Hazor 17: Another Clay Liver Model. *Israel Exploration Journal* 60: 133–145.

Invernizzi, Antonio
    1980   Excavations in the Yelkhi Area (Hamrin Project, Iraq). *Mesopotamia* 15: 19–49.

Jeyes, Ulla
    1989   *Old Babylonian Extispicy: Omen Texts in the British Museum*. Uitgaven van het

Nederlands Historisch-Archaeologisch Instituut te Istanbul Vol. 64. Nederlands Historisch-Archaeologisch Instituut te Istanbul, Istanbul.

Kalla, Gábor

1999   Die Geschichte der Entdeckung der altbabylonischen Sippar-Archive. *Zeitschrift für Assyriologie und Vorderasiatische Archäologie* 89: 201–226.

Khait, Ilga

2012   The Old Babylonian Omens in the Pushkin State Museum of Fine Arts, Moscow. *Babel und Bibel* 6: 31–60.

Koch-Westenholz, Ulla

2000   *Babylonian Liver Omens: The Chapters Manzāzu, Padānu and Pān tākalti of the Babylonian Extispicy Series Mainly from Aššurbanipal's Library.* Carsten Niebuhr Institute Publications Vol. 25. The Carsten Niebuhr Institute of Near Eastern Studies, University of Copenhagen and Museum Tusculanum Press, Copenhagen.

2002   Old Babylonian Extispicy Reports. In *Mining the Archives. Festschrift for Christopher Walker on the Occasion of his 60th Birthday, 4 October 2002,* edited by Cornelia Wunsch, pp. 131–146. ISLET, Dresden.

Koch, Ulla S.

2005   *Secrets of Extispicy: The Chapter Multābiltu of the Babylonian Extispicy Series and Niṣirti bārûti Texts Mainly from Aššurbanipal's Library.* Alter Orient und Altes Testament Vol. 326. Ugarit-Verlag, Münster.

2011   Sheep and Sky: Systems of Divinatory Interpretation. In *The Oxford Handbook of Cuneiform Culture,* edited by Karen Radner and Eleanor Robson, pp. 447–469. Oxford University Press, Oxford.

Kraus, Fritz R.

1985   Mittelbabylonische Opfterschauprotokolle. *Journal of Cuneiform Studies* 37: 127–218.

1987   Verstreute Omentexte aus Nippur im Istanbuler Museum. *Zeitschrift für Assyriologie und Vorderasiatische Archäologie* 77: 194–206.

Kuklick, Bruce

1996   *Puritans in Babylon: The Ancient Near East and American Intellectual Life, 1880–1930.* Princeton University Press, Princeton.

Larsen, Mogens Trolle

1996   *The Conquest of Assyria: Excavations in an Antique Land, 1840–1860.* Routledge, London.

Leiderer, Rosmarie

1990   *Anatomie der Schafsleber im babylonischen Leberorakel. Eine makroskopisch-analytische Studie.* W. Zuckschwerdt, Munich.

Leichty, Erle

1970   *The Omen Series Šumma Izbu.* Texts from Cuneiform Sources Vol. 4. J.J. Augustin, Locust Valley, New York.

Leichty, Erle, Jacob J. Finkelstein, and Christopher B.F. Walker

1988   *Tablets from Sippar 3.* Catalogue of the Babylonian Tablets in the British Museum Vol. 8. British Museum Publications, London.

Malamat, Abraham

   1986   "Doorbells" at Mari: A Textual-Archaeological Correlation. In *Cuneiform Archives and Libraries: Papers Read at the 30e Rencontre Assyriologique Internationale*, edited by Klaas R. Veenhof, pp. 160–167. Uitgaven van het Nederlands Historisch-Archaeologisch Instituut te Istanbul Vol. 57. Nederlands Historisch-Archaeologisch Instituut, Istanbul; Nederlands Instituut voor het Nabje Oosten, Leiden.

Marchetti, Nicolò

   2009   Divination at Ebla during the Old Syrian Period: The Archaeological Evidence. In *Exploring the Longue Durée: Essays in Honor of Lawrence E. Stager*, edited by J. David Schloen, pp. 279–295. Eisenbrauns, Winona Lake, Indiana.

Maul, Stefan

   2003   Omina und Orakel. A. Mesopotamien. *Reallexikon der Assyriologie und vorderasiatischen Archäologie* 10: 45–88.

Meyer, Jan-Waalke

   1985   Zur Herkunft der etruskischen Lebermodelle. In *Phoenicia and its Neighbours*, edited by E. Lipiński, pp. 105–120. Studia Phoenicia Vol. 3. Peeters, Leuven.

   1987   *Untersuchungen zu den Tonlebermodellen aus dem Alten Orient*. Alter Orient und Altes Testament Vol. 39. Verlag Butzon and Bercker, Kevelaer; Neukirchner Verlag, Neukirchen-Vluyn, Germany.

   1993a   Die Eingeweideschau im vor- und nachexilischen Israel. In *Religionsgeschichtliche Beziehungen zwischen Kleinasien, Nordsyrien und dem Alten Testament im 2. und 1. Jahrtausend*, edited by Bernd Janowski, Klaus Koch, and Gernot Wilhelm, pp. 531–546. Orbis Biblicus et Orientalis Vol. 129. Universitätsverlag, Freiburg, Switzerland; Vandenhoeck and Ruprecht, Göttingen.

   1993b   Ein Milzmodell aus Mari (AO 27906). *Mari, Annales de Recherches Interdisciplinaires* 7: 349–354.

   1994   Sonstige Tonobjekte. In *Die Kleinfunde von Tell Halawa A*, by Jan-Waalke Meyer and Alexander Pruß, pp. 193–204. Schriften zur vorderasiatischen Archäologie Vol. 6. Ausgrabungen in Halawa Vol. 2. Saarbrücker Druckerei und Verlag, Saarbrücken, Germany.

   2003   Beobachtungen zu den Tonlebermodellen aus dem Hamrin-Gebiet. In *Festschrift für Burkhart Kienast*, edited by Gebhard J. Selz, pp. 329–334. Alter Orient und Altes Testament Vol. 274. Ugarit-Verlag, Münster.

Michalowski, Piotr

   2006   How to Read the Liver – in Sumerian. In *If a Man Builds a Joyful House: Assyriological Studies in Honor of Erle Verdun Leichty*, edited by Ann K. Guinan, Maria de J. Ellis, A.J. Ferrara, Sally M. Freedman, Matthew T. Rutz, Leonhard Sassmannshausen, Steve Tinney, and M.W. Waters, pp. 247–257. Cuneiform Monographs Vol. 31. Brill, Leiden.

Oshima, Takayoshi

   2011   Ein altbabylonischer Omentext. In *Die Keilschrifttexte des Altorientalischen Instituts der Universität Leipzig*, edited by Michael P. Streck, pp. 83–85. Leipziger Altorientalistischen Studien Vol. 1. Harrassowitz Verlag, Wiesbaden.

Parrot, André

   1958   *Mission archéologique de Mari, volume II: Le palais, architecture*. Librairie Orientaliste Paul Geuthner, Paris.

Pedersén, Olof

2005   *Archive und Bibliotheken in Babylon: Die Tontafeln der Grabung Robert Koldeweys 1899–1917.* Abhandlungen der Deutschen Orient-Gesellschaft Vol. 25. Deutsche Orient-Gesellschaft, Berlin.

Richardson, Seth

2007   Omen Report No. 38. *Nouvelles Assyriologiques Brèves et Utilitaires* 2007: 56–57, No. 47.

2010   On Seeing and Believing: Liver Divination and the Era of Warring States (II). In *Divination and the Interpretation of Signs in the Ancient World*, edited by Amar Annus, pp. 225–266. Oriental Institute Seminars Vol. 6. The Oriental Institute of the University of Chicago, Chicago.

Robson, Eleanor

2011   Empirical Scholarship in the Neo-Assyrian Court. In *The Empirical Dimension of Ancient Near Eastern Studies / Die empirische Dimension altorientalischer Forschungen*, edited by Gebhard J. Selz, pp. 603–629. Wiener Offene Orientalistik Vol. 6. Lit Verlag, Vienna.

Robson, Eleanor, and Ruth Horry

2011   CT 06, pl. 01–03, Bu 1889–04–26, 238 [liver model]. Electronic document, http://oracc.org/cams/barutu/P365126, accessed February 27, 2011.

Rochberg-Halton, Francesca

1988   *Aspects of Babylonian Celestial Divination: The Lunar Eclipse Tablets of Enūma Anu Enlil.* Archiv für Orientforschung Beiheft Vol. 22. Ferdinand Berger und Söhne, Horn.

Rochberg, Francesca

2010   If P, then Q: Form, Reasoning and Truth in Babylonian Divination. In *Divination and the Interpretation of Signs in the Ancient World*, edited by Amar Annus, pp. 19–27. Oriental Institute Seminars Vol. 6. The Oriental Institute of the University of Chicago, Chicago.

Rouault, Olivier, and Claudio Saporetti

1985   Old Babylonian Texts from Tell Yelkhi (Hamrīn Project, Iraq). *Mesopotamia* 20: 23–52.

Rutten, Maggie

1938   Trente-deux modèles de foies en argile inscrits provenant de Tell-Hariri (Mari). *Revue d'assyriologie et d'archéologie orientale* 35: 36–70.

Saporetti, Claudio

1984   Cuneiform in Texts Discovered at Tell Yelkhi. *Sumer* 40: 245–259.

Shaffer, Aaron

2006   *Literary and Religious Texts, Part III.* With a contribution by Marie-Christine Ludwig. Ur Excavations Texts Vol. 6. The British Museum Press, London.

Starr, Ivan

1990   *Queries to the Sungod: Divination and Politics in Sargonid Assyria.* State Archives of Assyria Vol. 4. State Archives of Assyria, Helsinki.

Stommenger, Eva, and Peter Miglus

    2010   *Altorientalische Kleinfunde*. Ausgrabungen in Tall Biʻaʹ/Tuttul Vol. 5. Wissenschaftliche Veröffentlichungen der Deutschen Orient-Gesellschaft Vol. 126. Harrassowitz Verlag, Wiesbaden.

Tanret, Michel

    2011   Learned, Rich, Famous, and Unhappy: Ur-Utu of Sippar. In *The Oxford Handbook of Cuneiform Culture*, edited by Karen Radner and Eleanor Robson, pp. 270–287. Oxford University Press, Oxford.

Trigger, Bruce G.

    2006 [1989]   *A History of Archaeological Thought*. 2nd edition. Cambridge University Press, New York.

Trümpler, Charlotte (editor)

    2008   *Das Grosse Spiel: Archäologie und Politik zur Zeit des Kolonialismus (1860–1940)*. DuMont, Cologne.

van der Meer, L. Bouke

    1987   *The Bronze Liver of Piacenza: Analysis of a Polytheistic Structure*. Dutch Monographs on Ancient History and Archaeology Vol. 2. J.C. Gieben, Amsterdam.

van Dijk, Johannes

    1976   *Cuneiform Texts: Texts of Varying Content*. Texts in the Iraq Museum Vol. 9. Brill, Leiden.

Veldhuis, Niek

    2006   Divination: Theory and Use. In *If a Man Builds a Joyful House: Assyriological Studies in Honor of Erle Verdun Leichty*, edited by Ann K. Guinan, Maria de J. Ellis, A.J. Ferrara, Sally M. Freedman, Matthew T. Rutz, Leonhard Sassmannshausen, Steve Tinney, and M.W. Waters, pp. 487–497. Cuneiform Monographs Vol. 31. Brill, Leiden.

    2011   Levels of Literacy. In *The Oxford Handbook of Cuneiform Culture*, edited by Karen Radner and Eleanor Robson, pp. 68–89. Oxford University Press, Oxford.

Wasserman, Nathan

    2013   Treating Garments in the Old Babylonian Period: "At the Cleaners" in a Comparative View. *Iraq* 75: 255–277.

Woolley, Leonard, and Max Mallowan

    1976   *The Old Babylonian Period*. Ur Excavations Vol. 7. British Museum Publications, London.

The Ernest K. Smith Collection of Shang Divination Inscriptions at Columbia University and the Evidence for Scribal Training at Anyang

Adam Smith

The C.V. Starr East Asian Library at Columbia has a small but important collection of Late Shang (ca. 1300–1050 B.C.) divination inscriptions. The core of this collection was acquired in the 1930s by Ernest K. Smith and arrived at Columbia shortly afterwards. Smith's collection lacks a documented archaeological provenance, but the location where the inscriptions were discovered at the late Shang site near Anyang can nevertheless be precisely determined. The most important of Smith's 62 pieces is a densely inscribed divination scapula (US414–415 = YiCun266+257, for abbreviations, see References Cited) belonging to the so-called He Group of inscriptions (for abbreviations used for published corpora, see References Cited). This item is often referred to in the scholarly literature but rarely with reference to the context of its discovery, its relationship with other items in Smith's collection, or the fact that most of the inscriptions that appear on it are by scribal trainees. Its relevance to the question of late Shang scribal training has been overlooked. The presentation of these issues is preceded by a brief overview of divination and its written record at Anyang, and of late Shang scribal training.

Writing and Divination in Early China

The earliest extant remains of Chinese literacy are overwhelmingly dominated, numerically speaking, by records of divination incised into cattle scapulae and turtle plastrons (Keightley 1985, 1997). These bones and shells were themselves the materials with which the divinatory technique – pyro-osteomancy, the heat-cracking of animal bones or shells – was performed. This divinatory technique long predated writing, and its physical remains are distributed across a wide area of Northeast and Central Asia, from Tibet to Japan. The earliest examples date to the fourth millennium B.C., but in the third millennium pyro-osteomantic remains become attested in greater quantity. The practice reached a peak of intensity under elite patronage at the major sites of north China during the late second millennium B.C., where workshops of specialists performed divination on a daily basis (Flad 2008). During this period of intense investment in pyro-osteomancy, which was used to validate the performance of costly rituals directed at dead kin, written records began to be kept of the activity. The attestation of the Chinese writing system itself begins at the same period.

The earliest extant examples of pyro-osteomantic remains inscribed with written documentation were produced for members of the Shang royal family. With only a handful of exceptions, they are concentrated at a single site near the modern city of Anyang, the last seat of the dynasty during the final three centuries of the second millennium B.C. Approximately 50,000–100,000 of these inscribed objects (mostly fragments) have been published, of which about half were from controlled excavations (Wang Yuxin and Yang Shengnan 1999: 41–55). These figures reflect the intensity of both divination at Anyang and more than a century of excavation, uncontrolled as well as scientific, at the site.

To illustrate late-second millennium B.C. divination and its written documentation, consider HD17. This largely intact turtle plastron was repeatedly cracked in the performance of divination, and two of these cracks attracted written documentation into the surface:

> 甲辰，歲祖甲一牢，子祝。一。
> Day 41/60, perform a *sui*-sacrifice to Male Ancestor Day 1/10 with one *lao*-ox, and with the Child invocating. (Crack number) 1.

> 乙巳，歲祖乙一牢，叀祝。一。
> Day 42/60, perform a *sui*-sacrifice to Male Ancestor Day 2/10 with one *lao*-ox, and with [unknown name] invocating. (Crack number) 1.

These inscriptions contain the core formulae used to document divination at Anyang. The first of these is a record of the date, expressed according to a cycle of 60 days (Smith 2011a). The date is followed by the divinatory proposition, a statement of the course of action or future event to be validated or assessed. In the two cases above, the propositions concern the performance of a religious procedure and specify the procedure itself, the dead members of the patron's lineage who are the focus of the procedure, the livestock or other goods to be used, and the participatory roles of particular persons. Appended numerals count the heat cracks on the plastron associated with the inscription (only one in each of these cases). Dead kin are referred to using day-names based on a cycle of 10 days.

Distinct roles within the divination workshops were filled by scribes and bone-workers, as well as by the diviners themselves, whose names sometimes appear in the written records. During the latter part of the reign of Wu Ding (ca. 1250–1200 B.C.), the first Shang king whose divinations are known to have been documented in writing, at least three major divination workshops employing scribes were in simultaneous operation at separate locations at Anyang. Two of these, represented by the inscriptions of the so-called Bin and Li groups (Li Xueqin and Peng Yushang 1996: 105–128, 184–268), performed divination on behalf of Wu Ding himself. The patron of the third workshop, which produced the two records just cited, was almost certainly one of Wu Ding's sons (Yao Xuan 2006: 24–55). The locations where inscriptions by the three workshops have been found probably reflect their distinct locations of operation. However, the relationship between the pits in which the inscribed divination materials were deposited and the broader archaeological context is poorly understood.

The divination scapula discussed in this chapter is from a later Anyang workshop, operating two royal generations after Wu Ding, probably during the second quarter of the twelfth century B.C. The dating is clear from the mention in the inscriptions of a deceased king and son of Wu Ding, referred to as Father Jia (父甲 "Father Day 1/10"). The workshop produced the large class of inscriptions known as the He Group, so-called after one of several frequently occurring diviner names, He 何, that appears in the inscriptions. He Group inscriptions have been found concentrated in the northern area of the elite enclosure at Anyang, north of the modern village of Xiaotun. A trench excavated in 1929, known as the *da lian keng* 大連坑 "big extended trench," was a particularly rich source of He Group inscriptions and, as we shall see, is likely to have been the location where the Columbia scapula was found.

Divination record-keeping was not the only application of literacy during the late second millennium. Short inscriptions cast on ritual bronzes, involving little more than the descent-group emblem and day-name of the dedicatee, were common and widely distributed outside Anyang. Stone objects bearing brush-written texts are known in much smaller numbers. The divination records themselves contain numerous references to texts written on a writing medium ancestral to the later rolls of bamboo strips bound together with thread, the earliest physically preserved examples of which are from as late as the fifth century B.C.

It has been suggested that during the reign of Wu Ding literacy was far more geographically and socially widespread, and functionally more diverse, than the attested preponderance of royal divination records from Anyang would seem to imply (Bagley 2004). That remains an open question. However, there is no doubt that the ritual-administrative complex, of which the royal divination workshops were a central component, is the only Shang institution that on present evidence was demonstrably employing literacy on a routine, daily basis. Moreover, some divination workshops at Anyang appear to have been training their own scribes rather than employing previously literate individuals to keep divination records (Smith 2011b). Consequently, reconstructing the activities of the Anyang divination workshops, including their procedures for scribal recruitment and training, is central to understanding the emergence of literate institutions in China.

In sharp contrast to the study of the cuneiform tradition of the ancient Near East, in which scribal training is an intensely explored topic, there has been little work done on literacy acquisition and literate education in Bronze Age China. This is because it has not been generally recognized that relevant evidence, such as inscriptions produced by trainees acquiring literacy skills, has survived in sufficient quantity to shed light on the question. It has long been agreed that among the inscriptions from Anyang there are many examples of "practice engraving" (*xike* 習刻) inscriptions. However, these have been interpreted as the products of already literate individuals learning to engrave on bone, as they transfered their literacy skills from one medium to another (Venture 2002: 308; Wang 2007: 326; Zhang Shichao 2002: 27–28). The "practice engravings" are usually identified by evidently incompetent or disorderly graphs and inscription formulae. The "practice engravings" are treated as an anomalous phenomenon of minor interest – a distraction from the central business of interpreting "real" divination inscriptions. For example, one concordance to the Anyang inscriptions adopts a policy of excluding all instances of "practice engraving" inscriptions (Yao Xiaosui and Xiao Ding 1989: 16).

I have suggested that this consensus needs revision. The "practice engravings" were produced by individuals who were acquiring literacy as well as engraving skills. This is clearest from the errors that they make, which are incompatible with literate competence. It is also clear from the nature of the texts that they produce, many of which are copied from instructors' models or actual divination records. Although dramatically incompetent sign forms are distinctively associated with trainee inscriptions, many trainee texts are not immediately recognizable by this criterion, their engraving being in fact quite well executed. Other criteria need to be employed to identify the many trainee inscriptions that have previously gone unnoticed: evidence for the sight-copying of a model text, for example, or indications that what is ostensibly a divination record does not in fact document a divination performed using the object on which it is inscribed. From this fresh perspective, the trainee inscriptions cease to be a phenomenon of only marginal interest and become instead an important body of evidence relevant to the intergenerational reproduction of a nascent writing system.

In previous work on scribal training at Anyang, I have relied largely on inscriptions with a documented archaeological provenance and have tried to avoid items that entered museum collections through the antiquities market. Since trainee inscriptions are characterized by anomalous features (errors and incompetent engraving), it seemed wise to exclude the possibility of these traits being confused with those of fake inscriptions, which are not unusual in European and U.S. collections. For example, the Columbia Library collection includes a number of fake inscriptions (Hu Houxuan 1988: 119; Lee Yim [Li Yan] 1970: 319–320; Tong 1967: 13). However, having already established a foundational understanding of the characteristics of scribal training inscriptions from Anyang on the basis of exemplars with a secure archaeological provenance, attention can now be given to some of the more informative unprovenanced examples, like the Columbia scapula.

The Columbia University Collection

The Columbia University Library's collection of Shang divination inscriptions, though not large, is one of the more important collections of its kind in the United States. The collection was acquired from several donors during the mid-twentieth century. Most of the items in the collection have been published, sometimes several times, and appear in the standard reference corpora. Lee (1970: 257, 315–320), Chou (1976: 10–12, 17–18, Catalog Items 414–480), and Hu (1999: 118–125, Items 2, 3, 12, 17, 19, 20, 22, 23) have all published reproductions of items in the Columbia collection, and the Columbia University Office of the President (1937: 414), Baughman (1952: 24–25), and Goodrich (1959) give brief notices of Columbia's exhibition, acquisition, or holdings of this material.

The largest and most significant of Columbia's acquisitions was the collection of Ernest Ketcham Smith (1873–1954, Chinese name Shi Meishi 施美士). Smith's collection is important because many of the approximately 60 inscribed items are likely to have been excavated at the same time from a single location at Anyang. As with any items whose excavation was not documented, information about the archaeological context of Smith's inscriptions has been lost. In this case, however, we can recover some of that loss. We can determine with considerable confidence the precise location at Anyang where Smith's divination inscriptions were found. When they were first published in 1933, there were already suggestions regarding the source of Smith's collection and some sense of how the items had found their way onto the antiquities market (see below). There is now a great deal of additional evidence, in the form of joins that have been identified between items at Columbia from Smith's collection, and pieces currently in Taiwan whose excavation was scientifically recorded.

Smith lived in China from 1911 when he began working in Beijing at the newly founded Tsinghua College (later to become Tsinghua University) as a teacher of English (for Smith's biography, see Bunker 1997: 99, 104–105; Coryell 1970; Edwards 1959: 451; Su Yunfeng 2004: 43; Yanjing Yanjiuyuan 2001: 198–201). In 1914 he married Grace Goodrich, who had been born and grown up in the missionary community at Tongzhou west of Beijing, and whose brother Carrington Goodrich was to become the Dean Lung Professor of Chinese Studies at Columbia. Smith remained at Tsinghua until 1929, when he took up a similar position teaching English on the neighboring campus of Yenching University. The Smiths were interested in Chinese antiquities and knew many of the scholar-collectors active at this period (Goodrich 1957: 6). Their collection of 97 metalwork items was bought by Arthur M. Sackler in 1965 (Bunker 1997: 105). Ernest's acquisition of a collection of inscribed Shang divination bones seems to date to the early 1930s. According to Lee (1970: 257) and Chou (1976: 18), the acquisition was by purchase in 1932 in Beijing, but neither author provides a source for this information. Smith's daughter Dorothea variously states that he owned "about 80," or that his wife purchased "about 180 pieces" at a temple fair as a gift for Smith, who subsequently added to that collection (Coryell 1970: 84; Yanjing Yanjiuyuan 2001: 199). In any case, 62 of them received their first publication in 1933 (Shang Chengzuo 1933). Smith remained in Beijing after the closure of Yenching University by the Japanese at the end of 1941, and he was later interned for six months in 1943 before being repatriated to the United States. Ernest Smith's collection of inscriptions was already physically present at Columbia by 1937. After Smith's death in 1954, his collection, consisting of "62 excellent pieces," was given to Columbia by his widow (Tong 1967).

Smith's collection is far from being a random assortment of objects assembled from what was available on the market. Dong Zuobin, who led the earliest scientific excavations at Anyang in the late 1920s, was the first to notice the many He Group ("Period III" in Dong's terminology) inscriptions in Smith's collection (Shang Chengzuo 1933: 2–5). Dong noted that in this respect Smith's collection resembled the much larger body of inscriptions that Dong's team had excavated in 1929 from a unit referred to in the reports as the *da lian keng* "big joined-up trench". The "trench" refers to an excavator's trench rather than a feature of the Shang site, and the excavators were able to record very little in the way of archaeological context for the many inscribed divination bones that came from this unit. Nevertheless, the *da lian keng* is the source of the great majority of He Group inscriptions from recorded excavation. Of the 2,700 inscribed fragments from within the approximately 20 m × 20 m limits of the *da lian keng*, 1,350 were classified by Dong's team as "Period III," which for our purposes is synonymous with "He Group" (Shi Zhangru 1985: 57–96, figures 18–19, table 52). Presumably, the workshop of the He Group diviners and scribes was operating somewhere in the vicinity of the *da lian keng*. Dong also noticed that one of Smith's pieces (US418 = YiCun256) could be joined with a number of fragments that Dong himself had excavated from the *da lian keng* during the third season of excavations in 1929. Dong's join, which includes a substantial segment of the Shang king list probably by a scribal trainee, belongs to the Li Group and is thus a royal generation or two earlier than the majority of items from the *da lian keng*. Qiu Xigui (1992: 236, 239) subsequently added another fragment to the join. This physical join is a strong indication that some of the items in Smith's collection had come from the *da lian keng* or its immediate vicinity.

Dong Zuobin also outlined a sequence of events by which the inscriptions in Smith's collection may have found their way onto the market. During the excavations in 1929, there had been a dispute for control over the site between Dong's team, working for the newly founded Institute of History and Philology (IHP) and thus employees of the central government, and a provincial team led by the director of the Henan Museum, He Rizhang 何日章 (Wang Yuxin and Yang Shengnan 1999: 44). Accounts by IHP archaeologists portray the Henan team as exceedingly unscrupulous and incompetent. Certainly, their efforts resulted in no meaningful site report. Two of the Henan team's oddly-shaped trenches appear on the IHP site maps (Shi Zhangru 1985: 215, figure 52), though neither of these is especially close to the *da lian keng*. In the course of their efforts, the provincial team did recover a large number of divination inscriptions, many of which were published in the following decade (Sun Haibo 1937; Xu Jingcan and Guan Baiyi 1933; cf. Bai Yuzheng 1989: 313–314). None of these published collections has any obvious connection with Smith's. However, Dong Zuobin left the following remarks in his preface to the book in which Smith's collection was first published, and here he tries to account for how additional inscriptions unearthed by his provincial adversaries may have gone astray:

> I was the first to excavate in the vicinity of the *da lian keng*, during the third season of work. Then the dispute for control with the Henan Museum began, and that work was stopped for three weeks. Subsequently I returned to the excavation of the *da lian keng*, recovering many examples of Period III shells and bones. Before this there had certainly not been anyone digging in this area. The items collected by the Museum were, in no time at all, stolen: a small box covered in green cloth containing inscribed shells and bones was lost. The matter passed through the hands of Xuan and Qiu. The owner of the Five Continents Guest House ran away fearing punishment, and the establishment was closed for investigation for months. Those are the facts, and a case is on file with the county administration where they can be checked. This is most likely the source of Smith's bones [Dong Zuobin in Shang Chengzuo 1933: 6].

Comparison with other accounts (e.g., that of Dai Jun 2009: 69–78) seems to indicate that the "Xuan" named here is Xuan Zhongxiang 軒仲湘, brother-in-law of the Henan Museum director, police academy graduate, and would-be archaeologist. I do not know who Qiu 邱 is.

As we have seen, Dong Zuobin was already aware that YiCun256 could be joined with fragments that he had himself excavated, all of which are now among the IHP collections in Taiwan. In fact, there are six more items in Smith's collection that can be joined with items that Dong excavated from the *da lian keng* that year (Table 7.1). Joins are usually identified by comparing reproductions of rubbings with one another. In the case of the Columbia pieces, the actual fragments have not been close to one another since they were excavated 80 years ago. The joins appear in the tables by Hu Houxuan (1999), Zhongguo Shehuikexueyuan Lishi Yanjiusuo (1999), and Cai Zhemao (2004). The relevance to the provenance of Smith's bones does not appear to have been previously noted, except for the instance mentioned by Dong Zuobin. Zhang Juntao (2009a: Item 12, 2009b: 78, 82) proposed a further join between one of Smith's plastron fragments (HJ31477 = US437 = YiCun316) and six He Group fragments currently divided between the Royal Ontario Museum and the National Library of China. The seven pieces are certainly very closely related, and may well be pieces of the same object. However, the breaks around Smith's piece do not align directly with the others, and no single line of text can be traced across both sides of a break. None of the fragments is known to have come from the *da lian keng*. For these reasons, I have omitted Zhang's important discovery from Table 7.1.

Whether Smith's bones really were excavated by the Henan team, and whether they were stolen, is impossible to know with complete confidence.

Join Published as	E. K. Smith's Items	Items from da lian keng
HJ27456	US414 = YiCun266 + YiCun257	Jia2799
HJ26975	US416 = YiCun255	Jia2803
HJ32385 + HJ35277 = HJBB10436	US418 = YiCun256	Jia2282
HJBB7257	US425 = YiCun271	Jia2854 = HJ24377 Jia2828 = HJ24478
HJ31356 = HJ31365	US430 = YiCun282	Jia2513 + Jia2529 = HJ31330
HJ31406	US442 = YiCun278 = HJ31366	Jia2442 = HJ31395, Jia2561
HJBB6954	US453 = YiCun300 = HJ31886 = HJ20794	Jia2878–9 = HJ21475

Table 7.1.   Known Joins Involving Items from E.K. Smith's Collection.

Mysterious joins of excavated divination bones to unprovenanced items are certainly not confined to those from the *da lian keng*. Wei Cide (2008) lists 13 joins between unprovenanced items and bones excavated by the IHP in 1936. Wei suggests that they were excavated at the same time and became separated before most of the inscriptions were removed to Taiwan. However, the joins mean that the seven items in Table 7.1 were without a doubt from the immediate vicinity of the *da lian keng*, as Dong stated. Given the homogeneity of Smith's acquisitions, it is likely that most of the rest of his collection came from the same location.

Scapula HJ27456 as Evidence of Scribal Training

The first item in Table 7.1, HJ27456, is a join of two fragments from Smith's collection with a further fragment from the 1929 IHP excavations at the *da lian keng*, now in Taiwan (Figure 7.1). It was a product of the He Group workshop, as were many items from Smith's collection and from the *da lian keng*. Modern typologies of the Anyang inscription further subdivide the He Group, primarily on the basis of writing style, and different authors use different terms in their typologies of Anyang divination inscriptions, even when they agree on the membership of a type. The example to be discussed is a representative of the "He Group II" type (Li Xueqin and Peng Yushang 1996: 139–157), also referred to as "He Group I" by Huang Tianshu (1991) and Yang Yuyan (2005: 8). This chapter uses Li and Peng's terminology. The scapula HJ27456 shows obvious signs of having been used by a trainee for writing practice. The graphs on the reverse (not reproduced here) are indisputably incompetent. Many of those on the obverse are also less than fully secure, and the formulae they write are in several cases incomplete or otherwise anomalous. The presence of trainee inscriptions has been noted previously and interpreted as "engraving practice" (*xike* 習刻) (Zhang Juntao 2009b: 33–34). However, no attention has been paid to reconstructing the use-life of this complex object, or its implications for the question of literacy acquisition. Interestingly, Yim Lee (1970: 315–317), in his commentary on this scapula, disputed the join with Jia2799 (which he mistakenly referred to as Yi2799) on the grounds that the "chaotic and jumbled" inscriptions on the Columbia fragment and the orderly ones on the Taiwan piece "would not likely appear on the same object." In contrast, the interpretation of this chapter, in terms of scribal training exercises added to a used divination bone, turns the basis for this objection into additional evidence for making the join. There is no doubt that the Columbia and Taiwan fragments were originally parts of the same object.

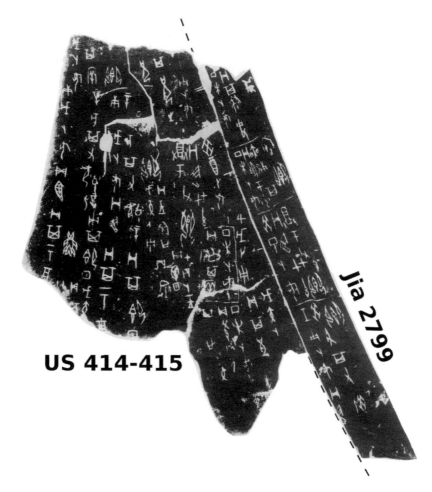

Figure 7.1. Scapula with divination records and scribal training exercises (HJ27456 = US414-415 + Jia2799).

Actual Shang records of pyro-osteomancy (as opposed to scribal training inscriptions or other texts that sometimes appear on shells and bones from Anyang) are by definition records of activity associated with particular heat-cracking events that took place on the bone or plastron. The Anyang divination scribes usually placed each divination record at a point on the bone or plastron close to the location where the heat crack appeared. The location corresponded to a gouged-out notch on the reverse surface where heat had been applied to produce the crack. This provides an important test for distinguishing divination records from other textual material, including trainee texts: a text is aligned with a crack on the obverse and a gouged-out notch on the reverse if and only if it is a real divination record (Smith 2011b: 191–196). The situation is made more complex by formats like the so-called "Bin Group big-character scapulae (*Binzu dazi guban* 賓組大字骨版)." The texts on these objects, written in large, clear graphs, are indistinguishable from divination records in terms of content yet do not correspond with the positions of divinatory cracks or notches. I have tentatively pursued Matsumaru's (2000) proposal that these may be some form of model text for scribal instruction (Smith 2008: 373–384). However, other interpretations exist (e.g., Sakikawa Takashi 2008) that would complicate spatial correspondence with cracks and notches as a criterion for distinguishing actual divination records from other categories of inscription.

Figure 7.2a maps the locations of cracks (obverse) and notches (reverse) on HJ27456 onto an outline of the obverse of the scapula. Since it is uninscribed, the reverse of the fragment in Taiwan (Jia2799) does not appear in HJ, but it can be inspected as a color photograph via an online database maintained by the IHP (http://archeodata.sinica.edu.tw/allindex. html, accessed December 14, 2011). There are six sets of notches and cracks, four running parallel to the right-hand edge, and two more at the proximal (top) end of the scapula. Note how the four collinear cracks were responsible for the break separating US414 from Jia2799. Although weakened at these points, the object remained intact while it was still in use and being inscribed, and it only fragmented when or after it was discarded and buried.

Since there are only six sets of notches and cracks on what remains of the scapula, we should expect to find no more than six records of divination events, written at positions adjacent to the cracks. Instead, the plastron surface is densely covered with inscriptions. There are 22 inscriptional units on the obverse of the scapula (Figure 7.2b). One or two of those units could be records corresponding to notches and cracks on missing fragments, but certainly there are many that, although they formally resemble divination records, cannot be actual records of divination performed using this bone. Some of the units are in an insecure hand, suggesting that the roughly 16 non-records represent some kind of exercise in scribal training.

Identifying the six records that correspond to the six cracks and notches is straightforward in most cases. The four records that run up the right-hand edge of the scapula, which ended up on the fragment in Taiwan, align with the run of four collinear cracks. They are neatly separated by dividing lines, and their corresponding cracks have been numbered by the scribe (on the Columbia side of the break). Each of these four records is dated in the normal way according to the sexagenary cycle of days. An established convention for

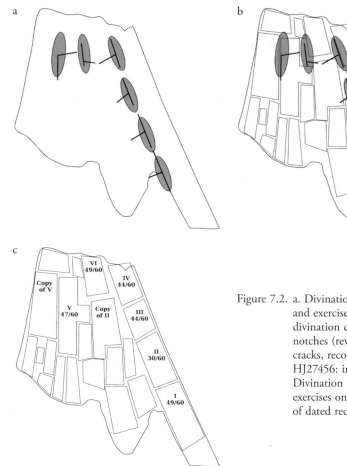

Figure 7.2. a. Divination cracks, records,
and exercises on HJ27456:
divination cracks (obverse) and
notches (reverse); b. Divination
cracks, records, and exercises on
HJ27456: inscription units; c.
Divination cracks, records, and
exercises on HJ27456: sequence
of dated records and copies.

scapulae belonging to this workshop is for a series of divinations running
along the edge of a scapula like this to be executed in bottom-to-top order.
Other He Group II items from the *da lian keng* that are most closely
comparable to the scapula under discussion include: Jia2484 + Jia2502 =
HJ27321; Jia2490 = HJ27138; Jia2748 = HJ27430; Jia2544 = HJ27564;
Jia2880 81 + Jia2692 93 + Jia2574 = HJ27042 + HJBB10209. Assuming
that the bottom-to-top order holds in this particular case, the sequence of
dates for the series of four divinations would then probably be: day 49 > day
30 (41 days later) > day 44 (14 days later) > day 44 (same day). Figure 7.2c
shows the location of these four records, labeled I to IV with their 60–cycle
dates. The record of the divination corresponding to the leftmost crack and
notch must be the one labeled V in Figure 7.2c, given its position relative

to the notch, and the fact that it has been used as a model for copying by a less confident hand. This divination took place on a cyclical day 47, most probably three days after divinations III and IV. The inscription labeled VI, dated to a day 49 and probably two days later than V, must be the record for the middle-top crack and notch: the only other inscription adjacent to the horizontal arm of the crack is, as we shall see, a trainee copy of II. The two inscriptions immediately to the left of VI, incomplete because of the break, may also have been actual records corresponding to cracks and notches on the missing proximal end of the scapula.

Divinations I–VI were all, according to their corresponding records, performed by the diviner He, after whom the He Group is named. Divinations I–III and V were for the purpose of validating offerings to dead members of the royal lineage, referred to by their posthumous day-names. Records II and V are of particular importance to the argument that follows, and they are transcribed and translated here:

> 癸巳卜，何貞：翌甲午蒸于父甲，饗。
> Day 30 cracking, He divined: "Tomorrow, day 31, make a *zheng*-offering to Father Day 1, feasting (?)." (Record II)

The reference to Father Day 1 is especially important as it allows the divination to be assigned to a particular royal generation, that of Father Day 1's sons (and Wu Ding's grandsons), Kang Ding 康丁 and Lin Xin 廩辛 (ca. 1150 B.C.).

> 庚戌卜，何貞：翌辛亥其又毓妣辛，饗。
> Day 47 cracking, He divined: "Tomorrow, day 48, the *you*-sacrifice will perhaps be performed to Recent Female Ancestor Day 8, feasting (?)." (Record V)

Recent Female Ancestor Day 8 is the posthumous name of Fu Hao (婦好 "Wife Hao"), one of Wu Ding's spouses and the grandmother (or possibly great aunt) of the reigning Kang Ding.

Besides the actual divination records I–VI and the one or two damaged inscriptions that may also have been real records, *all* the remaining inscriptional units appearing in Figure 7.2b are scribal exercises, added after the bone ceased to be used as a divinatory tool. First, they are written in a visibly less secure hand (or hands) than the actual records. Second, they include two close-to-verbatim copies of records II and V. Third, they include errors that no competent scribe would be likely to make. Finally, no other candidate explanation is available for the appearance of all these densely packed inscriptions with no corresponding cracks or hollows. The reasons for thinking that the trainee texts were added after the divination records are: first, that they are arranged simply so as to fill up remaining space and are somewhat jumbled as a consequence, while the positions of the records proper are orderly and constrained by the locations of the corresponding cracks and notches; second, as just mentioned, the trainee texts include two imperfect copies of actual records; and third, it seems intuitively more likely that a discarded divination bone would be made available for trainees to practice on, rather than that a practice scapula would be used for royal sacrifice divinations after scribal trainees had finished writing out exercises on it.

The visual contrast between what I describe as a less secure trainee hand (or hands) and the more secure hand responsible for records I–VI is a rather subjective one or, at any rate, one that is difficult to express concisely in words. Also, apart from the very poorly executed graphs on the reverse, which previous authors have agreed are "engraving practice" (Shang Chengzuo 1933: 41, Transcriptions; Yao Xiaosui and Xiao Ding 1988: 611), the engraving of the trainee inscriptions is not especially badly done. One can find many examples on other objects of real divination records being kept by hands that are similarly unsure (and which presumably belong to relatively inexperienced scribes). It is for this reason that relative competence in engraving is not, in isolation, an adequate criterion for distinguishing practice inscriptions from actual records. The other criteria mentioned above – absence of matching cracks and notches, errors and anomalies, signs of copying, and the overall use-history of the object – all need to be considered. The term *xike* 習刻, or "practice engraving," has typically been applied only to obviously incompetent hands, without reference to other criteria, and so has captured only the tail-end of a much larger body of evidence relating to scribal training.

That said, I invite the reader to consult reproductions of the scapula in question, together with other He Group II inscriptions, to test their intuition against mine as to what constitutes a more or less secure hand. Records II and V and their copies are reproduced in Figure 7.3. In all cases the text flows in columns from top to bottom. The columns flow from left to right, except for the copy of record II, in which they are arranged from right to left. Record V and its copy probably provide the clearer demonstration of the contrast in scribal competence. Readers familiar with the script will have little trouble noting in the copy of record V the weakness of the last two graphs of the first (leftmost) column of the copy (貞 and 翌), and of the fourth and fifth graphs in the next column (又 and 㲋), especially compared with the record that provided the model.

Besides the relative insecurity of the engraving technique, two errors made by the scribal trainee are also informative. The copy of record V is a faithful one. Not only is the text reproduced verbatim, but even the layout of the graphs in columns is preserved. In contrast, the copy of record II departs at two points from its model in such a way as to result in anomalies that

Figure 7.3. Divination records and trainee copies on HJ27456.

would be unlikely to occur in an actual divination record written by a fully competent scribe.

The first anomaly is the date. Recall from the transcription and translation above that record II was for day 30 of the 60-day cycle and concerned a ritual procedure to be performed the following day: "tomorrow, day 31." In the copy, one of the terms in the date of the divination has been changed, so that the text now begins, "Day 10 (癸酉) cracking, He divined: 'Tomorrow, day 31'." Clearly, an error has been introduced, and the two dates are no longer compatible. The word I translate as "tomorrow," *yi* 翌, can less commonly refer to other days in the upcoming 10–day Shang week. However, in the great majority of cases (including records I, II and V on this scapula) the day is the immediately subsequent one. It is sometimes claimed that it can refer to a day more than a 10-day week in the future. However, reported examples are rare enough for one to suspect that they are all anomalous in precisely the same way that the example considered here is. Among the examples tabulated by Chang Yuzhi (1998: 241), 73% refer to the immediately subsequent day, and only 1% seem to be referring to a day more than 10 days away. Note that Chang's only example from the He Group with a date at a remove of more than 10 days is the Columbia scapula itself. Thus, this kind of error in the scapula's text supports the contention that this inscriptional unit is not an actual record containing meaningful information but instead an inexact copy. It also suggests that the scribe was not used to the manipulation of common formulae involving cyclical dates.

The second anomaly indicates that the scribe making the copy of record II did not understand the text being copied. The scribe visually misunderstood the ligature (*hewen* 合文) for "Father Day 1" that occupies the third graph position in the third column of record II. The ligature combines the graph for "cyclical day 1" (which resembles our plus sign), with the graph for "father." The ligature should appear (as it does in record II) as ⼗⺈. Note that in record II, the graph for "cyclical day 1" also occurs in the third position in the middle column as part of the date, "day 31". It overlaps in a visually distinctive manner with its counterpart in the ligature. The trainee appears to have understood the two coincidentally overlapping "cyclical day 1" graphs as components of a single graph and the "father" component of the ligature as an independent graph, writing out the copy accordingly.

Both of these errors would be difficult to account for if this were a competent scribe merely transferring literacy skills onto the unfamiliar medium of bone. Ancestral day-name ligatures are exceedingly common in Shang inscriptions. By the end of the second millennium B.C., they had become a common feature in labels on cast bronze ritual vessels, sets of ritual equipment among the Shang-influenced elite across north China (Smith 2011a: 9–14). It is hard to imagine that a fully trained scribe working for a royal patron would have misunderstood this reference to his employer's dead father. Similarly, there is no known Shang graph resembling the paired "cyclical day 1" compound that the trainee has mistakenly written. It is inconceivable that even a modestly literate individual would have failed to recognize that an ordinary 60-cycle date was what was required in this context. We can thus conclude that the individual responsible for the copy, though capable of quite controlled and tidy engraving, was unfamiliar with some of the most common graphs and textual conventions. This trainee seems to have been in the process of acquiring a knowledge of literacy through the sight-copying of actual divination records produced by a scribe of the He Group.

Conclusions

As Dong Zuobin first stated, Smith's collection has important connections with the He Group inscriptions excavated in 1929 from the *da lian keng*, and it must have been unearthed at that location. Joins with excavated fragments now in Taiwan confirm Dong's original proposal. The link is strong enough that studies of either the He Group or the contents of the *da lian keng* should probably treat Smith's collection and the contents of the *da lian keng* as a single unit. Although both collections contain material from other groups, they are dominated by He Group inscriptions. It is likely that the workshop that produced the He Group inscriptions operated somewhere in the vicinity of the *da lian keng*.

Another trait that Smith's collection shares with the items excavated in 1929 is the significant presence of the remains of scribal training. Besides the scapula discussed in this chapter, the joins listed in the second, third, and last items in Table 7.1 all show clear signs of trainee hands, as do a number of Smith's other smaller fragments at Columbia.

HJ27456 is a complex example of a divination scapula that, after a period of use documented in writing on its surface, was turned over to scribal trainees for practice. The bone was in use for divination over a period of about 60 days. Six records corresponding to six heat cracks remain on the portions of the scapula that survive, dated to within that span of time. The remaining inscriptions (the substantial majority) were added subsequently by scribal trainees. In some cases they took actual records on the bone as their model, probably for the purpose of sight-copying. In others, they may have relied on records on other discarded divination bones that were made available to them. Errors made by the trainees imply that they were not fully literate individuals learning how to engrave, but rather reasonably competent engravers with a very imperfect grasp of the script. As with other evidence from the *da lian keng*, this item from Ernest Smith's collection suggests that the divination workshops at Anyang taught literacy skills to their own scribes.

Acknowledgements

I would like to thank Ria Koopmans-de Bruijn and Jim Cheng of the Starr East Asian Library, Columbia University, for providing access to and information about the inscriptions in their collection.

References

Abbreviations of standard corpora of inscriptions (numbers used with the abbreviations are serial numbers within the corpus, not page numbers):

CunYi   Shang Chengzuo 1933
HD   Zhongguo Shehuikexueyuan Kaogu Yanjiusuo 2003
HJ   Guo Moruo 1978
HJBB   Zhongguo Shehuikexueyuan Lishi Yanjiusuo 1999
Jia   Dong Zuobin 1948
US   Chou 1976

Bagley, Robert
    2004 Anyang Writing and the Origins of the Chinese Writing System. In *The First Writing: Script Invention as History and Process*, edited by Stephen Houston, pp. 190–249. Cambridge University Press, New York.

Bai Yuzheng 白玉崢

    1989 *Jiaguwen lu yanjiu* 甲骨文錄研究. Yiwen Yinshuguan 藝文印書館, Taibei.

Baughman, Roland (editor)

    1952 Our Growing Collections. *Columbia Library Columns* 1(2): 22–26.

Bunker, Emma C.

    1997 *Ancient Bronzes of the Eastern Eurasian Steppes from the Arthur M. Sackler Collections*. Arthur M. Sackler Foundation, New York.

Cai Zhemao 蔡哲茂

    2004 *Jiagu zhuihe xuji* 甲骨綴合續集. Wenjin Chubanshe 文津出版社, Taibei.

Chang Yuzhi 常玉芝

    1998 *Yin Shang lifa yanjiu* 殷商歷法研究. Jilin Wenshi Chubanshe 吉林文史出版社, Changchun.

Chou, Hung-hsiang

    1976 *Oracle Bone Collections in the United States*. University of California Press, Berkeley.

Columbia University Office of the President

    1937 *Annual Report of the President and Treasurer to the Trustees with Accompanying Documents for the Year Ending June 30, 1937*. Columbia University, New York.

Coryell, Dorothea Smith

    1970 *Small Mouse Person in China*. Dorothea Smith Coryell, Santa Barbara, California.

Dai Jun 岱峻

    2009 *Li Ji zhuan* 李濟傳. Jiangsu Wenyi Chubanshe 江蘇文藝出版社, Nanjing.

Dong Zuobin 董作賓

    1948 *Yinxu wenzi jia bian* 殷虛文字甲編. Guoli Zhongyang Yanjiuyuan Lishi Yuyan Yanjiusuo 國立中央研究院歷史語言 研究所, Nanking.

Edwards, Dwight

    1959 *Yenching University*. United Board for Christian Higher Education in Asia, New York.

Flad, Rowan

    2008 Divination and Power: A Multiregional View of the Development of Oracle Bone Divination in Early China. *Current Anthropology* 49(3): 403–437.

Goodrich, L. Carrington

    1957 Archaeology in China: the First Decades. *The Journal of Asian Studies* 17(1): 5–15.

    1959 Chinese Oracle Bones. *Columbia Library Columns* 8(3): 11–14.

Guo Moruo 郭沫若 (editor)

    1978–1982 *Jiaguwen heji* 甲骨文合集. 13 vols. Zhonghua Shuju 中華書局, Beijing.

Hu Houxuan 胡厚宣

    1988 *Su De Mei Ri suo jian jiagu ji* 蘇德美日所見甲骨集. Sichuan Cishu Chubanshe 四川辭書出版社, Hubei Cishu Chubanshe 湖北辭書出版社, Chengdu.

Hu Houxuan 胡厚宣 (editor)

    1999 *Jiaguwen heji cailiao laiyuanbiao* 甲骨文合集材料來原表. Zhongguo Shehui Kexue Chubanshe 中國社會科學出版社, Beijing.

Huang Tianshu 黃天樹

  1991   *Yinxu wang buci de fenlei yu duandai* 殷墟王卜辭的分類與斷代. Wenjin Chubanshe 文津出版社, Taibei.

Keightley, David N.

  1985   *Sources of Shang History: The Oracle-bone Inscriptions of Bronze Age China*. University of California Press, Berkeley.

  1997   Shang Oracle-bone Inscriptions. In *New Sources of Early Chinese History: An Introduction to the Reading of Inscriptions and Manuscripts*, edited by Edward Shaughnessy, pp. 15–55. Society for the Study of Early China and the Institute of East Asian Studies, University of California Berkeley, Berkeley.

Li Xueqin 李學勤 and Peng Yushang 彭裕商

  1996   *Yinxu jiagu fenqi yanjiu* 殷虛甲骨分期研究. Shanghai Guji Chubanshe 上海古籍出版社, Shanghai.

Lee Yim (Li Yan) 李棪

  1970   *Bei Mei suo jian jiagu xuancui kaoshi* 北美所見甲骨選粹考釋. Chinese University Press, Hong Kong. (Reprinted from the *Journal of the Institute of Chinese Studies of the Chinese University of Hong Kong*, Vol. 3[2], 1970.)

Matsumaru Michio 松丸道雄

  2000   Indai no gakusho ni tsuite: kôkotsubun no okeru "shûkoku" to "hôkoku" 殷代の学書について—甲骨文字における'習刻'と'法刻'. *Shogaku shodôshi kenkyu* 書学書道史 10: 3–17. Electronic document, http://dx.doi.org/10.11166/shogakushodoshi1991.2000.3, accessed December 14, 2011.

Qiu Xigui 裘錫圭

  1992   Jiagu zhuihe shi yi 甲骨綴合拾遺. In *Guwenzi lunji* 古文字論集, pp. 236–248. Zhonghua Shuju 中華書局, Beijing.

Sakikawa Takashi 崎川隆

  2008   Yinxu chutu dazi guban keci de shiliao xingzhi kaobian 殷墟出土大字骨版刻辭的史料性質考辨. In *Dongfang kaogu di si ji* 東方考古第四集, edited by Shandong Daxue Dongfang Kaogu Yanjiu Zhongxin 山東大學東方考古研究中心, 248–252. Kexue Chubanshe 科學出版社, Beijing.

Shang Chengzuo 商承祚

  1933   *Yin qi yi cun* 殷契佚存. Jinling Daxue Zhongguo Wenhua Yanjiusuo 金陵大學中國文化研究所, Nanjing.

Shi Zhangru 石璋如

  1985   *Jiagu kengceng zhi yi (yi ci zhi jiu ci chutu jiagu)* 甲骨坑層之一（一次至九次出土甲骨）. Zhongyang Yanjiuyuan Lishi Yuyan Yanjiusuo 中央研究院歷史語言研究所, Taiwan.

Smith, Adam D.

  2008   *Writing at Anyang: The Role of the Divination Record in the Emergence of Chinese Literacy*. Ph.D. dissertation, Cotsen Institute of Archaeology, University of California, Los Angeles. http://www.cangjie.info/files/ads_diss_complete.pdf.

  2011a The Chinese Sexagenary Cycle and the Ritual Foundations of the Calendar. In *Calendars and Years, Vol. 2: Astronomy and Time in the Ancient and Medieval World*, edited by John M. Steele, pp. 1–37. Oxbow Books, Oakville, Connecticut.

2011b The Evidence for Scribal Training at Anyang. In *Writing and Literacy in Early China*, edited by Li Feng and David Branner, pp. 173–205. University of Washington Press, Seattle.

Su Yunfeng 蘇雲峰

2004 *Qinghua Daxue shi sheng minglu ziliao huibian, 1927–1949* 清華大學師生名錄資料彙編, 1927–1949. 中央研究院近代史研究所 Zhongyang yanjiuyuan jindai shi yanjiusuo, Taibei.

Sun Haibo 孫海波

1937 *Jiaguwen lu* 甲骨文錄. Henan Tongzhi Guan 河南通志館, Henan.

Tong, Te-kong

1967 The Tortoise Shell that Set Off a Mighty Chain Reaction. *Columbia Library Columns* 16(3): 11–18.

Venture, Olivier

2002 Étude d'un emploi rituel de l'écrit dans la Chine archaïque (XIII\u1d9c–VIII\u1d9c siècle avant notre ère): réflexion sur les matériaux épigraphiques des Shang et des Zhou occidentaux. Unpublished PhD dissertation, Études de l'Extrême-Orient, Université Paris 7, Paris.

Wang Yuxin 王宇信 and Yang Shengnan 楊升南 (editors)

1999 *Jiaguxue yibai nian* 甲骨學一百年. Shehui kexue wenxian chubanshe 社會科學文獻出版社, Beijing.

Wang, Haicheng

2007 Writing and the State in Early China in Comparative Perspective. Unpublished PhD dissertation, Department of East Asian Studies, Princeton University, Princeton.

Wei Cide 魏慈德

2008 Tan yi er qi keng jiagu yu qita zhulu jiagu xiang zhuihe de xianxiang 談一二七坑與其它著錄甲骨相綴合的現象. In *Jinian Yinxu YH127 jiagukeng Nanjing shinei fajue 70 zhounian lunwenji* 紀念殷墟YH127甲骨坑南京室內發掘70周年論文集, edited by Song Zhenhao 宋鎮豪 and Tang Maosong 唐茂松, pp. 73–89. Wenwu Chubanshe 文物出版社, Beijing.

Xu Jingcan 許敬參 and Guan Baiyi 關百益

1933 *Yinxu wenzi cun zhen* 殷虛文字存眞. Henan Bowuguan 河南博物館, Kaifeng.

Yang Yuyan 楊郁彥

2005 *Jiaguwen heji fenzu fenlei zongbiao* 甲骨文合集分組分類總表. Yiwen Yinshuguan 藝文印書館, Taibei.

Yanjing Yanjiuyuan 燕京研究院

2001 *Yanjing Daxue renwu zhi* 燕京大學人物志. Beijing Daxue Chubanshe 北京大學出版社, Beijing.

Yao Xiaosui 姚孝遂 and Xiao Ding 肖丁

1988 *Yinxu jiagu keci moshi zongji* 殷墟甲骨刻辭摹釋總集. Zhonghua Shuju 中華書局, Beijing.

1989 *Yinxu jiagu keci leizuan* 殷墟甲骨刻辭類纂. Zhonghua Shuju 中華書局, Beijing.

Yao Xuan 姚萱

 2006 *Yinxu Huayuanzhuang dong di jiagu buci de chubu yanjiu* 殷墟花園莊東地甲骨卜辭的初步研究. Xianzhuang Shuju 線裝書局, Beijing.

Zhang Juntao 張軍濤

 2009a He zu jiagu xin zhui shjiu zu 何組甲骨新綴十九組. Electronic document, http://www.xianqin.org/blog/archives/1460.html, accessed October 12, 2011.

 2009b Hezu buci de zhengli yu yanjiu 何組卜辭的整理與研究. Unpublished MA thesis, Zhengzhou Daxue, Zhengzhou.

Zhang Shichao 張世超

 2002 *Yinxu jiagu ziji yanjiu: Shi zu buci pian* 殷墟甲骨字迹研究：師組卜辭篇. Dongbei Shifan Daxue Chubanshe 東北師範大學出版社, Changchun.

Zhongguo Shehuikexueyuan Kaogu Yanjiusuo 中國社會科學院考古研究所

 2003 *Yinxu Huayuanzhuang dong di jiagu* 殷墟花園莊東地甲骨. Yunnan Renmin Chubanshe 雲南人民出版社, Kunming.

Zhongguo Shehuikexueyuan Lishi Yanjiusuo 中國社會科學院歷史研究所 (editor)

 1999 *Jiaguwen heji bubian* 甲骨文合集補編. Yuwen Chubanshe 語文出版社, Beijing.

Tracing Networks of Cuneiform Scholarship with Oracc, GKAB, and Google Earth

Eleanor Robson

Oracc: Facilitating the Online Dissemination of Cuneiform Text

Since the cuneiform script began to be deciphered in the mid-nineteenth century, it has by and large remained the preserve of a small group of specialists. A few writings from the ancient Middle East have penetrated popular consciousness – the Laws of Hammurabi, the Epic of Gilgamesh, and perhaps the Babylonian Epic of Creation – and, particularly since James B. Pritchard's pioneering *Ancient Near Eastern Texts Relating to the Old Testament* (1st edn. 1950 and still in print today), print anthologies have disseminated larger bodies of translations to academic, educational, and wider readerships, especially through series such as Writings from the Ancient World, The Context of Scripture, and State Archives of Assyria in English, Texte aus der Umwelt des Alten Testaments in German, and Littératures anciennes du Proche-Orient in French, as well as in a number of stand-alone works (e.g., recently, Black et al. 2004; Chavalas 2006; Foster 2005). But anthologies are necessarily selective, subject as they are to the constraints and conventions of the commercially viable book, which makes them relatively intractable as research resources for those without access to, or expertise in, the original sources.

Since the mid-1990s there have been various attempts to create online corpora of cuneiform texts, but even the most long-lived and successful – namely the *Cuneiform Digital Library Initiative* (CDLI, cdli.ucla.edu) and *The Electronic Text Corpus of Sumerian Literature* (ETCSL, etcsl.orinst. ox.ac.uk) – have their drawbacks as well as their strengths. By the end of 2010 CDLI contained records of some 250,000 cuneiform tablets, but its primary focus is providing basic reference transliterations of inscribed objects, rather than offering a scholarly working environment for the development of analytic tools or easy comprehensibility for non-expert users. The ETCSL project (1996–2006), by contrast, produced text editions of some 400 works of Sumerian literature from the period 2100–1600 B.C., in alphabetic transliteration and English translation, with sophisticated textual search and linguistic analysis tools. There, though, the emphasis was on the reconstruction of whole compositions rather than the documentation of individual manuscript witnesses. Both projects have been addressed primarily to cuneiformists rather than to a wider public.

Over the past few years, a new consortium of online projects has grown up, steered by a small group of us, who had been (and still are) closely involved with CDLI and ETCSL in various ways and wished to retain or develop the best practices of both projects, while offering new facilities for the widest possible range of users, in order to complement CDLI's central archival role as a catalogue, image database, and transliteration repository. Oracc – *The Open, Richly Annotated Cuneiform Corpus* (oracc.org) – went public in mid-2010. Developed by Steve Tinney and steered by him, Niek Veldhuis, and myself, it comprises a workspace and toolkit for the development of a complete corpus of cuneiform whose rich annotation and open licensing are designed to support the next generation of scholarly research and online dissemination of data and findings. Let us look at each of those features in turn.

Oracc is *open* in several senses.[1] Most obviously, the data and tools it provides are released under a Creative Commons Attribution Share-Alike license (http://creativecommons.org/licenses/by-sa/3.0/), meaning that all users and developers are free to access, create, and re-use Oracc material without formal permission, as long as they attribute the original work to its creator(s) and funders, and release their derived work under a similarly open licensing agreement. Just as fundamentally, the Oracc Steering Committee is committed to principles of co-operative, collaborative, responsive working. Our goal is to provide standards-based, well-documented resources that are as simple, flexible, and adaptable to user needs as possible, and supported by free server space, backup, and personal contact with Oracc liaison staff (for more information, see http://oracc.org/doc/about/aboutoracc/index.html).

Oracc aims to encourage the development of a comprehensive *cuneiform corpus*, as inclusive and exhaustive as possible, across languages (Sumerian, Akkadian, Hittite, Elamite, Aramaic, Old Persian, etc.), script type, time (ca. 3300 B.C.–A.D. 100), place (across the Middle East from Anatolia to Egypt to Iran), and genre (from mundane administrative records to arcane scholarly works). It does so by facilitating individual corpus-based projects across the world, each with their own aims, objectives, and funding. By the end of 2010 it comprised seven major public corpora, plus a further 15 in development. While some, such as *The Digital Corpus of Cuneiform Lexical Texts* (DCCLT, oracc.org/dcclt), track particular genres through time, others, such as *The State Archives of Assyria online* (SAAo, oracc.org/saao), provide access to multiple genres of texts from particular times or places. Some, such as SAAo, are re-presentations and developments of print publications; others, such as DCCLT, are born digital. Further projects, currently under development, will be released online and in print simultaneously. Minimally, projects consist of alphabetic transliterations of cuneiform text corpora, with associated catalogue metadata (which may be drawn from CDLI), but Oracc also encourages the provision of translations, in any modern language – or more than one – as well as various types of annotation.

Oracc corpora can be *richly annotated* in several senses. Oracc provides various tools for the linguistic annotation of cuneiform texts, from lemmatisation (the association of individual spellings of words to dictionary head-words for the generation of language glossaries), to the analysis of number systems (in economic, mathematical, or astronomical contexts, for instance), orthography (spelling habits), prosopography (patterns of naming), and social networks (who trades or trains or communicates with whom). We are also in the process of developing a range of infrastructure projects, currently planned to include super-glossaries of Sumerian and Akkadian, and a global sign list of cuneiform. Finally, we also offer facilities for creating portal websites which serve as the introductory front-end to individual projects. These sites – such as the SAAo portals *Assyrian Empire Builders* (www.ucl.ac.uk/sargon) and *Knowledge and Power in the Neo-Assyrian Empire* (K&P, oracc.org/saao/knpp) – enable projects to present explanatory or supplementary material to non-specialist audiences, whether background essays, glossaries of technical terms, summaries of the project's aims and findings, or any other content.

We provide all Oracc corpora and Oracc-hosted portal sites with visitor access statistics so that project directors can report to their funders or institutions on the range and depth of their online outreach. For instance, in January 2011 SAAo had some 370 unique visitors from 32 countries, making nearly 1,300 visits between them and accessing an average of 20 pages each. During the same month one of its portals, K&P, had nearly 3,300 visitors from 105 different countries, who made a total of 4,500 visits and accessed around 3 pages each time. Given that 370 would be a generous estimate of the number of professional cuneiformists worldwide, and 3,300 a similarly generous estimate of the number of their graduate students, it is clear that Oracc corpora and associated portal sites are enabling cuneiform texts to reach a more global – and educationally diverse – audience than ever before.[2]

GKAB: Researching the Ancient Dissemination of Cuneiform Scholarship

One of Oracc's core projects is *The Geography of Knowledge in Assyria and Babylonia, 700–200 B.C.* (GKAB, oracc.org/cams/gkab), funded by the U.K. Arts and Humanities Research Council (2007–2012), and jointly directed by Tinney and myself at the Universities of Pennsylvania and Cambridge. Its core aim was to investigate the generation, replication, dissemination, and consumption of scholarly knowledge in cuneiform culture. Questions about the ownership and accessibility of knowledge, the circumstances and environments in which it flourishes or perishes, the socio-political influences and impacts of its transmission and reception, are all central to the history and sociology of science. GKAB addressed these ideas in relation to ancient Assyria and Babylonia in the first millennium B.C., while exploring the potential and limitations of applying and adapting methodologies designed to analyse modern techno-science for the study of ancient scholarship (Robson 2011). GKAB's central dataset comprises online editions of nearly 1,500 scholarly manuscripts, a major component of the Oracc-hosted *Corpus of Ancient Mesopotamian Scholarship* (CAMS, oracc.org/cams). Learned writings are probably (almost) as old as cuneiform script itself (Veldhuis 2006), but GKAB focused on the tablets found in and around just four discrete buildings from a 500-year period of the first millennium B.C., all formally excavated and at least minimally published, but none hitherto subjected to holistic study and analysis. Such collections are commonly called "libraries" in Assyriological parlance (e.g., Clancier 2009; Pedersén 1998). I have addressed the thorny question of what constitutes a cuneiform library elsewhere (Robson 2013; Robson and Stevens in press); here I shall simply avoid the term wherever possible.

From the ninth to seventh centuries B.C., Assyria was by far the most powerful empire of the Mediterranean and Middle East. The ideology of empire centred on the symbiotic relationship between the king and the great god Aššur: military conquest was both an act of devotion and confirmation of Aššur's support. But Assyrian kingship depended not solely on piety and military might. A retinue of scholarly advisors guided royal decision-making through the observation and analysis of omens, and the performance of appropriate rituals (Radner 2011). The scholars in turn depended on a wide range of scholarly works written on cuneiform tablets, from astronomy to mythology, kept both in private households and in institutions such as temples and palaces. Two of the GKAB corpora stem from seventh-century Assyria, one belonging to a temple in the royal city of Kalhu, close to the capital Nineveh, and the other deliberately hidden outside a private house in the western provincial town of Huzirina several hundred miles away.

After Assyria fell in 612 B.C., Babylonian scholarly activity continued to flourish and develop under the patronage of wealthy urban temples in the south. Here scholarship was adapted to new purposes of maintaining the intellectual integrity and social status of native religion in the face of new ways of thinking and believing. The courts of Achaemenid (ca. 540–330 B.C.) and Seleucid (ca. 330–130 B.C.) rulers no longer supported cuneiform scholarly traditions. New genres came into being; others were adapted or survived relatively unchanged; still others disappeared completely. Temples were the last bastions of cuneiform scholarship until at least the final centuries B.C. The GKAB project focused on three assemblages of scholarly tablets from the southern city of Uruk. Two are from successive strata of a well-to-do house in the southeastern corner of the city, occupied consecutively by two apparently unrelated families of *mašmaššu*s ("incantation priests") in the late-fifth and late-fourth centuries B.C. The third, which I shall not discuss further here, has been reconstructed from tablets excavated from a second-century storeroom in one of the city's central temples, together with tablets stemming from illicit diggings in the vicinity in the early twentieth century (on the tablets from this temple, see Robson 2013).

By looking at similarity and difference across the five groups of tablets, and by drawing on appropriate comparanda from other places and periods, the GKAB project addressed some fundamental questions about the changing meanings and functions of literate scholarship in first-millennium cuneiform culture. Of particular relevance to the geography of knowledge are questions concerning the relationship(s) between scholarly practice, familial inheritance, and royal power, as well as the survival, adaptation, and development of learning in face of political change.

These are novel topics for Assyriological study. Since A. Leo Oppenheim's articulation of the notion of a "stream of tradition" (Oppenheim 1960), it has been commonplace to posit a stable corpus of scholarly writings which was relatively accessible to all learned men, through copying and commentary, as part of their formal education throughout the first millennium B.C. At mid-century this was a reasonable inference from the evidence then available, which was weighted heavily to the famous and gargantuan "Library of Assurbanipal" from seventh-century Nineveh in the absence of the large number of smaller, formally excavated assemblages that have since become available. This is not the place for a longer discussion of the relevant historiography and excavation/publication history of the material (Robson 2011) or an up-to-date survey of excavated assemblages of cuneiform scholarship from the first millennium B.C. (Robson and Stevens in press). However, it is now clear that this apparently archetypal "Library of Assurbanipal" is in fact atypical in several key ways (Robson 2013). First, containing tens of thousands of manuscripts, it was about 50 times the size of any other scholarly tablet collection now known. For example, the so-called *āšipus'* house in seventh-century Assur and the Ebabbar temple in sixth-century Sippar each held a collection of about 800 tablets (Pedersén 1998: 135–136, 194–197). Second, it was assembled, at least in part, through coercion and conquest, while most scholarly communities – without world-class armies at their disposal – had to rely on the more normal means of inheritance, collection, and copying. Third, at its apogee, it was directly shaped by the close involvement of two of the most powerful men in the ancient world: the Assyrian king Esarhaddon (r. 681–669 B.C.) and his son Assurbanipal (r. 669–ca. 630 B.C.).

Further, it is only since Oppenheim's day that the mechanisms and motivations behind the dissemination of knowledge have been the subject of sustained academic study. Most relevant for our purposes here is the work of the sociologist of science Bruno Latour, who articulated several related concepts that have opened up new lines of geographical research:

> If techno-science may be described as being so powerful and yet so small, so concentrated and yet dilute, it means it has the characteristics of a *network*. The word network indicates that resources are concentrated in a few places – the knots and the nodes – which are connected with one another – the links and the mesh: these connections transform the scattered resources into a net that may seem to extend everywhere [Latour 1987: 180; emphasis added].

If we in turn understand the scholars of cuneiform culture as actors in a Latourian network, it becomes apparent why earlier generations of Assyriologists perceived the intellectual world those scholars created as ubiquitous, monolithic, and self-sustaining.

But for Latour, people are not the only actors in the network; objects are too, and in particular inscriptions (whether computer printouts or cuneiform tablets) are "immutable and combinable *mobiles* … conveniently at hand and combinable at will, no matter whether they are twenty centuries old or a day old" (Latour 1987: 227; emphasis added). In other words, writing travels as much as people do, taking established knowledge to new places, and enabling new knowledge to be created through acts of editing and rewriting. In order for this to happen the messy observables of the real world have to be reduced and simplified into manageable scientific (or scholarly) data: "*Metrology* is the name of this gigantic exercise to make of the outside a world inside which facts and machines can survive" (Latour 1987: 251; emphasis added). The final act in the transformation of new knowledge into established truth is to "black box" it, or erase all traces of the process of production: "The word black box is used by cyberneticians whenever a piece of machinery or a set of commands is too complex. In its place they draw a little box about which they need to know nothing but its input and output" (Latour 1987: 2). According to the *Oxford English Dictionary Online,* the term "black box" was originally Royal Air Force slang for "a navigational instrument in an aircraft," later extended to denote any "device which performs intricate functions but whose internal mechanism may not readily be inspected or understood" (OED Online 2013). Cuneiform scholars, we can now see, were masters of black-boxing: almost no evidence remains of how their learned writings came to be.

By taking a Latourian view of the production and dissemination of scientific knowledge, and by plotting the origins of people, writings, and deities on Google Earth, we are able to see afresh the means and routes by which scholarship travelled around the buildings and communities studied by the GKAB project. Here I focus on just three of them, which – as we shall see – are sufficient to challenge the old assumption that all cuneiform "libraries" served essentially the same functions for essentially the same sorts of people.

Kalhu: An Assyrian Royal City

The city of Kalhu on the Tigris (biblical Calah, modern Nimrud) was the Assyrian imperial capital for much of the ninth and eighth centuries, and continued to function as a royal city until its fall in 614 B.C. (on the archaeology of Kalhu, see Curtis et al. 2008; Mallowan 1966; Oates and Oates 2001). A short walk from the palace was a temple named Ezida, dedicated to the god of wisdom Nabu. Fully half of the 250-odd scholarly tablets found in a room immediately opposite his shrine bear omens, incantations, and rituals – for advising the Assyrian king on political decision-making and for helping him to maintain his relationship with the gods. A further quarter comprise hymns and lexical works (standardised lists of words and cuneiform signs), while the majority of the remainder comprise medical, literary and calendrical writings (on the scholarly tablets from Kalhu, see Black 2008; Pedersén 1998: 151–152; Wiseman and Black 1996; and http://oracc.org/cams/gkab/kalhu). The generic profile of the collection is very similar to that of the libraries at Nineveh (Robson 2013).

Some 30 scholarly tablets of the Kalhu Ezida corpus have extant or partially surviving colophons, from which at least 15 names of scholars can be identified. Many of them belong to just two dynasties of Assyrian royal scholars. The earliest comprises several generations of the descendants of Ištaran-šumu-ukin, a tenth(?)-century *āšip šarri* ("royal exorcist"):

- Ištaran-mudammiq, *šaggamaḫḫu* ("senior exorcist") of king Assurnaṣirpal II (r. 883–859 B.C.), son of Tappuya, *šatammu* ("temple administrator") of Der and grandson of the *šatammu* Huzalu; owner of an ominous calendar for the month of Tašritu (CTN 4, 58; duplicate KAR 147, with the same colophon, found in Assur);

- Ištaran-mudammiq's grandson (name missing), son of Nabu-mudammiq; owner or copyist of a compendium of incantations called *Utukkū lemnūtu* "Evil demons" (CTN 4, 103); possibly Babilaya (see below) or a brother of his;
- Ištaran-mudammiq's great-grandson Marduk-[...], the *ṭupšar šarri* ("royal scribe"), and *ummânu* ("scholar") of king Adad-nerari III (r. 811–783 B.C.); son of the *āšip šarri* Babilaya; owner of a tablet of celestial omen series *Enūma Anu Ellil* (CTN 4, 8, dated 787 B.C.).

By the late eighth century, it appears that the Ištaran-šumu-ukin family had been ousted or superseded by the descendants of Gabbu-ilani-ereš, *ummânu* of Assurnaṣirpal II (and thus Ištaran-mudammiq's contemporary):

- Adad-šumu-uṣur, chief *āšipu* of king Esarhaddon and son of the famous scholar Nabu-zuqup-kena; owner of a tablet from the terrestrial omen series *Šumma ālu* (CTN 4, 45);
- a son (name missing but possibly Šumaya) of his brother Nabu-zeru-lešir (?), Esarhaddon's chief scribe; copyist of an ominous calendar (CTN 4, 59) "for the prolongation of his life;"[3]
- further sons or descendants of Nabu-zuqup-kena are mentioned in colophons of two tablets of physiognomic omens *Alandimmû* and another of unidentified omens (CTN 4, 74; 78; 89).
- Nabu-le'i, son of Adad-šumu-uṣur's close associate, Esarhaddon's chief lamenter Urad-Ea; scribe of a hitherto unidentified ritual (CTN 4, 187), which he "copied like its original for him to see".

Nabu-zuqup-kena himself, chief scribe to kings Sargon II (r. 721–705 B.C.) and Sennacherib (r. 704–681 B.C.), wrote over 60 surviving scholarly tablets, nearly two-thirds of which explicitly state that they were written in Kalhu (Hunger 1968: 90–95, nos. 293–311, of which nos. 293–294 and 305 name Kalhu). However, the tablets themselves belong to the Kuyunjik collection of the British Museum, most likely meaning that they were excavated by Layard and his associates from the royal citadel of Nineveh. Likewise, his sons Adad-šumu-uṣur and Nabu-zeru-lešir are well attested in Assyrian court correspondence from Nineveh, sometimes in collaboration with Urad-Ea and other colleagues.[4] Adad-šumu-uṣur also worked at Kalhu, where he is documented performing a ritual against two types of fungi that had infested Ezida (SAA 13, 71). Coincidentally or not, a tiny fragment of *Šumma ālu* ("If a city") Tablet XIII, containing omens about fungus growths, is amongst the extant scholarly tablets from the Kalhu Ezida (CTN 4, 36).

By contrast, the only other well-documented scholar in the temple conspicuously never mentions his family:[5]

- Banunu, an *āšipu*, is copyist and/or owner of four scholarly tablets: a prayer of divination "from a Babylonian original" (CTN 4, 61); the ritual *Mīs pî* "Mouth opening" (CTN 4, 188); medical recipes (CTN 4, 188); and the medical plant list *Uruanna* (CTN 4, 192). In the colophons of the second and third he exhorts, "Do not disperse the *gerginakku* (library); taboo of Ea, king of the Apsu". The copyist of a cultic commentary (CTN 4, 185), whose name is now missing, also asks for that tablet [not to be removed] "from the *gerginakku* (library) of the temple."

It is possible, but by no means certain, that this is the same Banunu who, in the aftermath of Assurbanipal's conquest of Babylonia, was assigned oversight of the governor of Nippur's son in the Succession Palace at Nineveh after he had finished copying out *Enūma Anu Ellil* ("the Series") (SAA 11, 156; Parpola 1983).

The Ezida at Kalhu was not the only Assyrian royal temple to Nabu, god of wisdom. In 717 B.C. Sargon began construction work on a new capital city, Dur-Šarruken (modern Khorsabad), some 30 miles upriver of Kalhu. Within the citadel, adjacent to the palace and linked to it by a private walkway, he commissioned a bigger and better Ezida. This new temple was furnished with two rooms fitted with pigeonholes for storing tablets, one in the outer courtyard and one in the courtyard closest to Nabu and Tašmetu's shrines (Loud and Altman 1938: 56–64, pls. 2, 12–29). Sargon endowed the temple with 4,000 homers of land, regular offerings of sheep, and daily provisions of bread and beer for an *āšipu* and *laḫḫinu* ("temple steward") (SAA 1: 88, no. 106, and 102–105, nos. 128–129). At least one set of new writing boards was commissioned, containing the celestial omen series *Enūma Anu Ellil* (Wiseman 1955), and further library holdings may also have been moved there from Kalhu.

Dur-Šarruken was functional and occupied by 707 B.C. but abandoned just two years later, following Sargon's inauspicious death in battle. His son and successor Sennacherib moved the court to Nineveh, an ancient Assyrian city between Dur-Šarruken and Kalhu, where a temple of Nabu had been founded by Adad-nerari III in 788 B.C. and restored by many successive kings (Reade 1998–2001: 410). Almost nothing of it now survives except the 60 m-square foundation platform. However, a number of scholarly tablets in the Kuyunjik Collection of the British Museum bear colophons dedicated by Assurbanipal to the *gerginakku* ("library") of the Ezida "that is in the middle of Nineveh" (Hunger 1968: 101–102, nos. 327–328, 105–107, nos. 338–339), so it is clear that it had a significant scholarly function. Presumably the holdings of the abandoned Dur-Šarruken Ezida were moved here, or back to Kalhu, or both, for Kalhu remained a royal city – and its Ezida remained active – until the very end of empire. For instance, one Nabu-sakip made

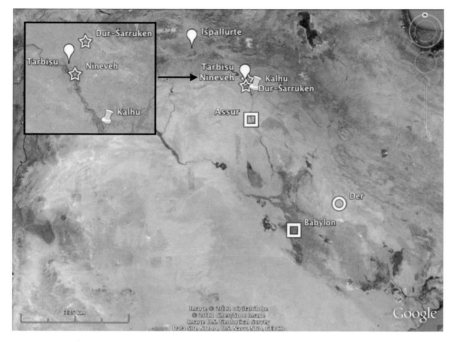

Figure 8.1. The scholarly knowledge network around seventh-century Kalhu. Key: ▣ =
origins of tablet originals or duplicates; ◎ = origins of ancestors; ☆ = locations
of other Ezida temples in the network; ♀ = locations of activities of Kalhu-
based scholars.

a private benefaction of two slaves and seven homers of land to the Kalhu
Ezida in 621 B.C. (SAA 12, 96), just seven years before it fell to the Medes
and Babylonians.

In sum, the scholars of the Kalhu Ezida were – perhaps unsurprisingly
– deeply embedded in a tightly-knit Assyrian royal knowledge network
(Figure 8.1). For the most part descended from eminent scholarly dynasties,
they were so closely tied to their divine and royal patrons that they and their
writings, indeed their very institution, moved as the court relocated following
political imperatives. Coincidentally or not, it was only Banunu, with no
family to speak of, who copied a text "from a Babylonian original" – the sole
extant acknowledgement of scholarship beyond the Assyrian court.

Huzirina: A Provincial Town in the Assyrian West

The nearly 400 tablets found buried outside a domestic dwelling in the
provincial Assyrian town of Huzirina (modern Sultantepe), near Harran,

comprise a striking contrast to those found in contemporary royal cities such as Kalhu (on the archaeology of Huzirina, see Lloyd 1954; Lloyd and Göçke 1953). As well as hymns, incantations, and rituals, there is a preponderance of literary works in the assemblage, but very few omen collections (on the tablets, see Gurney 1952; Gurney and Finkelstein 1957; Gurney and Hulin 1964; Pedersén 1998: 178–180; http://oracc.org/cams/gkab/huzirina). Compared to the Kalhu tablets, the Huzirina manuscripts tend to be very poorly executed (Gurney 1952: 26). Nearly 60 of them have surviving colophons, together attesting to the activities of around 25 different scribes (Hunger 1968: 110–120, nos. 351–408). As in Kalhu, they can be differentiated into two distinct groups. The first is a priestly family, descended from one Nur-Šamaš (Gurney 1997), and their associates:

- Qurdi-Nergal, *šangû*-priest of the gods Zababa and Bau of Arbela, Harran, and Huzirina; a *šamallû agašgû* ("novice apprentice") in 701 B.C., when he wrote a bilingual listing of the incantation series *Utukkū lemnūtu* (STT 2, 192);
- his son Mušallim-Bau, a *šamallû* (*agašgû*), who copied various incantations and rituals, an ominous calendar, and a medical text (STT 2, 179; 199; 299; 305 and maybe STT 1, 64);
- his descendant Ninurta-[..], a *šamallû ṣeḫru* ("junior apprentice"), son of the *šamallû ṣeḫru* Nabu-zer-kitti-lešir, who copied a calendar for incantations (STT 2, 300) in 619 B.C.;
- the *šamallû* ("apprentice") and eunuch Nabu-ah-iddin, copyist of four incantations and rituals (STT 2, 161; 172; 237; 247) who sometimes writes *ana tāmarti* ("for the viewing of") Qurdi-Nergal;
- Nabu-ah-iddin's *mār mummu* ("pupil"), the *šamallû ṣeḫru* Nabu-rehtu-uṣur, who copied the literary work *The Poor Man of Nippur* (STT 1, 38) in 701 B.C. *ana tāmarti* ("for the viewing of") Qurdi-Nergal, writing: "Do not disperse the library (*gerginakku*); taboo of Ea, king of the Apsu," just like Banunu of Kalhu.

Apart from Qurdi-Nergal's family and immediate associates, tablets from the Huzirina cache record over 20 further writers, including:

- Adad-mušammer, a *šamallû šubultinbi* ("young apprentice"), son of the scribe Nergal-tukulti; copyist of the literary *Gilgamesh Letter* (STT 1, 40);
- Bel-le'u-uṣur, a *šamallû šubultinbi*, son of Marduk-ban-apli, scribe of the *turtannu* ("field marshal"), who copied out a now unidentifiable text (STT 2, 342);
- Iddi-Meslamtaea, a *šamallû*, son of the *šangû*-priest Ašu, copyist of three manuscripts of *Utukkū lemnūtu* (STT 2, 159; 174; 177), a god list (STT 2, 377), and Tablet 2 of the literary work *Ludlul bēl nēmeqi* "Let me praise the lord of wisdom" (STT 1, 33) in and around 701 B.C.;

- Mutaqqin-Aššur, a *šamallû daqqu* ("tiny apprentice"), son of a scribe from Assur, grandson of the *šamallû šubultinbi* Šamaš-šum-iddina, and great-grandson of Nabu-kabit-ahhešu, a scribe from the Babylonian city of Kutha; copyist of a blessing for the city of Assur (STT 1, 87);
- Nabu-ibni, a *šamallû ligimû* ("youthful apprentice"), son of the Assyrian scribe Aplaya, who wrote out an unidentified medical work (STT 1, 92);
- Nabu-šum-iškun, son of Kandalanu, senior scribe of the *turtannu*, who copied Tablet 1 of the myth *Erra and Išum* (STT 1, 16), and a set of *namburbû*-incantations and rituals against ants and other pests (STT 2, 242);
- Šum-tabni-uṣur, a *šamallû ṣehru*, son of Nabu-tukulti, *asû* ("physician") and servant of the crown prince, who copied a literary work (STT 1, 36) and *Abnu šikinšu*, a treatise on the healing properties of stones (STT 1, 108) in the late eighth century.

It is notable that all but one of these men (Nabu-šum-iškun) describes himself as a *šamallû* ("apprentice") of some sort; and that at least nine more such apprentices are attested amongst these tablets,[6] plus five whose names are now missing.[7] Two men, Iddi-Meslamtaea and Šum-tabni-uṣur, are contemporaries of Qurdi-Nergal, writing in the late eighth century B.C. Almost all have good connections to the scholarly or administrative life of the empire. Bel-le'u-uṣur and Nabu-šum-iškun are sons of scribes of the *turtannu*, Assyria's senior military officer and governor of a neighbouring province whose capital was Til-Barsip (Radner 2006–2008: 48). Šum-tabni-uṣ ur is the son of a crown prince's (i.e., Sennacherib's?) *asû* ("physician"); Iddi-Meslamtaea is a *šangû*-priest's son; Mutaqqin-Aššur and Nabu-ibni trace their descent to scribal families of the cities of Assur and/or Kutha. Their now-anonymous fellow-copyists seem to have similar pedigrees, including descent from a *šangû*-priest and a *bārû* ("diviner").

While it is of course possible that Qurdi-Nergal and his descendants acquired some or all of these men's tablets through purchase, inheritance, or exchange, their social homogeneity and mediocre scribal ability together suggest an alternative explanation. Stefan Maul (2010: 208) has recently used colophons from an assemblage of several hundred scholarly tablets, found in a seventh-century house in the imperial city of Assur, to show that it accrued during the course of scholarly training of four generations of a family of *mašmaššus* ("incantation priests") associated with the temple of the city god Aššur. In the second generation, for instance, Kiṣir-Aššur's titles evolved from *šamallû ṣehru* through *šamallû*, *šamallû mašmaššu ṣehru* ("junior apprentice incantation priest"), *mašmaššu ṣehru* ("junior incantation priest"), and *mašmaššu* to *mašmaššu bīt Aššur* ("incantation priest of Aššur's temple"). He also notes the presence of 13 tablets with colophons of men that apparently do not belong to Kiṣir-Aššur's family, but who are all designated as *šamallû* or *šamallû ṣehru*

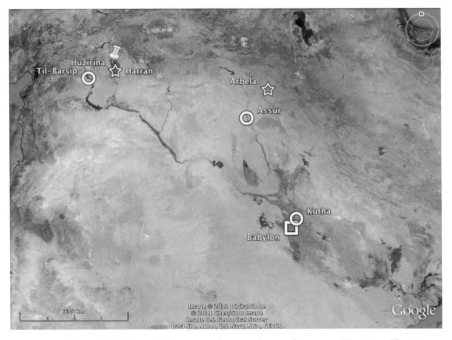

Figure 8.2. The scholarly knowledge network around seventh-century Huzirina. Key: ▣ =
origins of tablet originals; ◎ = origins of fathers and ancestors; ☆ = locations
of other temples to Zababa and Bau in the network.

too (Maul 2010: 216). Many further tablets without colophons are written
in immature script, replete with errors and erasures (Maul 2010: 217). The
parallels with Huzirina are compelling. Both houses, it appears, were centres
of scholarly apprenticeship which attracted advanced (but not always entirely
competent) learners from outside the resident family. It may be that Qurdi-
Nergal's family took in paying pupils to supplement their temple income that
is documented by two fragmentary records of endowments to the temples of
Zababa and Bau, and Ištar, found at Huzirina (SAA 12, 48; 91 = STT 1, 44; 2,
406+407). The Huzirina students were predominantly the sons of provincial
officials, priests and scholars who – with the possible exception of Šum-tabni-uṣ
ur – had no direct connections to the Assyrian royal family or the inner circle
of court scholars of the Ezida at Kalhu, although some belonged to families
from the city of Assur (Figure 8.2).

It is not only the human actors in the Huzirina network that were not
integrated into contemporary royal scholarship. While four Huzirina tablets
are said to be copies from Babylon, or from the goddess Gula's temple there

(STT 1, 73; STT 2, 136; 232; 323), none claims to be from any city of the Assyrian imperial heartland. And while Nabu was clearly central to the royal scholarly network, in Huzirina it was the divine couple Zababa and Bau of Arbela, Harran, and Huzirina, the deities served by Qurdi-Nergal and his family. However, the colophons do invoke a similar range of gods to curse or bless those who would steal or protect the tablets. In the very fragmentary Kalhu tablets only Ea and Šamaš are currently legible (CTN 4, 27; 116; 188). At Huzirina, Šamaš is invoked five out of fifteen times (STT 1, 71; 84; 92; 2, 215, 394) and Ea three times, always in conjunction with Nabu (STT 1, 38; 40; 192). Nabu is summoned a further three times, once together with Marduk (STT 1, 108; 2, 247; 256), while Iddi-Meslamtaea calls twice on Lugalira (STT 1, 33; 2, 159), and there are single occurrences of Adad and Zababa (STT 1, 56; 2, 199). But with the exception of the last, these deities do not seem to have particular geographical significance here but rather stand for the general or specific realms of learning with which the colophon writers wished to be associated.

Uruk: A Venerable Babylonian City under Achaemenid Rule

When the Achaemenid Persians conquered Babylonia in 539 B.C., Uruk was already about 3,000 years old. At its economic, social, and intellectual heart was a huge temple complex which had served the great sky-god An (later Anu) and his daughter the irresistible Inana (Ištar) since at least the fourth millennium B.C. Substantial property, investments, and commercial activity, as well as a flourishing offering culture, meant that – in the medium term at least – the Uruk temples could withstand the loss of royal interest and favour that came with the end of indigenous rule. Indeed, they continued to support a substantial community of learned men for several hundred years. A family of *mašmaššu*s ("incantation priests") associated with the temples, the descendants of one Šangi-Ninurta, occupied a house in southeast Uruk until about 420 B.C., when they left behind a handful of legal records and some 190 scholarly tablets, including 56 with colophons (on the archaeology of this house, see Schmidt 1979). Medical recipes, healing rituals and incantations, and medical, terrestrial, and birth omens predominate, as might be expected of a family of healers, but mathematical and metrological works also feature (on the tablets, see Clancier 2009: 47–72, 387–405; Hunger 1976; Pedersén 1998: 212–213; von Weiher 1982, 1988, 1993, 1998; http://oracc.org/cams/gkab/achaemenid). As in Huzirina, we can clearly identify a core group of family men plus their direct associates:

- Šamaš-iddin, *mašmaššu*, writer of nine scholarly tablets: four incantations and rituals, including *Lamaštu* and *Bīt rimki* ("Bath house"); two collections of medical recipes; two commentaries on the medical omen series *Sakikkû* ("Ailments"); and the mathematical compilation *Zēru u qanû* ("Seed-measure and reed-measure") (SpTU 1, 44; 48; 3, 66; 84; 100; 4, 127; 128; 5, 254; and Friberg et al. 1990: no. 483);

- Šamaš-iddin's son Anu-ikṣur, *mašmaššu (ṣeḫru)* ("[junior] incantation priest") of Anu, writer of 24 scholarly tablets: 18 for himself – 11 commentaries, three ritual series, three sets of medical recipes and a list of ingredients (SpTU 1, 28; 31–33; 38; 45, 47; 49–51; 56; 60; 72; 83; 2, 8; 3, 99; 5, 241; 248) – plus four for his father: two incantation series, the lexical text *An = Anum*, and a collection of medical recipes (SpTU 1, 59; 126; 3, 69; 5, 242);

- Anu-ikṣur's son Anu-ušallim, scribe of two tablets from the omen series *Šumma izbu* and *Alandimmû* (SpTU 3, 90; 4, 151) for his father;

- Šamaš-iddin's other son Rimut-Anu, a *mašmaššu*; copyist of a list of diseases, a set of metrological tables, and the so-called *Āšipu's Handbook* (SpTU 4, 152; 172; 5, 231) some time during the reign of Darius II (r. 423–405 B.C.);

- Belu-kaṣir, son of Balaṭu, apparently not a family member, who copied a list of diseases (SpTU 1, 43) for Rimut-Anu;

- Nadin, family relationship unclear, who compiled a set of arithmetical tables (SpTU 4, 174), also for Rimut-Anu;

- and two tablets – part of the lexical commentary *Mur-gud* and an extract from the birth omen series *Šumma izbu* (SpTU 1, 60; 23, 116), written by members of the Šangi-Ninurta family whose names are now lost.

A further five tablets, which are probably to be associated with this tablet collection on stratigraphic grounds, bear colophons of men who cannot be directly linked to members of the Šangi-Ninurta family:

- Anu-apal-iddin, son of Anu-šum-lišir, descendant of Kuri, copyist of a tablet of the anti-witchcraft ritual *Maqlû* ("Burning") (SpTU 3, 47A);

- GUBšu-Šamaš, a *mašmaššu ṣeḫru* and son of Ibni-Ištar, descendant of Gimil-Nanaya, who copied a tablet of the purification ritual *Bīt rimki* (SpTU 3, 67) for the *mašmaššu* Ištar-nadin-ahi, son of Arad-Gula, descendant of Gimil-Ištaran;

- Sin-banunu, a *mašmaššu* and son of Ile''i-Marduk, copyist of a *namburbû*-ritual against the evil of birds entering the home (SpTU 3, 80);

- Šamaš-ah-iddin, writer of a commentary on the medical omen series *Sakikkû* (SpTU 1, 39);

- UB-ia-[…], writer of a commentary on celestial and physiognomic omens (SpTU 1, 84).

Whether or not these tablets were produced in the Šangi-Ninurta family's house or elsewhere, it is clear from their contents, and from the professions of their copyists, that they were kept or acquired because they were all directly relevant to the family's core intellectual interests, namely healing and purification. Presumably this is how they earned their livelihood as well, but

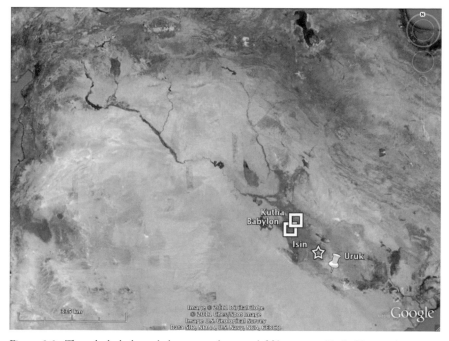

Figure 8.3. The scholarly knowledge network around fifth-century Uruk. Key: ▣ = origins
of tablet originals; ☆ = location of the goddess Gula's main temple.

it is also possible that the Šangi-Ninurta family held prebends, or rights to
shares in temple income. Unfortunately none of the legal documents found
in their house (many of which are fragmentary) mentions any of our men.

It is striking that whereas the Huzirina scribes tend to emphasize their
geographical origins and/or their relationships to politically powerful patrons,
the Uruk *mašmaššu*s give only their paternity and profession. This may
suggest that their scholarly network operated on a much smaller geographical
scale, an impression also given by the origins of the tablets and writing boards
from which they copied. Two of Šamaš-iddin's *Bīt rimki* tablets are said to be
"a copy of a writing-board, property of the Eanna temple" in Uruk (SpTU 3,
66; 4, 127) and Anu-ikṣur and Rimut-Anu both had occasion to work from
"Urukean copies" (SpTU 1, 59; 3, 90; 4, 172; plus SpTU 1, 71, unsigned).
There are just two extant exceptions to this localism: Anu-ikṣur copied a
section of *Maqlû* from "a tablet from among the old tablets of Meslam," a
temple at Kutha (SpTU 5, 241), and Sin-banunu's *namburbû* stems from "a
writing board from Babylon" (SpTU 3, 80) (Figure 8.3).

The divine world in which the *mašmaššu*s operated was also much reduced.
Sixteen of the 17 tablets that invoke deities in colophons call on the city

god Anu, plus the goddess Ištar of Eanna (mostly written by Šamaš-iddin and non-family men) or Anu's divine spouse Antu (mostly by Anu-ikṣur).[8] Only one, by Anu-ikṣur, summons Gula, the goddess of healing traditionally associated with the Babylonian city of Isin (SpTU 1, 47). Nabu, the god of wisdom so prevalent in Assyrian scholarly life, is nowhere to be seen.

Conclusions

By taking a Latourian view of cuneiform scholarship – widened to include divine as well as human and inanimate actors – and by mapping it with tools such as Google Earth, we begin to glimpse the complexities and variety under the apparently smooth surface of the "stream of tradition." The three ancient knowledge networks surveyed here each have their own distinctive characteristics, stemming from their very different scholarly and socio-political functions. The Ezida temple in seventh-century Kalhu was but one node in a network of scholarly repositories serving an elite group of learned men who guided Assyrian royal decision-making, and who followed king and court from city to city in the imperial heartland. The priestly household at Huzirina, by contrast, offered a gentlemanly education to the young men of empire: the offspring of scholars and provincial officials, who were proud of their origins but who aspired, perhaps, to climb further up the Assyrian social scale through acquisitions of the classics of Babylonian literature. Their network is conspicuously excluded from access to the royal cities, although it is otherwise impressively extensive. In the *mašmaššus*' house in fifth-century Uruk, however, we see a dramatic shrinking of the intellectual landscape that may be the outcome of late Achaemenid attitudes to Babylonian autonomy (Waerzeggers 2003–2004). While family-based learning continued in much the same way as before, scholars, apprentices, and their writings seem to have travelled rarely beyond the city limits or across professional divides. However, the Urukeans' geographical horizons were to open up again to some extent during the Seleucid period, when the Ekur-zakir family of *mašmaššus*, who by then were occupying the Šangi-Ninurta family's house, had access to originals from the Babylonian cities of Nippur and Der (SpTU 2, 34; 4, 125; 185) and even possessed a 300-year-old tablet from Nineveh, bearing a colophon of Assurbanipal (SpTU 2, 46).

It has also become clear that the distinction Assyriologists have traditionally made between familial and institutional tablet collections (e.g., recently Clancier 2009: 17, 319; Pedersén 1998) is not particularly meaningful: scholarly dynasties could be associated with particular institutions over many generations, and it is likely that tablets and writing boards moved as freely as their owners between homes and workplaces. Indeed, we now see that people, objects, and institutions were all surprisingly mobile. Individuals and groups could travel for long distances in pursuit of teachers, clients, and patrons, taking memorised as well as recorded knowledge with them. Perhaps too they travelled in search of particular learned works, for, as I have discussed elsewhere (Robson 2011, 2013), access to scholarly writings was patchy and unreliable. Instead, the composition of learned collections, while demonstrably shaped by the core intellectual interests of their creators (and deformed by the subsequent loss of perishable media), is decidedly uneven. This appears to reflect the eclectic, opportunistic acquisition of tablets and writing boards across a wide range of genres which rarely, if ever, resulted in ownership of a complete run of multi-tablet series.

Our sobering conclusion must then be that no person or community in the first millennium B.C., even the royal scholars of Nineveh, had access to as much of the so-called "stream of tradition" as we do today. And our understanding of it will only grow with the expansion of online corpora such as those that Oracc facilitates. But while previous generations understandably took their panoptic view of the whole to be a fair reflection of ancient knowledge worlds, Oracc's annotational and analytical power facilitates a more nuanced chronological, geographical, and social partition of first-millennium intellectual space. At the same time, it breaks down the genre-based barriers erected by Assyriology over the twentieth century, allowing us new glimpses of the interrelations between different types of scholarly endeavour and some of the means by which intellectual communities cohered. But this is just the beginning: as the online Assyriological knowledge network grows and strengthens, we will be afforded many further insights – many as yet unimaginable – into the fragility and power of cuneiform scholarship in the ancient Middle East.

Acknowledgements

It is a pleasure to express my gratitude to all GKAB staff: senior research associate Graham Cunningham, research associates Marie Besnier, Philippe Clancier, Frances Reynolds, and Greta Van Buylaere, website consultant Ruth Horry, research assistant Kathryn Stevens, and the members of our editorial and historical advisory panels (see oracc.org/cams/gkab/abouttheproject). I particularly thank Heather D. Baker for her help with the Kalhu colophons discussed here (new readings now incorporated into her updates to *The Prosopography of the Neo-Assyrian Empire* at http://homepage.univie.ac.at/heather.baker/pna.html), and most of all Steve Tinney, not only for his careful and perspicacious proofreading of this article but for everything he does to make our collaboration so enjoyable and rewarding.

Notes

1. Oracc's name is a tongue-in-cheek homage to the BBC TV science fiction series Blake's 7 (1978–81), about a small group of renegade freedom fighters and their portable super-computer Orac, who battle against the evil and oppressive Terran Federation.

2. The USA and UK each accounted for 31% of visits to K&P in January 2011. But also in the top ten countries were the Philippines (no. 8, at 1.3%) and India (no. 10, at 1.1%), where no Assyriology is taught at university level. For SAAo, by contrast, the top ten for January 2011 were all North American or European countries where Assyriology is a university subject. However, the total of 33 countries included Singapore, Croatia, Brazil, Syria, Slovakia, Greece, Yemen, and Iran.

3. Šumaya son of Nabu-zeru-lešir is attested as an *āšipu* at Nineveh late in Esarhaddon's reign (SAA 10, 257; 291). Some time in 671–669 B.C. he petitioned crown prince Assurbanipal to let him take over his dead father's scholarly work at Kalhu, having established himself in a similar role in Tarbiṣu (SAA 16, 34). He and Adad-šumu-uṣur witnessed a legal document together in the northern Assyrian town of Išpallure in 666 B.C. (SAA 6, 314).

4. Adad-šumu-uṣur alone: SAA 8, 160–163; SAA 10, 185–204; 206–208; 210–211; 213–215; 217–220; 222–230; SAA 16, 167; with Nabu-zeru-lešir and/or Urad-Ea (and others): SAA 10, 1; 3; 212; 232; with other colleagues, SAA 10, 24; 205; 209; 216; 221 231; 256; 259; Nabu-zeru-lešir alone: SAA 10, 2; SAA 16, 50; Urad-Ea alone or with others: SAA 8, 181–183; SAA 10, 25; 338–344.

5. The two remaining extant names are both very fragmentary: Bel-[..], copyist of birth omens (CTN 4, 31); Nabu-[..], mentioned in the colophon of an unknown incantation (CTN 4, 125); there is also a *šamallu ṣeḫru* ("junior apprentice"), copyist of the astronomical compendium *Mul-apin* "Plough star" (CTN 4, 27), whose name is now missing.

6. The other named scribes are the *šamallû ṣeḫrūtu* ("junior apprentices") Aššur-šumu-iddina, Bel-ašaredu, Išdi-ilu, Marduk-ban-[..], Nabu-eṭir, Nabu-šabši, [..]-ereš, and [..]-šum-ikṣur (STT 1, 57; 73; 84; 85; 2, 136; 256; 340; 368); the *šamallû* [..]-zer-ibni and Sin-šumu-iddin, both sons of scribes (STT 1, 82; 109); and – with no titles given – Mannu-ki-Babili, Nabu-eṭir-napšate, Nabu-eṭiranni, Nabu-ahhe-šallim, and Sin-iddina (STT 1, 3; 10; 2, 215; 232; 241; 301; 330). In addition Bel-šar-ahhešu, a [priest] of Aššur's temple in Assur, and Marduk-šapik-zeri, an *āšipu* from Babylon, are mentioned in one colophon each, but apparently not as copyists or owners (STT 1, 69; 89).

7. A *šamallû ṣeḫru*, son of a *šangû*-priest (STT 2, 394); a *šamallû ṣeḫru* [with some relationship to] Iddi-Meslamtaea (STT 2, 390); a *šamallû ṣeḫru*, son of the scribe and *bārû* ("diviner") Marduk-ban-apli (STT 1, 70); and one or more further *šamallû* (*ṣeḫr[ūt]u*) (STT 1, 55; 66; STT 2, 343).

8. Anu and Ištar: SpTU 1, 48; 59; 3, 69, 84 (Šamaš-iddin), SpTU 1, 45; 5, 241 (Anu-ikṣur), SpTU 1, 39 (Šamaš-ah-iddin) and SpTU 3, 74A (Anu-apal-iddin); Anu and Antu: SpTU 1, 126; 5, 254 (Šamaš-iddin), SpTU 1, 33; 2, 8; 3, 90; 5, 242; 248 (Anu-ikṣur); Anu and [..]: SpTU 4, 152 (Rimut-Anu).

References

Black, Jeremy

    2008   The Libraries of Kalhu. In *New Light on Nimrud: Proceedings of the Nimrud Conference, 11th–13th March 2002*, edited by John E. Curtis, Henrietta McCall, Dominique Collon, and Lamia al-Gailani Werr, pp. 261–266. British Institute for the Study of Iraq, London.

Black, Jeremy, Graham Cunningham, Eleanor Robson, and Gábor Zólyomi

    2004   *The Literature of Ancient Sumer.* Oxford University Press, Oxford.

Chavalas, Mark W. (editor)

    2006   *The Ancient Near East: Historical Sources in Translation.* Blackwell, Oxford.

Clancier, Philippe

    2009   *Les bibliothèques en Babylonie dans la deuxième moitié du Ier millénaire av. J. C.* Ugarit-Verlag, Münster.

CTN 4 = Wiseman and Black 1996

    Editions of individual texts online at http://oracc.org/cams/gkab/ctn_4_0 (replacing 0 with the text number).

Curtis, John E., Henrietta McCall, Dominique Collon, and Lamia al-Gailani Werr (editors)

    2008   *New Light on Nimrud: Proceedings of the Nimrud Conference, 11th–13th March 2002.* British Institute for the Study of Iraq, London.

Ebeling, Erich

1919–1923   *Keilschrifttexte aus Assur religiösen Inhalts.* 2 vols. J.C. Hinrichs, Leipzig.

Foster, Benjamin R.

    2005   *Before the Muses: An Anthology of Akkadian Literature.* 3rd edition. CDL Press, Bethesda, Maryland.

Friberg, Jöran, Hermann Hunger, and Farouk N. H. Al-Rawi

    1990   "Seed and Reeds": A Metro-Mathematical Topic Text from Late Babylonian Uruk. *Baghdader Mitteilungen* 21: 483–557. Edition online at http://oracc.org/cams/gkab/bagm_21,_483/.

Gurney, Oliver R.

    1952   The Sultantepe Tablets: A Preliminary Note. *Anatolian Studies* 2: 25–35.

    1997   Scribes at Huzirina. *Nouvelles Assyriologiques Brèves et Utilitaires* 1997(1): 18, no. 18.

Gurney, Oliver R., and Jacob J. Finkelstein

    1957   *The Sultantepe Tablets,* Vol. 1. British Institute of Archaeology at Ankara, London.

Gurney, Oliver R., and Peter Hulin

    1964   *The Sultantepe Tablets,* Vol. 2. British Institute of Archaeology at Ankara, London.

Hunger, Hermann

    1968   *Babylonische und assyrische Kolophone.* Butzon and Bercker, Kevelaer; Neukirchener Verlag des Erziehungsvereins, Neukirchen-Vluyn.

    1976   *Spätbabylonische Texte aus Uruk*, Vol. 1. Mann, Berlin.

KAR   = Ebeling 1919–1923

Latour, Bruno

    1987   *Science in Action: How to Follow Scientists and Engineers through Society.* Harvard University Press, Cambridge.

Lloyd, Seton
  1954   Sultantepe, Part II. Post-Assyrian Pottery and Small Objects Found by the Anglo-Turkish Joint Expedition in 1952. *Anatolian Studies* 4: 101–110.

Lloyd, Seton, and Nuri Göçke
  1953   Sultantepe: Anglo-Turkish Joint Excavations, 1952. *Anatolian Studies* 3: 27–47.

Loud, Gordon, and Charles B. Altman
  1938   *Khorsabad, Part 2: The Citadel and the Town.* The Oriental Institute of the University of Chicago, Chicago.

Mallowan, Max Edgar Lucien
  1966   *Nimrud and Its Remains.* 2 vols. Collins, London.

Maul, Stefan M.
  2010   Die Tontafelbibliothek aus dem sogenannten "Haus des Beschwörungspriesters." In *Assur-Forschungen: Arbeiten aus der Forschungsstelle "Edition literarischer Keilschrifttexte aus Assur" der Heidelberger Akademie der Wissenschaften,* edited by Stefan M. Maul and Nils P. Heeßel, pp. 189–228. Harrassowitz, Wiesbaden, Germany.

Oates, Joan, and David Oates
  2001   *Nimrud: An Assyrian Imperial City Revealed.* British School of Archaeology in Iraq, London.

Oxford English Dictionary Online
  2013   black box, n. *OED Online,* September 2013, Oxford University Press, electronic document, http://www.oed.com/view/Entry/282116?redirectedFrom=black+box&, accessed September 25, 2013.

Oppenheim, A. Leo
  1960   Assyriology: Why and How? *Current Anthropology* 1: 409–423.

Parpola, Simo
  1983   Assyrian Library Records. *Journal of Near Eastern Studies* 42: 1–29.

Pedersén, Olof
  1998   *Archives and Libraries in the Ancient Near East, 1500–300 B.C.* CDL Press, Bethesda, Maryland.

Pritchard, James B.
  1950   *Ancient Near Eastern Texts Relating to the Old Testament.* Princeton University Press, Princeton.

Radner, Karen
  2006–2008   Provinz. C. Assyrien. In *Reallexikon der Assyriologie,* Vol. 11, edited by Michael P. Streck, pp. 42–68. De Gruyter, Berlin.
  2011   Royal Decision-Making: Kings, Magnates and Scholars. In *The Oxford Handbook of Cuneiform Culture,* edited by Karen Radner and Eleanor Robson, pp. 358–379. Oxford University Press, Oxford.

Reade, Julian E.
  1998–2001   Ninive (Nineveh). In *Reallexikon der Assyriologie,* Vol. 9, edited by Dietz O. Edzard, pp. 388–433. De Gruyter, Berlin.

Robson, Eleanor
  2011   The Production and Dissemination of Scholarly Knowledge. In *The Oxford*

Handbook of Cuneiform Culture, edited by Karen Radner and Eleanor Robson, pp. 557–576. Oxford University Press, Oxford.

2013   Reading the Libraries of Assyria and Babylonia. In *Ancient Libraries,* edited by Jason König, Katerina Oikonomopoulou, and Greg Woolf, pp. 38–56. Cambridge University Press, Cambridge.

Robson, Eleanor, and Kathryn Stevens

in press   Tablet Collections in First-Millennium Assyria and Babylonia. In *The Earliest Libraries: Library Tradition in the Ancient Near East from the Dawn of History until the Roman Era, ca. 3200 B.C.–200 A.D.*, edited by Kim Ryholt and Gojko Barjamovic. Oxford University Press, Oxford.

SAA   = *State Archives of Assyria*
       Editions of individual texts online at http://oracc.org/saao/saa_n_m (replacing "n" with the volume number and "m" with the text number).

Schmidt, Jürgen (editor)

1979   *XXIX. und XXX. vorläufiger Bericht über die von dem Deutschen Archäologischen Institut aus Mitteln der Deutschen Forschungsgemeinschaft unternommenen Ausgrabungen in Uruk-Warka 1970/71 und 1971/72*. Mann, Berlin.

SpTU   = Hunger 1967; von Weiher 1982, 1988, 1993, 1998
        Editions of individual texts online at http://oracc.org/cams/gkab/sptu_n_m (replacing "n" with the volume number and "m" with the text number).

STT   = Gurney and Finkelstein 1957; Gurney and Hulin 1964
       Editions of individual texts online at http://oracc.org/cams/gkab/stt_n_m (replacing "n" with the volume number and "m" with the text number).

Veldhuis, Niek

2006   How Did They Learn Cuneiform? "Tribute/Word List C" as an Elementary Exercise. In *Approaches to Sumerian Literature in Honour of Stip (H.L.J. Vanstiphout)*, edited by Piotr Michalowski and Niek Veldhuis, pp. 181–200. Brill, Leiden.

Weiher, Egbert von

1982   *Spätbabylonische Texte aus Uruk*, Vol. 2. Mann, Berlin.

1988   *Spätbabylonische Texte aus Uruk*, Vol. 3. Mann, Berlin.

1993   *Spätbabylonische Texte aus Uruk*, Vol. 4. Verlag Philipp von Zabern, Mainz am Rhein.

1998   *Spätbabylonische Texte aus Uruk*, Vol. 5. Verlag Philipp von Zabern, Mainz am Rhein.

Waerzeggers, Caroline

2003–2004   The Babylonian Revolts Against Xerxes and the "End of Archives." *Archiv für Orientforschung* 50: 150–173.

Wiseman, Donald J.

1955   Assyrian Writing-Boards. *Iraq* 17: 3–13.

Wiseman, Donald J., and Jeremy Black

1996   *Cuneiform Texts from Nimrud, Vol. 4: Literary Texts from the Temple of Nabû*. British School of Archaeology in Iraq, London.

Ancient Relationships, Modern Intellectual Horizons: The Practical Challenges and Possibilities of Encoding Greek and Latin Inscriptions

Lisa Anderson and Heidi Wendt

Introduction to the U.S. Epigraphy Project

The U.S. Epigraphy Project (http://usepigraphy.brown.edu) was started in 1995 at Rutgers University by John Bodel (then at Rutgers) and Steven Tracy (then director of the American School of Classical Studies at Athens). The first manifestation of the project was a print volume by the project directors, *Greek and Latin Inscriptions in the USA: A Checklist*, which appeared in 1997. The *Checklist* provided short entries on the epigraphic collections, including some 2,300 inscriptions (720 Greek and 1,575 Latin) reported to Bodel and Tracy that were held by museums, universities, private individuals, and other institutions throughout the United States. Inasmuch as all ancient Greek and Latin inscriptions in the U.S. are originally from elsewhere in the world, this publication aimed to track what has come to this country and to follow inscriptions that have been split into several different collections.

While the *Checklist* brought together material whose historical, and in some cases even topographical, relationships were either not well known or had been lost, its digital supplement, in the form of a web-based project at Rutgers, permitted fuller recording and distribution of information about these texts. In 2003, the U.S. Epigraphy Project (hereafter, USEP) came to Brown University with Bodel, where it was converted from its original HyperText Markup Language (HTML) markup to a more detailed and versatile eXtensible Markup Language (XML) format by the Brown University Library's Scholarly Technology Group (now Center for Digital Scholarship), with the help of classics and archaeology graduate students. This painstaking process also provided an opportunity to discover and correct errors and inconsistencies in existing scholarly publications of the materials. More inscriptions have been added to the database by graduate student epigraphists under the supervision of John Bodel, and over 1,000 of these are illustrated with photographs and drawings provided by the owners. The present archives comprise digital files of texts, images, and metadata for nearly 3,000 inscribed objects housed in more than 80 museum, university, and private collections of ancient art and artifacts in North America, which represents perhaps 95% of the known material held here. USEP also provides up-to-date bibliographies (along with links to documents available online) for many of these texts. Its searchable database is both a powerful research tool as well as a training resource for a rising generation of epigraphists and art historians.

The following paper provides a basic orientation to the practical and intellectual advantages of digital humanities scholarship through the lens of this project's development. In particular, it calls attention to new possibilities for engaging with epigraphic materials at multiple levels of academic inquiry. First, with respect to individual examples, digital encoding practices disambiguate information about the components of a given inscription in a manner that forces the scholar to consider each of them seriously without relying on categorical assumptions. This exercise results in a subtler account of an object's complex components that moves beyond conventional generalizations about, for instance, the relationship between the intention of a text and the type of object that bears the inscription. It also pinpoints where interpretive ambiguities occur and necessarily explicates editorial decisions. Second, while a single datum, or even a sizeable collection of texts, may offer limited contributions to the study of antiquity, the ability to examine unlimited types of relationships across multiple sets of materials increases the explanatory potential of such evidence for research questions about ancient societies. This is true not only with respect to the opportunity that digital resources offer to understand better the original context of texts that now reside in disparate modern collections – a point to which we will return using the example of material originating from the Via Salaria necropolis in Rome. It is also true for broader patterns in epigraphic evidence that exceed the immediate frames of reference for a specific object or set of objects (namely, commemorative practices from a certain historical period, as opposed to relationships between monuments from the same archaeological site). Finally, USEP's participation in an EpiDoc peer community holds the potential to demonstrate affinities not only between texts represented in federated collections of epigraphic materials, but also to compare epigraphic data points to other forms of ancient evidence (e.g., manuscripts and papyri) encoded using the same conventions. The ability to consider so many types of material from antiquity, and with such specificity, augments the importance of even the most insular datum, irrespective of the medium on which it survives.

EpiDoc XML, Metadata, and Controlled Vocabularies

In order to appreciate how each of these larger points is borne out by digital encoding practices, we will begin with a basic orientation to the language and methods that define text encoding as part of the digital humanities and our EpiDoc peer community specifically.

XML stands for eXtensible Markup Language, a flexible language that can be used to encode or "mark up" texts in order to enrich the information that can be adduced from and made available about them. For those unfamiliar with XML, it describes a process whereby users add descriptive information to a text by demarcating it using a set of predefined extensible tags. The names and relationships among the tags are defined by a schema, and the semantics of the tags are defined primarily by community practice and guidelines. XML is not limited in its encoding possibilities by existing encoding "tag sets," as other programming languages are limited, but can develop and vary its encoding vocabulary as necessary. In 2005, when USEP moved its data to an XML format, the encoding process followed, in general, the conventions of the EpiDoc project, which was adapting the Text Encoding Initiative (TEI) XML schema (www.tei-c.org) to work with inscribed documentary texts. EpiDoc (http://epidoc.sourceforge.net/) was spearheaded by Tom Elliot, then at the University of North Carolina, Chapel Hill, and Charlotte Roueché of King's College, London. The focus of the components that EpiDoc adapted from the TEI is mostly on the encoding of text from manuscripts, and it has not always been simple to adapt TEI, which has the richest metadata developed for texts on paper, accurately for the representation and description of texts on non-paper materials. Many online epigraphic projects use some form of EpiDoc to encode their inscriptions because it provides a starting point for new projects and makes data more consistent (which may lead to federated searching). For example, the Electronic Archive of Greek and Latin Epigraphy (EAGLE) can search texts in the major databases of the Epigraphische Datenbank Heidelberg (EDH), Epigraphic Database Roma (EDR), Epigraphic Database Bari (EDB), and Hispania Epigraphica (HE) (http://www.eagle-eagle.it). In addition, the fields of numismatics and sigillography have recently shown interest in developing search capabilities of this kind, and there is a similar trend in papyrology (e.g., the Duke Databank of Documentary Papyri, among others). While one of the great benefits of XML is its adaptability to any particular project, standard tags and encoding practices are necessary for different databases of ancient texts to be able to access the information stored in others.

Most EpiDoc-based projects have focused on the encoding of text transcriptions, and indeed most EpiDoc conventions deal with text issues. The thought processes that develop encoding practices are often informed

Figure 9.1. The epitaph of Philargyrus L. Sullae (MI.AA.UM.KM.L.1428).

by the highly sophisticated and standardized editorial practices that scholars have used to represent various textual features – disparities in letter size, stylistic flourishes, scribal errors or corrections, and so forth – that would not be apparent in a simple transcription. Beyond these sorts of features, as with a standard print epigraphic edition, encoding a text with EpiDoc also allows one to expand abbreviations, to supply missing text, to indicate the certainty of the reconstruction, and most recently, to tag details of interest beyond the immediate inscription, such as prosopographical data. A "person" tag, for instance, can capture the complete name of an individual mentioned in an inscription, as well as the specific elements that comprise this name, such as, for Roman names, the *praenomen, nomen gentilicium, cognomen*, filiation or libertination, and sometimes tribal membership.

The marked-up epitaph of Philargyrus, who was the slave of a Lucius Sulla, illustrates many of these features (Figure 9.1). This inscription, identified in USEP as MI.AA.UM.KM.L.1428, was found in the Porta Salaria necropolis of Rome and is currently part of the collection of the Kelsey Museum of Archaeology in Ann Arbor, Michigan. We will discuss our classification system and the Porta Salaria necropolis further below, but first let us look at an example of a marked-up text.

```
<persName key="PhilargyrusSullae">
    <name type="cognomen" key="Philargyrus">Philargyrus</name>
    <name type="praenomen" key="Lucius">
        <expan><abbr>L</abbr><ex>ucii</ex></expan></name>
    <name type="gentilicium" key="Sulla">Sullae</name></persName>
    <expan><abbr>horre<hi rend="apex">a</hi>r</abbr><ex>ius</ex></expan>
    <expan><abbr>vix</abbr><ex>it</ex></expan>
    <expan><abbr>an</abbr><ex>nis</ex></expan>
    <num valuc="25">XXV</num>
```

<ab type="translation">Philargyrus, slave of Lucius Sulla, private granary keeper. He lived 25 years. </ab>

A computer will not display the text tags – they are only for classifying the information available in the inscription and supplied by the editor. The marked-up text will show only the text supplied between the tags:

> Philargyrus
> L(ucius) Sullae
> horreár(ius) vix(it) an(nis) XXV

Here the "person" is understood to be "Philargyrus L. Sullae." Other inscriptions that name this Philargyrus can be linked to the "person" tag's unique key attribute "PhilargyrusSullae." The elements of his name and of his master's name, Lucius Sulla, are also tagged to indicate their presence in the inscription and can be searched to find other slaves in the possession of the same owner. Key attributes in the nominative are added to each name element in order to standardize the lists for searching, i.e., the computer will search for "Lucius" rather than "L" (the standard abbreviation) or "Lucii" (the genitive form) in order to find all instances of this particular *praenomen*. While the "person" tag itself allows for the connection of all inscriptions that mention the same individual, the separate components isolate occurrences of name elements that may indicate family relationships, slave ownership patterns, ethnicity, and other social information.

Although USEP complies with EpiDoc editing practices as it adds transcriptions of Latin texts to its database, the main information provided by the project has always been so-called metadata rather than transcriptions. For example, the entry in the *Checklist* for the same inscription is as follows:

> Marble columbarium slab, Porta Salaria (mid I)   epitaph of Philargyrus L. Sullae, *horrearius*
> > Sheldon, *LIKMDennison* 119–20 no. 92, Pl. 17 (ph)
> > MI.AA.UM.KM.L.1428

The *Checklist* provided very brief information for each inscription following a set pattern. In the example of the columbarium slab of Philargyrus L. Sullae, the entry includes a description of the object shape (broken stele), material (marble), date (mid-first century A.D.), findspot (Porta Salaria), type of inscription (epitaph), name or names of the subject or subjects (Philargyrus L. Sullae) and perhaps occupation (*horrearius*), publication history and whether a photo appears in the publication (relatively rare in early epigraphic publications), and a unique number assigned to each inscription by the project. Publication references from non-canonical volumes are given abbreviations that often combined the name of the author with that of the publication, since authors of works on epigraphy often have multiple publications, even in a single year. The list of abbreviations appears in the *Checklist*. The inscription used as an example here has been published by R.M. Sheldon (in Baldwin and Torelli 1979: 119–120, no. 92) and more recently by Tuck (2005: 197, no. 335). The USEP numbers are formed by aggregating current geographic information from general to specific: in the case of MI.AA.UM.KM.L.1428, the inscription is in Michigan, in the city of Ann Arbor, in the University of Michigan's Kelsey Museum collection, it is in Latin, and 1428 is the museum's accession number for the object. Although sparse, the highlighting of the non-textual information or metadata available for each inscription in the *Checklist* was a departure from canonical epigraphic volumes like the *Corpus Inscriptionum Latinarum* (*CIL* 1853–present, http://cil.bbaw.de/) or the *Inscriptiones Latinae Selectae* (*ILS*, 1892–1916), which do not prioritize such details. To an even greater extent than the *Checklist* was able, USEP tried to represent a complete snapshot of items in U.S. collections and to start doing more in-depth description, adding texts and perhaps ultimately historical and textual commentary.

Because USEP was concerned almost exclusively with metadata over text, this meant that more of the tag set in the TEI conventions needed to be adapted for use in USEP, which could then help set the standard for metadata in EpiDoc. When the TEI upgraded its conventions from its fourth version (P4) to its fifth version (P5) in 2007, USEP was a leader in adapting TEI P5 tag sets and controlled vocabulary for use in describing inscriptions. Our revised metadata scheme was subsequently circulated throughout the EpiDoc community and forms the basis for sections of the TEI P5-compliant EpiDoc schema.

Types of metadata that USEP has concentrated on include dates, materials, types of inscriptions, and object forms. We use a hierarchical controlled vocabulary to encode the objects in order to make them more easily searchable and also to highlight more clearly the connections that can be made amongst various objects. Developing this hierarchy exemplified some of the intellectual reorientation that such a minute parsing of text information encourages. Developing controlled vocabulary to make decorative elements easily describable and searchable remains a desideratum of the project. Due to the large variety of decorative elements on inscribed objects, it has been difficult to develop a logical but flexible hierarchical scheme of classification. Going forward, the standards set by the Getty Vocabulary Program may help with this problem (see the Getty Research Institute's Art and Architecture thesaurus: http://www.getty.edu/research/tools/vocabularies/aat/; Harpring 2010). In any case, whereas print publications tend to categorize epigraphic texts thematically (e.g., as funerary inscriptions), the process of describing an inscription using the categories that we devised parses the inscription into various parts, from the text itself to other kinds of information present in the object, such as material or object type. An object's material properties can perhaps tell us about the origin of the inscription (through the location of the marble quarry), its date (certain materials were used in specific periods), or even the relative status of the object (depending on the scarcity of the material). Its type can tell us something about how it was used or where it was placed in antiquity (a columbarium marker, for instance, would only be used in a columbarium and would by definition be funerary in nature). Perhaps the most fruitful distinction that we make is between inscription type, which is the category of text without reference to the type of object or the manner of writing, and the object type, which refers specifically to the object onto or into which a text is inscribed or imprinted. Although the relationship between these two fields may seem self-evident, our separation of the intention of the text (the inscription type) from the object type challenges modern assumptions about such relationships in light of the variability of the texts, the patrons, and the original contexts (e.g., an epitaph carved into a building wall, an agonistic text carved upon a tomb slab, and so on). Our controlled vocabulary also specifies an object's constitutive materials and the type of writing that produced its text, the latter of which is useful for identifying specific styles, manners, and tools of writing (e.g., impressed, protruding, painted, inset, and subsets thereof). We pair these controlled vocabularies with free text "glosses" that allow an epigraphist to take advantage of the power and standardization of the controlled vocabularies, but also to provide more individual detail about a feature, which will appear when the full description of an object is displayed.

While a human being can read a paragraph of information and make connections, understand if a known person/object is being discussed, or if it is someone or something entirely new, a computer cannot do so on its own. By adding in all of that information, categorizing every name element, every individual, every piece of decoration, etc., in a known way with controlled vocabularies, we can research the data more effectively. The scope can be as broad or as narrow as we need (all inscriptions in Europe vs. all inscriptions from Porta Salaria), although narrower slices of data throw into relief the sorts of textual ambiguities and problematic categories that we have indicated. The inscription of Philargyrus L. Sullae provides further examples of how markup renders individual items more searchable and easier to classify into groups.

In the description of the inscription itself (msContents), the inscription type can be noted as well as the language or, in the case of bilingual inscriptions, languages used. Note that the main tag for describing the intent of the inscription stands for "manuscript contents," due to the TEI's focus on manuscripts when developing its tag set. USEP uses these TEI tags that, at first glance, seem inappropriate to describe inscribed objects, because the intent is similar to what is needed for inscriptions and because keeping the tag name aids in cross-searching of data sets. Several aspects of the physical description (physDesc) of the inscribed object can be detailed, including the type of object (objectDesc) and material (supportDesc), which can be further subdivided to provide more specific information about the material (here, gray marble), dimensions and units of measurement, the number of lines on the surface, and details about the decorative elements or lack thereof. As with the "person" example above, the computer uses the tags to search and classify each marked-up section, but it only displays the free-text glosses typed between the elements, with the arrangement and display of each part on a web browser determined by style sheets.

```
<msContents>
    <textLang mainLang="lat" otherLangs="">Latin</textLang>
        <msItem class="#funerary.epitaph">
            <p>Epitaph of Philargyrus L. Sullae</p>
        </msItem>
</msContents>
<physDesc>
    <objectDesc ana="#tablet">
    <supportDesc ana="#stone.marble">
        <support>
            <seg type="material">The material is gray marble.</seg>
            <dimensions type="surface" unit="m">
                <height>0.15</height>
                <width>0.028</width>
                <depth>0.04</depth>
            </dimensions>
        </support>
    </supportDesc>
    <layoutDesc>
        <layout columns="1" writtenLines="3">The text is in three lines, one
        column.</layout>
    </layoutDesc>
    </objectDesc>
    <decoDesc>
        <decoNote type="ansata">
        <p>The inscription is within a tabula ansata.</p>
        </decoNote>
    </decoDesc>
</physDesc>
```

The history of an object includes information about its provenance and date. The standardized place reference (europe.italy.rome) allows for hierarchical searching from most general (Europe) to most specific (Porta Salaria cemetery). The number attributes in the date tag are essential for browsing date ranges of multiple objects. One can combine a search of provenance and date to see when a cemetery was in use; a search of family name, date, and place will indicate when a family group made use of a place.

```
<history>
    <summary>
        <note>Excavated from the Porta Salaria necropolis in Rome.</note>
    </summary>
    <origin>
        <date notBefore="0025" notAfter="0075"> mid first century CE</date>
    </origin>
    <provenance>
        <placeName ref="europe.italy.rome.salaria">Porta Salaria, Rome, Italy</placeName>
    </provenance>
</history>
```

One of the most valuable implications of this careful indexing is that our data are now separated into several classificatory facets. With the incorporation of powerful faceted browsing capabilities in the design of our site, users are able to tailor their searches and investigate multiple relationships between objects and epigraphic texts. Most importantly, these relationships will be apparent in different collections, which can foster comparative academic work and stimulate dialogue between scholars and collection curators. To the extent that a large proportion of epigraphic material held in the United States shares a common provenance – Rome's Porta Salaria cemetery region – the ability to engage with these objects digitally as a related group is invaluable for any number of intellectual projects. The shared genealogy of epigraphic materials in U.S. collections is presently under-appreciated, and the capabilities of our site, including our image repository, will allow for virtual approximations of their original context.

"Re-placing" the Porta Salaria Necropolis Inscriptions

The digital capabilities we have outlined above have even greater repercussions with respect to investigating multiple relationships across aggregate data sets. While one might use nuanced browsing to isolate patterns of specific epigraphic or object features, our encoding practices also allow the reunion of objects that were found together and subsequently separated into different collections. For instance, in our database of approximately 3,000 objects, around 650 found their way into U.S. collections from a specific archaeological area, the Porta Salaria necropolis in Rome, Italy.

The Porta Salaria necropolis was discovered outside of Rome's Aurelian Gate around the end of the nineteenth century and was excavated through the beginning of the twentieth century (Bodel 1992; Egbert 1908: 263–264). Approximately 2,500 inscriptions and tombs, still in their original archaeological context, were unearthed during the residential development of the area over several years. A hasty but professional excavation of the site generated a number of new epigraphic publications and inundated the antiquities market with related objects that were then parceled out to disparate locations. Concurrently, a number of important American antiquities collections were being formed, with the result that about one-fifth of these inscriptions were acquired by institutions such as the Speed Art Museum (Louisville, Kentucky), the Sackler Museum collections of Harvard Art Museums (Cambridge, Massachusetts), the Smith College Department of Classical Languages and Literatures and the Museum of Art (Northampton, Massachusetts), the University of Michigan's Kelsey Museum (Ann Arbor, Michigan), the Johns Hopkins University Archaeological Museum (Baltimore, Maryland), Columbia University's Rare Book and Manuscript Room of the Butler Library (New York, New York), and New York University's Department of Classics (New York, New York). In the Speed Art Museum alone there are over 550 inscriptions from the Porta Salaria necropolis (Gigante 2008), all of which are illustrated on USEP's website.

When the Porta Salaria inscriptions were first uncovered, transcriptions and short descriptions of their texts were recorded, although not systematically, in *CIL* VI and several editions of *Notizie degli Scavi* (*NSc*). After this the inscriptions were dispersed, and unless they were subsequently published, no other easily locatable information indicated their object histories or present whereabouts. Distributed in small, often inaccessible groups throughout the country, they can seldom be seen, let alone examined, except in isolated and often unfavorable circumstances. Much of the inscribed material held in American collections has not been properly studied, and many of these pieces now lie buried in the storerooms of these same museum and university collections. While this problem obtains for epigraphic materials in the U.S. writ large, it is especially striking for the scattered Porta Salaria materials, to the extent that they share a common provenance and could be studied profitably in the fashion of *in situ* monument groups like the Isola Sacra cemetery near Ostia (Hope 2007) or the clusters of funerary monuments at Pompeii (Koortbojian 1996).

We are now able to begin to bring these items together again, albeit virtually, and more work can be done to study them as forming part of a shared original context. As Linda Gigante (2008: 29 n. 8) indicates, it would be helpful to compile a complete inventory of all items originally from the Porta Salaria necropolis. The paths of dispersal of the Porta Salaria materials are also pertinent to analyses of American antiquities collecting and alert us to items that may have been lost completely. For instance, Gigante (2008: 28 n. 3, 31 n. 11) lists several inscriptions published in *CIL* that remain unaccounted for – they might have been sold or possibly left in Italy, but are presently undocumented. In addition to the studies that could be done with the transcriptions that appeared in the late nineteenth and early twentieth centuries, we can now begin to formulate questions about trends in materials, decorative elements, and even the hands of carvers, inquiries that are enriched further by the access that USEP provides to images of its objects. These, in turn, can tell us more about the people who used the necropolis, how it was used, and the carvers whose inscriptions are now all that remain of the cemetery. New research trajectories hold promise not only for the relationship between monuments whose spatial relationships can be approximated (particularly texts that were viewed contemporaneously, in roughly the same topographical location), but in some cases even within the bounded context of a single monument. For example, the Speed Art Museum houses the complete inventory of texts from a single *columbarium* excavated from the Porta Salaria area.

Collaborative Work

A project like the USEP makes several intellectual contributions, not the least of which is training a new generation of epigraphists who make explicit, critical editorial and classificatory decisions as they encode epigraphic materials. Projects like USEP and EpiDoc are necessarily collaborative in nature, bringing together a wide range of scholars from the humanities and computer science, none of whom could accomplish this sort of work without collaborators from other fields.

EpiDoc has set the standard in the development of markup projects of other ancient text-bearing objects, such as papyri (e.g., http://papyri.info/) and coins. Feedback from USEP resulted in refinements and improvements to The Chapel Hill Electronic Text Converter (CHET-C: http://eds.library. brown.edu/projects/chet-c/chetc.html), which Hugh Cayless (University of North Carolina, Chapel Hill) developed to take texts that have been marked up with the standard Leiden epigraphic diacritical marks and convert them into EpiDoc-compliant XML files that can be combined with the existing XML file for a particular inscription.

The encoding standards and vocabularies that the digital humanities community works to implement facilitate the coordination of numerous collections and databases of materials ranging from inscribed objects to manuscripts and papyri. When viewed in isolation these forms of evidence reveal relatively modest amounts of information about antiquity, but digital, corpus-based approaches can greatly expand the implications of even a single datum. In other words, although specific items offer some value on their own, a far greater value emerges from the quantity of evidence that digital corpora are able to collate and then make available for comparison and analysis.

Acknowledgments

The content of this paper was reviewed and commented upon usefully by Elli Mylonas of the Brown University Library's Center for Digital Scholarship, to whom we are both indebted in every aspect of the USEP's development.

References

Baldwin, Martha W., and Mario Torelli (editors)
  1979   *Latin Inscriptions in the Kelsey Museum: The Dennison Collection*. Kelsey Museum Studies Vol. 4. University of Michigan Press, Ann Arbor.

Bodel, John
  1992   Thirteen Latin Funerary Inscriptions at Harvard University. *American Journal of Archaeology* 96.1: 71–100.

Bodel, John, and Stephen Tracy
  1997   *Greek and Latin Inscriptions in the USA: A Checklist*. American Academy in Rome, New York.

Egbert, James C.
  1908   Inscriptions of Rome and Central Italy. *Supplementary Papers of the American School of Classical Studies in Rome* 2: 263–290.

Gigante, Linda M.
  2008   A Collection of Inscriptions from the Via Salaria Necropolis Now in the Speed Art Museum, Louisville, Kentucky. *Memoirs of the American Academy at Rome* 53: 27–78.

Harpring, Patricia
  2010   *Introduction to Controlled Vocabularies: Terminology for Art, Architecture, and Other Cultural Works*. Getty Research Institute, Los Angeles.

Hope, Valerie
  2007   *Death in Ancient Rome: A Sourcebook*. Routledge, London.

Koortbojian, Michael
  1996   In Commemorationem Mortuorum: Text and Image along the "Street of Tombs." In *Art and Text in Roman Culture*, edited by Jaś Elsner, pp. 210–234. Cambridge University Press, New York.

Tuck, Steven
  2005   *Latin Inscriptions in the Kelsey Museum: The Dennison and De Criscio Collections*. Kelsey Museum Studies Vol. 9. University of Michigan Press, Ann Arbor.

Forging History:
From Antiquity to the Modern Period

Christopher A. Rollston

Introduction: Basic Facts About Forgeries

As an *Ausgangspunkt*, it is useful for certain foundational factors to be emphasized: (1) Epigraphic forgeries have been produced in many ancient and modern cultures. (2) Some forgeries are of poor quality, but some forgeries are of very high quality. (3) Many trained scholars are able to detect poor quality forgeries, but high quality forgeries have sometimes duped even the best of scholars. (4) Some forgers are gifted and assiduous, some are not; even the best of forgers make mistakes. (5) Some scholars are gifted and assiduous, some are not. (6) Scholars without formal training in epigraphy are rarely good at detecting epigraphic forgeries. (7) Some scholars trained in epigraphy are bad at detecting epigraphic forgeries. (8) Epigraphic forgeries often have sensational content. (9) Epigraphic forgeries are often reported to have come from a named site, so as to augment the alleged authenticity of the inscription. (10) Disinterested scholars are better at detecting forgeries than are scholars that have a vested interest in the content; forgers know this. (11) Forgers and those marketing forgeries are most apt to contact scholars that are known normally to confirm the authenticity of documents; forgers and those marketing forgeries normally avoid scholars who debunk forgeries. (12) Many of the reasons scholars have sometimes used to "authenticate" a forgery are transparently false, or at best, specious. (13) Forgers often attempt to model their forgeries on genuine texts. (14) Some forgeries are detected rapidly and exposed as forgeries. (15) Some forgeries have been considered genuine for long periods of time. (16) The motivations of forgers are varied, but are often (but not always) discernible. (17) Forgeries are often sold on the market for large sums of money. (18) Forgeries are sometimes produced for ideological, political, religious reasons. (19) Generally speaking, forgeries are becoming easier to produce as well as more sophisticated (Rollston 2003, 2004, 2005). At this juncture, I shall turn to a discussion of various forgeries from antiquity to the modern period, with emphasis on the basic content of the forgeries, probable purposes and motivations, putative dates, and the means of detection. Implicit through all of this will be a demonstration of the fact that the production of forgeries has a long history in the past and a presence in the modern period as well.

An Ancient Mesopotamian Forgery of the Neo-Babylonian Period

Manishtushu (late third millennium B.C.) was the son of Sargon of Akkad, the brother of Rimush (who preceded him on the throne), and the father of Naram-Sin. Manishtushu is often referred to as the third king of Akkad. A text that purports to come from the reign of Manistushu is the "Cruciform Monument." It ostensibly details some of the achievements of Manishtushu, including building activities and the smiting of enemies. Various components of this inscription are of particular interest. For example, within the text, Manishtushu states: "I renewed the rites and ordinances of the (temple) É-babbar; I added offering upon offering" (Sollberger 1967–68: 63). Moreover, Manishtushu also says the following: "I lifted my hand to (the sun-god) Shamash, my master: he heard my prayer, he opened to me the way of justice. On that very day I returned that field in perpetuity" (Sollberger 1967–68: 64). He also notes "from Abshan to Akshak east of Durdanum, thirty-eight townships were released unto Shamash. Indeed, I did not covet their corvée, one did not call them up to service: they perform corvée for the É-babbar only" (Sollberger 1967–68: 64). Much of the remainder of this text records, among various things, the fact that Manishtushu basically doubled the provisions for the temple. The text then concludes with an oath formula and curses:

> I swore (by) Shamash and Aya, Enki, Nin-hursaga, (and) Adad: this is not a lie, it is indeed the truth! ... He who will damage this document, let Enki fill up his canals with slime. Let Nin-hursaga stop child-birth in his land! Let him plan, (and) let Adad smite (it), and gather all his descendants! [Sollberger 1967–68: 64].

The Cruciform Monument of Manishtushu was originally understood by the author of the *editio princeps* (L. King) to be a text that actually hailed from the reign of Manishtushu and recorded the numerous privileges (e.g., no corvée) and revenues (e.g., large donations) bestowed upon the É-babbar Temple of Sippar, during the Old Akkadian Period (i.e., late third millennium B.C.). These privileges and revenues were associated in particular with renovations that occurred at the Sippar Temple. Significantly, however,

I. J. Gelb argued that this document was a *"fraus pia,"* produced during the Old Babylonian Period (i.e., early second millennium B.C.) to suggest that the privileges accorded the Sippar Temple were of great antiquity (Gelb 1949: 346–348). The arguments that he marshaled were philological and palaeographic in nature. Subsequently, Sollberger wrote a particularly detailed article, augmenting Gelb's arguments in various ways. Although Sollberger believed that a date of the Old Babylonian Period was (basically) permissible philologically, he made a convincing case for an origin in the Neo-Babylonian Period. Sollberger's argument was based on two major pillars: (1) There was a Neo-Babylonian fragment (known as Si 3) that had long been recognized as a "duplicate" of Manishtushu's Cruciform Monument (even King had noted this, as early as 1910). Of course, this fragment was assumed to be a (much) later copy of the Cruciform Monument. However, although the fragment contained the same text as the Cruciform Monument (normally, *verbatim*), there was a striking difference. Namely, Sollberger noted that the fragment (given the siglum Si 3) "shows none of the archaisms or pseudo-archaisms of the Cruciform Monument: it is written in 'correct' Neo-Babylonian." Along those lines, there is also a difficult colophon at the conclusion of the fragment (Si 3) that states that it was a copy of an inscription from Babylon. Sollberger concluded that the fragment (Si 3)

> far from being a copy of the Cruciform Monument, is the original text composed by officials of the É-babbar for a scribe to turn into the 'antique document' they needed to reinforce their claims. The 'copy from Babylon' may well have been that of an authentic historical inscription, such as, for example, BM, which supplied our 'forgers' with the historical background to Manistushu's alleged donation [Sollberger 1967–68: 52; "BM" = BM78290].

Of great import is the fact that the archaeological context of the Cruciform Monument at Sippar had not been discussed prior to Sollberger, but must be factored into the assessment. Namely, the Cruciform Monument was found in an archaeological context with two large terracotta cylinders (barrel-shaped) from the Neo-Babylonian King Nabonidus (r. 556–539 B.C.). Based on the convergence of the cumulative data (summarized above), the Cruciform Monument of Manishtushu text is considered to be a pious forgery, dating to the Neo-Babylonian Period (see also Al-Rawi and George 1994: 139–148).

Regarding this forgery, therefore, the following can be stated with a high degree of certitude: the Cruciform Monument of Manistushu purports to come from King Manishtushu of the Old Akkadian Period (third millennium B.C.), but it actually hails from the Neo-Babylonian Period (and probably the sixth century B.C.). That is, the setting (third millennium) is quite realistic, but fictive. The language of this document is archaizing, not actually archaic. The Cruciform Monument's use of earlier historical materials made it seem to be a straightforward document from deep antiquity, that is, a "real" historical document, and this was the intent of the forger(s). Ultimately, the actual purpose of the document was to give an aura of great antiquity to the privileged status of the É-babbar Temple of Sippar, with the primary beneficiaries being those associated with the temple. Therefore, the forger(s) of this document can arguably be considered to have been elites (e.g., priests) who had much to gain (economically, religiously, and politically) from the privileged status. That is, the forger(s) can be said to have produced this document very deftly, and because of a strong vested interest. Fortunately, modern scholarship has been able to determine its actual date of composition and its purpose.

An Ancient Egyptian Forgery of the Ptolemaic Period

The Famine Stele (Lichtheim 1980: 94–103) was found on Sehel Island, not far from Aswan, and purports to hail from the reign of King Djoser of the Old Kingdom's Third Dynasty (ca. 2700–2600 B.C.). There is a relief on this stele that depicts King Djoser giving offerings to the gods Khnum-Re, Satis, and Anukis. Near the beginning of the text, the following statement occurs:

> I was in mourning on my throne, those of the palace were in grief, my heart was in great affliction, because Hapy had failed to come in time. In a period of seven years, grain was scant, kernels were dried up, scarce was every kind of food [Lichtheim 1980: 95–96].

King Djoser then tells the "Governor of the domains of the South" that a priest of Imhotep had told him that there was a Temple of the god Khnum at Elephantine and that Khnum controlled the flooding of the Nile. Soon the god Khnum appears in a dream to King Djoser and promises him an end to the famine. Because of King Djoser's gratitude to Khnum of Elephantine, Djoser states that he will broaden the borders of the Temple of Khnum and that the produce of the fields in the region of the Temple of Khnum will be brought not into royal coffers, but into the Temple's granary. Furthermore, game that was hunted, and precious stones that putatively belong to the throne, will also be given to the Temple of Khnum in abundance. According to the narrative of the Famine Stele, Djoser states that all of this is done "in return for what you have done for me." Moreover, so as to solidify the new arrangement, it is stated that "no officials are to issue orders in these places or take anything from them, for everything is to be protected for your sanctuary." Finally, it is decreed that someone is to engrave this decree on a stele of the sanctuary in writing for it happened as said, (and) on a tablet, so that divine writings shall be on them in the temple twice. He who spits (on it) deceitfully shall be given over to punishment [Lichtheim 1980: 100].

Lichtheim (1980) has stated that "in its present form, the text is undoubtedly a work of the Ptolemaic period." She notes that some scholars have argued that it was based on a genuine Old Kingdom decree from the time of Djoser. However, some scholars understand it to be a complete fiction (Lichtheim 1980: 94). In terms of the probable forgers, Lichtheim herself concludes

the most plausible hypothesis… is the one that sees the inscription as the work of the priesthood of the Khnum Temple, who were anxious to strengthen their privileges in the face of the encroaching claims made by the clergy of Isis of Philae [Lichtheim 1980: 95].

Haiying (1998: 515–521) has come to the same basic conclusions, stating first and foremost that "it is generally accepted that the famine stela, dated to year 18 of Djoser, is a Ptolemaic inscription," and then arguing in some detail that of the possible composers of this stele, it was probably "the priests of Khnum who made this pious forgery" during the Ptolemaic Period, for political and religious reasons. After all, they were the primary beneficiaries of the statements made within this stele.

In sum, the consensus of the field is that the Famine Stele is a forgery. It purported to have hailed from King Djoser of the Third Dynasty of the Old Kingdom, but it was actually a product of the Ptolemaic Period (i.e., late first millennium B.C.). The primary beneficiaries of the Famine Stele were those associated with, and benefiting from (economically, religiously, and politically) the Temple of Khnum; therefore, it would be reasonable to posit that those associated with the Khnum Temple were responsible for the forgery. Of course, the forger(s) were very careful to produce a text that seemed to have hailed from the Old Kingdom, but this too was a ruse. Ultimately, it was a forgery, written two millennia after its purported date, and its purpose was to attempt to create and fortify a privileged status for elites associated with a particular temple and god.[1] Again, because of careful philological and historical analysis, the fictive nature of this inscription has been discovered and thus can be factored into the interpretation of the totality of this Ptolemaic text.

A Latin Forgery of the Middle Ages:
The *Donation of Constantine*

According to a document known as the *Donation of Constantine*, the Emperor Constantine the Great, on the fourth day after his baptism (ca. A.D. 337), "yielded his crown, and all his royal prerogatives in the city of Rome, and in Italy, and in Western Parts, to the Apostolic see" (Coleman 1922: 11). Within the *Donation of Constantine* itself, it is stated that Constantine's conferral is noted in the "Acts of the Blessed Sylvester," that is, Pope Sylvester I (A.D. 314–335). Significantly, the wording of the *Donation of Constantine* readily conveys the document's import and purpose. For example, it is stated that "Constantine... conferred this privilege on the Pontiff of the Roman church: that in the whole Roman world priests should regard him as their head, as judges do the king" (Coleman 1922: 12–13). The *Donation* continues with words such as the following:

> the Sacred Seat of the Blessed Peter shall be gloriously exalted... we ordain and decree that he shall have the supremacy as well of the four principal seats, Alexandria, Antioch, Jerusalem, and Constantinople, as also over all the churches of God in the whole earth.

Furthermore, the *Donation* notes that

> we have granted him [Peter] of our property in the east as well as in the west, and even in the northern and southern quarter; namely, in Judea, Greece, Asia, Thrace, Africa, and Italy and the various islands [Coleman 1922: 15].

Along those same lines, the *Donation of Constantine* also states that

> We give over and relinquish to the aforesaid our most blessed Pontiff, Sylvester, the universal Pope, as well our palace, as has been said, as also the city of Rome, and all the provinces, places and cities of Italy and the western regions, and we decree by this our godlike and pragmatic sanction that they are to be controlled by him [Pope Sylvester] and by his successors, and we grant that they shall remain under the law of the holy Roman Church ... and we decree that all these things we have established and confirmed, remain inviolate and unshaken unto the end of the world [Coleman 1922: 17].

The *Donation* concludes by stating that

> all the emperors our successors, and all the nobles, the satraps also, the most glorious senate, and all the people in the whole world, now and in all times still to come shall not be allowed to "break these decrees." Those that do "shall be subject and bound over to eternal damnation" (Coleman 1922: 18–19).

Thus, according to the *Donation of Constantine* the Church was to govern the Roman Empire.

The fact that the *Donation of Constantine* came to be understood (within the Church) as authoritative is demonstrated by the fact that Pope Leo IX (A.D. 1002–1054) actually cited the *Donation* (in a letter written in 1054 to Michael Cerularius), in order to argue for the supremacy of the Church; furthermore, the successors of Leo IX used the *Donation* for the same purposes. That is, this letter, with its grandiose assertions regarding the supremacy of the Church, was considered both authentic and binding.[2] For several centuries this continued to be the case, with no one seriously contesting its authenticity.

Nevertheless, the brilliant Italian humanist scholar named Lorenzo Valla (A.D. 1406–1457) was convinced that it was a forgery, that it was not from Constantine, and that it did not hail from the fourth century A.D. Valla's devastating critique of the *Donation of Constantine* is entitled *De falso Credita et Ementita Constantini Donatione Declamatio* (written ca. A.D. 1440), translated into English as "The Discourse of Lorenzo Valla on the Forgery of the Alleged Donation of Constantine" (Coleman 1922). The dating of Valla's document is based on the fact that the assassination of Vitelleschi occurred in March 1440, and Valla mentions this event (Coleman 1922: 163). Valla begins his historical-critical analysis with the following words:

> I have published many books, a great many, in almost every branch of learning. Inasmuch as there are those who are shocked that in these I disagree with certain great writers already approved by long usage, and charge me with rashness and sacrilege, what must we suppose some of them will do now! How they will rage against me, and if opportunity is afforded how eagerly and how quickly they will drag me to punishment! For I am writing against not only the dead, but the living also, not this man or that, but a host, not merely private individuals, but the authorities. And what authorities! Even the supreme pontiff. [Coleman 1922: 21].

Although the words of Valla may seem to be laden with hubris, one could also frame them as an *apologia* of sorts. After all, he is about to besiege a font of power and wealth, and he anticipates that he will endure the ire of those who wish to cast doubt on his demolition of the *Donation's* authenticity. In any case, at that juncture, Valla throws down the gauntlet in a decisive fashion:

> I know that for a long time now, men's ears are waiting to hear the offense with which I charge the Roman pontiffs. It is indeed, an enormous one, due either to supine ignorance, or to gross avarice which is the slave of idols, or to pride of empire of which cruelty is ever the companion. For during some centuries now, either they have not known that the Donation of Constantine is spurious and forged, or else they themselves forged it, and their successors walking in the same way of deceit as their elders have defended as true what they knew to be false. [Coleman 1922: 27].

Valla then begins in earnest to argue against the authenticity of the *Donation of Constantine*. As a point of departure, Valla delineates the essence of his critique:

> I shall show that (1) Constantine and Sylvester were not such men that the former would choose to give, would have the legal right to give, or would have it in his power to give those lands to another, or that the latter would be willing to accept them or could legally have done so; (2) the latter did not receive, nor the former give possession of, what is said to have been granted, but that it always remained under the sway and empire of the Caesars; (3) Nothing was given to Sylvester by Constantine, but to an earlier Pope (and Constantine had received baptism even before that pontificate), and that the grants were inconsiderable, for the mere subsistence of the Pope; (4) It is not true either that a copy of the Donation is found in the Decretum [of Gratian], or that it was taken from the History of Sylvester; for it is not found in it, or in any history, and it is comprised of contradictions, impossibilities, stupidities, barbarisms and absurdities [Coleman 1922: 27, 29].

Valla's arguments throughout his treatise are varied and particularly cogent. At the beginning of his treatise, his arguments are general. Thus, he begins by noting that it is not reasonable to believe that Constantine the Great would simply give the empire to the Church. Kings, after all, attempt "to increase empires and kingdoms… and to extend authority as far and wide as possible" (Coleman 1922: 27, 29, 31). He refers to the fact that kings often commit many "crimes" and "horrors" in order "to attain and extend power"; therefore, "if domination is usually sought with such great resolution, how much greater must be the resolution to preserve it!" (Coleman 1922: 31). Furthermore, he also affirms that Constantine's surrendering of the empire would have encountered substantial opposition from various sectors of his empire. For example, he notes that those within the Roman Empire that had "stood so often in line of battle, who have seen brothers, fathers, sons, pierced and writhing under hostile acts" would have been dismayed (Coleman 1922: 39). Moreover, those that held high office within it, for example, "the senate," would have been disturbed at Constantine for surrendering the Empire to the Church. Furthermore, Valla notes also that many within the empire would have refused to embrace major religious tenets of the Church. That is, the non-Christians of the empire would have said

> You [Constantine] have the power, indeed to do with your empire what you will, and even with us, one thing however excepted, which we will resist to the death; we will not give up the worship of the immortal gods [Coleman 1922: 39].

At that juncture, Valla focuses on the fact that there is no textual evidence from the fourth century that records Sylvester's acceptance of the *Donation of Constantine*. Thus he writes: "to make us believe in this 'donation' which your document recites, something ought still to be extant concerning Sylvester's acceptance of it." Then Valla plunges the dagger, noting that "there is nothing concerning it extant." He concludes that "the fact that there is no mention [anywhere] of an acceptance is reason for saying that there was no donation" (Coleman 1922: 61). He then also queries: "where is any taking possession, any delivery?" (Coleman 1922: 63). The necessary conclusion, argues Valla, is that there never was a transfer of property, because the *Donation of Constantine* is a forgery that post-dates Constantine by centuries. Moreover, Valla notes that the *Donation of Constantine* is not contained in the detailed documents of Gratian (died ca. A.D. 1159). To be sure, Valla notes that someone had interpolated a manuscript of the Decretum of Gratian with some sections of the *Donation*, but Valla immediately notes that "the well-informed have never thought" that the sections of the *Donation* were present in the original Decretum.[3] That is, as a good textual critic, Valla sagely notes that no portion of the *Donation* is present in "any of the oldest copies of the Decretum" (Coleman 1922: 75). With a judicial flourish, Valla declares that he wishes he could "drag the forger into court" and interrogate him regarding the fact that the "Donation" is not even mentioned in the "Acts of Sylvester," the very Pope that was supposed to be the first recipient of the *Donation*.

Valla also notes numerous linguistic problems in the *Donation*. For example, he states that the forger put in the same sentence "extiterit" and "existat," creating a semantic morass (because of the usage of different moods and tenses). Furthermore, Valla declared that the forger actually confused the words "ordain" and "decree" (Coleman 1922: 93). In addition, rather than using the term "Byzantium," the forger used the name "Byzantia" (Coleman 1922: 97). Additionally, Valla criticizes the forger for "using the gerundive, 'permanendas,' for the future infinitive (permansuras)" (Coleman 1922: 127). Furthermore, he mentions that although the forger assumed that the "diadem" was made of "purest gold and precious gems," in reality the royal diadem was made of "coarse cloth, or perhaps silk" (Coleman 1922: 105). That is, Valla is arguing that the *Donation of Constantine* is riddled with historical and linguistic problems, something that would not be the case for an official document that actually hailed from the fourth century A.D. Ultimately, the *Donation of Constantine* is a forgery, probably produced during the ninth century A.D., with the intent of enfranchising the Church, further enriching and empowering those already most powerful within it. To be sure, the author(s) attempted (as forgers always do) to make the document seem as ancient and historical as possible, but Valla's penetrating analysis demonstrates that the *Donation of Constantine* was a certain forgery, crafted several centuries after the time from which it purports to hail.

A Forgery of the Nineteenth Century A.D.:
The Brazilian Phoenician Inscription

During the late nineteenth century, a Phoenician inscription had surfaced purporting to be an account of Sidonians from the region of (biblical) Ezion-geber, who circled the "land belonging to Ham" (i.e., Africa) during the reign of King Hirom [III] (r. 552–532 B.C.), but were blown far off course to a "distant shore." This inscription was reported to have been found at a place called Pauso Alto near the Paraíba River in Brazil. Hand-copies of it were circulated, and it was agreed that Ladislau de Souza Mello Neto would publish it. Although many were jubilant about the inscription's contents, some doubts were also voiced. Lidzbarski declared it a definite forgery, and the inscription was forgotten (Lidzbarski 1898: 132; for an early analysis, see Schlottmann 1874: 481–487). Gordon (1968), however, published an article in the late 1960s discussing this inscription, and argued that it was certainly genuine.

Cross was not convinced (Cross 1968). He began by stating that the clarity of the inscription aroused concerns. Moreover, he also found it "striking and suspicious" that so many features of the inscription had parallels of various sorts in classical and biblical sources (especially Herodotus and the biblical book of Jonah). However, he then marshaled a substantial amount of very damning evidence against it. For example, several words were written with the *'alep mater lectionis* (and thus an anomaly for Phoenician of this period). Thus, *nhn'* is used for the first person common plural independent personal pronoun. Gordon considered this to be an "Aramaism," but Cross correctly noted that "the borrowing of elements as fundamental as the pronoun is a phenomenon so rare in linguistic data that it may be dismissed on methodological grounds." In addition, the *hiph'il* was employed within the inscription as well, something that is anomalous for a Phoenician inscription of this period.[4] Another problematic aspect was the use of the article *h* on the *nomen regens* of a construct chain, hence, *mhqrt hmlk* ("from *the* city of the king").[5] Cross's argument is careful, thorough, and cogent. The cumulative data about content and orthography demonstrate beyond a reasonable doubt that this "Phoenician inscription from Brazil" is a nineteenth-century forgery. In this context, it should be remembered that during the late nineteenth century there was discussion in the scholarly world about whether or not the Phoenicians had actually sailed all the way to the New World. This inscription would have, for some, confirmed just such a notion. I suspect that this inscription was indeed forged for this very purpose. I should note in this connection that, although this inscription was said to have been on stone, to the best of my knowledge no scholar has ever actually seen it. Moreover, my attempts to locate it in Brazil have not been successful. In fact, there is not even complete certainty about the precise location of the place where it was found. Therefore, it may very well be that this inscription itself never existed in any place, other than the hand-copy that the forger produced. Of course, the forger certainly made an attempt to make this inscription seem historical, but careful philological analysis unmasked it as a modern forgery. Also of significance in this regard is that – as is so often the case – a respected scholar (Cyrus Gordon) continued to assert that he believed the inscription to be authentic and ancient, and he continued to believe this even after Cross's devastating article. The lesson here is that sometimes even a rather obvious forgery will find credentialed defenders. Alas, I would contend that a major reason for this is that sometimes a scholar will so earnestly desire for a text to be genuinely ancient (sometimes because a text might confirm a cherished belief of theirs), that they will suspend the necessary hermeneutic of suspicion.

Greek and Latin Forgeries and Coleman Norton's Mid-Twentieth Century Forgery

Peerless New Testament textual critic Bruce Manning Metzger of Princeton has noted (largely following Abbott 1908: 27) that there have been numerous forged Greek and Latin documents through the centuries. He states that "the most prolific forger during the late Renaissance period seems to have been Pirro Ligorio, the successor to Michelangelo in supervising the work at St. Peter's in Rome" (Metzger 1972: 24–24). Metzger goes on to note that Ligorio was responsible for 2,995 of the 3,645 spurious inscriptions in the *Corpus Inscriptionum Latinarum*. Many of these forgeries Ligorio pretended to have found in gardens (e.g., lapidary inscriptions) and libraries (e.g., manuscripts) of well-known homes in Rome, and he often mentioned the exact location. A number of his forgeries were produced for his trusting patron, the cardinal of Carpi. Significantly, the "true character" of many of his forgeries was not discovered for some time, and in the meantime, many were copied into new collections by scholars throughout the world (Metzger 1997: 125–126). Similarly, during the nineteenth century, Metzger notes that a Greek named Constantine Simonides began producing manuscripts of Greek texts professing to be of "fabulous antiquity." For example, he produced a copy of Homer in an almost prehistoric style of writing, a copy of the Gospel according to Matthew written within two decades after the "ascension." Because museums and collectors were willing to pay high prices for ancient documents, Constantine Simonides was enjoying the fruits of many of his manuscript "finds." Ultimately, scholars such as Tischendorf (who found the

Codex Sinaiticus, a fourth century uncial, at the Monastery of St. Catherine in the Sinai) exposed Constantine Simonides, who in retaliation said that he had forged one manuscript: the Codex Sinaiticus (an obvious lie).

One of the most intriguing twentieth-century forgeries was, according to Metzger, produced by Paul R. Coleman-Norton, a classicist at Princeton who was sometimes accustomed to enlivening his classes with a humorous anecdote or wisecrack. Coleman-Norton claimed to have found a copy of a Greek translation of a portion of the Latin *Opus Imperfectum in Matthaeum* (a collection of some fifty-four homilies on the canonical Gospel of Matthew) in a mosque in the North African town of Fedhala in 1943 during his time in the United States Army. Especially significant was the fact that this Greek text contained a unique saying regarding weeping and gnashing of teeth. Here is Coleman-Norton's translation:

> And behold, a certain one of his disciples standing by said unto him, "Rabbi" (which is to say, being interpreted, Master), "how can these things be, if they are toothless?" And Jesus answered and said, "O thou of little faith, trouble not thyself: if haply they will be lacking any, teeth will be provided" [Coleman-Norton 1950].

It is imperative to note that this "plus" is not only absent from the Latin text of the *Opus*, but is also without parallel in patristic literature. In any case, after returning to the States, Coleman-Norton prepared an erudite discussion of the Greek text and its plus. Although a specialist in Latin, he submitted his article to *Harvard Theological Review*, then the *Journal of Biblical Literature*, and Chicago's *Journal of Religion*. The article was rejected by these journals. Ultimately, it was published in *Catholic Biblical Quarterly* (Coleman-Norton 1950). Metzger, however, has noted that, before World War II (and thus before the "manuscript discovery" with the unique plus), he had been in class when Coleman-Norton told the students about a query of someone who had been puzzled by Jesus' announcement that the wicked would suffer amid weeping and gnashing of teeth. "But Master," asked a disciple, "what if a man has no teeth?" The response of Jesus was "teeth will be provided." Metzger concludes by stating that he "is convinced that this is a pia fraus" (Metzger 1997: 136–139).

There is much that can be said about Metzger's discussion of forgeries. Among those things are the following: Metzger has candidly stated that there have been literally thousands of forgeries in Greek and Latin, many of which were accepted as genuine for a time and even made it into the standard collections and reference works. Furthermore, some of these forgeries were written in very archaic scripts (and thus many were duped into believing that they were genuinely ancient texts), and often these forgeries were said to be "found" in particular places (thus ostensibly creating an aura of authenticity for the discovery). Striking also is the fact that the forgers can be scholars, as was the case with Coleman-Norton of Princeton University. Finally, it should also be emphasized that the motives for the various forgeries detailed by Metzger are often discernible as primarily economic in nature. However, in the case of Coleman-Norton, it is tenable to suggest that it was in part simply a *Witz* (joke), while in part it was also originally intended as reflective of a desire to embarrass a rival institution and program (i.e., if Coleman-Norton of Princeton had succeeded in getting the faux discovery published in a journal from Harvard, it seems he would have arguably felt it to be a particularly pungent prank).

A Forgery of the Mid- to Late Twentieth Century: The Philistine Hebron Documents

During December of 1970, non-provenanced documents "reported to have been found in the region of Hebron" were announced. Brownlee and Mendenhall considered them ancient and even argued that they were "Philistine" (Brownlee and Mendenhall 1970; Mendenhall 1971). During Brownlee's presentation of the documents at the Society of Biblical Literature meeting in 1971, Cross declared that these documents were forgeries, noting parallels between the Siloam Tunnel Inscription and the "Hebron Documents." Brownlee accepted Cross's conclusion. Mendenhall, however, persisted with arguments in print. He countered that some of the laboratory tests were consistent with antiquity (Mendenhall stated that the C^{14} tests yielded a modern date, but he argued that the C^{14} tests were compromised because of variable storage and handling practices). Mendenhall (1971: 99) stated that "ultra-violet examination (both short-wave and long-wave) yielded absolutely no evidence of inauthenticity. Exhaustive examination of the documents under the microscope and analysis of the ink and leather with a scanning electron microscope brought a number of surprises for which there is no known published parallel, but no evidence against their authenticity." He noted that attempts at decipherment continued, and he was able to affirm that progress had been made. He also indicated that the alphabetic signs used in these "Hebron Inscriptions" numbered approximately 31. Regarding orthography, he stated that there was not a "rigidity of alphabetic forms and rules of spelling," but attributed this to the fact that the documents were early, non-professional exemplars of the alphabet. Computer analyses were employed and were said to be very helpful in isolating morphemes (Mendenhall 1971: 99–100). Mendenhall was, of course, aware of the fact that some questioned the documents' authenticity. He replied in the following way:

The question of the authenticity of the documents has of course been raised concerning these as well as every other new discovery from the Stone Age cave paintings of France and Spain to the Qumran scrolls. Allegations of forgery seem to be a predictable defense mechanism of those elements of the scholarly world that have made up their minds about what the ancient world was supposed to produce, and do not want to be confused with new facts. It is curious that the only scholars who are convinced of their authenticity are those who have worked seriously with the original documents, including the extremely productive computer analysis [Mendenhall 1971: 101].

He went on to note that

it is very difficult to believe that scholars capable of putting such an enormous range of information into these documents would also be capable of such irresponsible misuse of learning. Those who perpetuate the rumors have the obligation of common decency to produce the evidence concerning those alleged forgeries if in fact they do exist [Mendenhall 1971: 101–102].

That is, he assumed (falsely) that no one who was capable of producing a forgery would actually do so, certainly a Panglossian philosophical position.

During the early 1980s, Naveh accepted Mendenhall's challenge and did a detailed analysis of one of the "Hebron Documents," demonstrating at length that it was a modern forgery. In fact, he demonstrated that the forger had, in essence, simply copied large portions of the Siloam Tunnel Inscription, but had done so (essentially) from left to right, that is, basically "backwards" (Naveh 1982: 53–58)! Naveh also affirmed that the document (he analyzed one in particular) had been done by a "clumsy hand," an incisive reference to the poor forger. Because all of the documents were similar (in terms of medium, script, and content), it was readily apparent that all were forgeries. Naturally, it can be stated that the purported "find spot" of Hebron was smoke and mirrors, intended to give these documents a legitimate pedigree, fictive though it was. It should be emphasized that Mendenhall was a gifted scholar, but his defense of the antiquity of these texts was simply wrong: they were forgeries, and rather poor ones at that. Moreover, it is also striking (and tragic) that Mendenhall minimized the results of the C^{14} (as these showed that the texts were not ancient). Furthermore, his dismissive manner with regard to those suggesting these documents were modern forgeries was, obviously, understandable, but certainly misguided. Of course, the "extremely productive computer analysis" Mendenhall touted was inconsequential. The "Hebron Documents" were, in my opinion, a prank and the fact that some had considered these documents genuine for a full decade must have been a source of enormous satisfaction and pleasure for the forger.

A Forgery of the Late Twentieth Century:
The Moussaieff Ostraca

During the late 1990s, Naveh and Eph'al argued that the contents of the non-provenanced "Moussaieff Ostraca" published by Bordreuil, Israel, and Pardee were suspicious (Bordreuil et al. 1996, 1998; Eph'al and Naveh 1998). Naveh and Eph'al did not state definitively at that time that these ostraca were to be considered modern forgeries, but they did cite a striking number of parallels between biblical and Iron Age epigraphic phrases and those employed in the Moussaieff Ostraca. Ultimately, they concluded that "such a high degree and frequency of similarity, which can hardly be regarded as accidental, raises serious doubts about the authenticity of the ostraca" (Eph'al and Naveh 1998: 271–272).

Pardee (2003) responded by arguing that many of the biblical and epigraphic words and phrases discussed by Eph'al and Naveh are quite common or formulaic; therefore, their presence in non-provenanced epigraphs proves nothing. He goes on to note that "unless inaccuracies are present, such arguments are equally valid in favor of authenticity." Finally, he also avers that to believe that the Moussaieff Ostraca are forgeries

> requires the hypothesis that the forger was a master epigrapher, a master grammarian…, a master of biblical law, and a master chemist… The forger would also, however, have had to be cunning enough to produce some unexpected forms [Pardee 2003: 86].

Subsequently, I argued in detail that the forger had made a number of damning palaeographic errors that demonstrated that these ostraca were indeed forgeries. To be precise, basically the forger had produced an inscription with a mélange of letter forms from the eighth through the sixth centuries B.C., and he had also made some serious mistakes regarding the relative positioning of certain letters, especially the *samek* and *pe* (Rollston 2003). The forger was quite good, and had largely modeled his Hebrew forgeries on ancient Hebrew grammar and syntax, but his understanding of the Old Hebrew script had some marked deficiencies, so it was possible for me to detail these at some length. Again, a number of scholars had contended that these ostraca were genuine, ancient ostraca, but ultimately they were shown to be modern forgeries.

A Forgery of the Early Twenty-first Century:
The Jehoash Inscription

During early 2003, the "Jehoash Inscription" surfaced, allegedly having been found in the region of the Temple Mount in Jerusalem and purchased on the antiquities market. Although the first line is not extant, it is readily apparent that the inscription purports to have been commissioned by the late ninth-century Judean King Jehoash (Joash). Cross (2003), Rollston (2003), Naveh (personal communication), and McCarter (personal communication) analyzed this inscription and concluded that it was a definite modern forgery. Some scholars (e.g., Barkay, Lemaire), however, concluded that it might indeed be authentic (see Shanks 2003: 22–23 for his citation of the views of these scholars). Cross (2003) published a brief, but detailed analysis of the Jehoash inscription, noting some of the severe problems with its orthography and content. Eph'al (2003) wrote a short, but compelling article detailing the striking similarities between the Jehoash Inscription and the material in Kings and Chronicles about the reforms of Jehoash. And I (Rollston 2003: 175–180) wrote an article detailing the fact that there were serious palaeographic problems in this inscription, many of which were very similar to the palaeographic problems in the Moussaieff Ostraca (I believe the same forger, or pair of forgers, produced all three of these modern forgeries). It should be noted that laboratory tests had been performed on the Jehoash Inscription (much as they had been performed on the Moussaieff Ostraca), but those conducting the tests were arguably intent on declaring the Jehoash Inscription to be ancient and so suspended critical faculties, ignored significant problems, and declared the inscription to be ancient (for additional information on the extensive problems with the laboratory tests, see Rollston 2003: 182–189).

Cross's analysis of the orthography is of fundamental importance. For example, he noted that *lwlm* (line 12) is spelled with an internal *mater lectionis*. Cross affirmed that

> we would expect in ninth-century spelling *llm* without the internal *mater lectionis*. However, in the eighth and seventh centuries there are rare cases in which an internal *mater lectionis* is used in a one-syllable word [Cross 2003: 121; see also Greenstein 2003: 29–30, 2012].

An even more problematic orthographic anomaly, however, is *'mw* (line 15). Pre-Exilic orthography for this form is *'mh*. Cross notes that this is "an astonishing mistake for the forger to make, given his adherence to pre-Exilic orthography in most of the inscription" (Cross 2003: 121).

Within the Jehoash Inscription, there are also lexical problems. For example, the following phrase occurs: *w's̆ t . bdq . hbyt* (lines 9, 10), with the *intended meaning* "and I made the repair(s) of the Temple." However, within Standard Biblical Hebrew, the noun *bdq always* means something akin to "breach," "fissure," "hole" (i.e., a sign of structural weakness that requires repair).[6] A standard biblical Hebrew idiom is *ḥzq bdq hbyt* (with the verb *ḥzq* in the D or H stem), and means "to repair the breach(es) of the Temple." The idiom occurs in 2 Kings 12: 6, 7, 8, 9, 13; 2 Kings 22: 5 (cf. the Septuagint's rendering: *krateō … to bedek* and cognate idioms meaning "to strengthen/repair the *bedeq*"). Finally, the noun *bdq* (with the verb *ḥzq*) also occurs in the book of Ezekiel as well (Ezekiel 27: 9, 27), meaning "to repair the breaches" of a ship. The point is that *bdq* is a word that refers to *damage* and it can be accurately translated as "fissure," "breach," "hole" in Standard Biblical Hebrew, not "repairs." Ironically, therefore, the phrase *w"š 't . bdq . ḥbyt* of the Jehoash Inscription would mean (in ancient Hebrew) "and I made the fissures of the Temple."

Significantly, within Late Biblical Hebrew, the extant evidence suggests that the semantic domain of the root *bdq* had begun to evolve; hence, the Chronicler uses the G infinitive construct of *bdq* with the meaning "to inspect" or "to repair" (2 Chronicles 34: 10; cf. Septuagint *episkeuasai* "to make preparations" or perhaps "to repair"; with regard to the terms "Standard Biblical Hebrew" and "Late Biblical Hebrew," see Hackett 2002). This same basic meaning is also attested in the Late Biblical Hebrew of Ben Sira (Sir 50: 1 MsB with *bdq* in the N stem; cf. the Septuagint's rendering: *huperrapsen* "to fix up," "repair").[7] Post-Biblical Hebrew (e.g., the Mishnah) uses the term *bdq byt* in the sense of "(setting) the house in order" (Greenstein 2003: 29). Within Modern Hebrew, the noun *bdq* means "repair" and *bdq ḥbyt* means "house repairs." The verb *bdq* is attested in Modern Hebrew with the meaning "inspect," "examine" (see also Eph'al 2003: 126). In any case, the point remains that the semantic domain for the nominal /bdq/ in Standard Biblical Hebrew is damage resulting in a "fissure," "breach," "hole." There are no attested exceptions. Cross summarizes the data by stating that "the forger has committed a howler in using the modern sense of *bdq* in an 'ancient' inscription" (Cross 2003: 121, citing P.K. McCarter, Jr.). Ultimately, the modern forger of the Jehoash Inscription had created a nice *Sitz im Leben* (the temple repairs of King Jehoash) for his logia, and he had been quite successful in doing his lexical, orthographic, and palaeographic homework; however, the convergence of certain philological, orthographic, and palaeographic errors were sufficient to allow scholars to unmask this modern forgery as well. To be sure, some scholars have argued that this inscription may be ancient (Cohen 2007), but the arguments against its authenticity are damning. At this juncture, it is difficult to determine if the primary motivations for the forgery of the Jehoash Inscription were monetary (it was offered for sale to the Israel Museum at a seven-figure sum) or religious and political (with its alleged find-spot being near the Temple Mount in Jerusalem). Perhaps the most convincing argument is that it was convergence of such motives.

Conclusion

It can be stated that forgeries have a very long history, from antiquity to the modern period. Moreover, forgeries are not limited to any particular language or place. And, of course, it must be remembered that forgeries have sometimes duped the best of scholars during the course of the centuries. Furthermore, it should be emphasized that in many ways a forgery (once discerned as such) becomes part of the historical record for the period during which it was forged. That is, the Cruciform Monument of Manistushu is part of the history of the Neo-Babylonian Period, the Famine Stele is part of the history of the Ptolemaic Period, and the *Donation of Constantine* is part of the Middle Ages. Similarly, therefore, I would contend that the forgeries produced during the nineteenth, twentieth, and twenty-first centuries are part of the historical record for those periods (and not, of course, part of the historical record for the periods of antiquity from which they purport to hail).

Finally, I should emphasize that, during the modern period, most forgeries surface on the antiquities market (and this has often been the case for forgeries since the time of the Renaissance). I wish that there were no black market for antiquities, but the fact of the matter is that there is one. For this reason, I would emphasize that those scholars who wish to utilize epigraphic materials from the antiquities market in their research must be very cautious. After all, the forgers are becoming better with each passing decade, and I believe that the future could witness the production of rather perfect forgeries (at least in Northwest Semitic, Greek, and Latin). Therefore, the scholar that relies heavily on the antiquities market for some of the data for his or her research may be foolishly (if blithely) using materials that are modern forgeries, and thus not at all relevant for reconstructions of antiquity.

Acknowledgements

I would like to thank Morag Kersel and Matthew T. Rutz for the invitation to be part of this symposium and for the invitation to contribute to this volume. It was a distinct honor to be part of the symposium. Moreover, I would like to thank my research assistants Travis Weeks and Jared Poznich for bibliographic assistance with this article.

Notes

1. For a very useful discussion of similar motifs in ancient texts, see Na'aman (2011). Furthermore, it should be noted that the Hebrew Bible arguably contains similar

forgeries as well, with most scholars embracing De Wette's contention (first articulated in 1806) that "the Book of the Law" discovered during the Josianic Reforms was a pious forgery of some sort (see Childs 1979: 202–210). Similarly, it has long been the consensus of the field (albeit with a vocal minority protesting it) that the Pastoral Epistles of the Greek New Testament are also forgeries, much as F. Schleiermacher (1807) had argued, regarding 1 Timothy in particular, already some two centuries ago. For the thrust of the arguments and reference to some of the voluminous literature, see B. Ehrman (2011: 79–141).

2. The earliest manuscript of the *Donation of Constantine* is at the Bibliothèque nationale de France in Paris, Ms Latin 2777, normally dated to the ninth century A.D. References to the *Donation of Constantine* are first attested in the second half of the ninth century A.D.; for example, both Ado, Bishop of Vienne, and Aeneas, Bishop of Paris, refer to it in their writings.

3. Gratian was an Italian figure of the twelfth century A.D., who is often considered to be the "Father of Canon Law." His work entitled *Concordantia Discordantium Canonum* (i.e., *Decretum Gratiani*) is a collection of ca. 4,000 Patristic texts, conciliar texts, and papal decrees.

4. The active causative conjugation in Phoenician is the *yip'il*. Within Late Punic, the preformative *h* is used, and the forger was probably basing his form upon this datum (or perhaps it was simply a mistake, deriving from his knowledge of Hebrew). Significantly, Cross has noted that during the nineteenth century, widely used treatments of Phoenician actually posited the *hip'il* in Phoenician (Cross 1968: 446).

5. Cross deals with the issue of the article on the *nomen regens* in some detail, noting that the article on the *nomen regens* "goes against the overwhelming usage of Phoenician and Hebrew, and is most easily described as a blunder." Of course, he does cite those very rare examples of the article on the *nomen regens* in the Hebrew Bible (e.g., Ezekiel 9:3; 1 Samuel 26:22), noting that most other examples in the Hebrew Bible are textually corrupt. He also dismisses Gordon's citation of an alleged example from Karatepe: *hbrk b'l 'bd b'l*, noting that *hbrk* is probably a loanword from Akkadian *abarakku*, "temple steward," "chief steward" (Cross 1968; Oppenheim 1964: 32–35). Note that Röllig has concurred with understanding *hbrk* as a title, and states that "the translation: 'the blessed of Ba'al', although often used, is problematic since Semitic syntax does generally not allow a *status constructus*, which is already determined within itself, by a noun preceded by the article h- standing first" (Röllig 1999: 58).

6. Compare Ugaritic *bdqt*, "opening." See also Greenfield (1958: 221) and Hurowitz (1986: 293). Note that Cohen (2007) has attempted to argue, based on the philology, that the Jehoash Inscription may be ancient, but the fact of the matter is that the philological arguments of Cross and Greenstein are simply more convincing, the philological and palaeographic problems with the Jehoash Inscription too great.

7. Note the synonymous parallelism in the Hebrew with *ḥzq* (arguably) in the Dp stem (cf. also 2 Chronicles 34:10 for the same pairing). For text-critical discussion, see Smend (1906: 479). I concur with Smend's textual assessment.

References

Abbott, Frank Frost
  1908   Some Spurious Inscriptions and Their Authors. *Classical Philology* 3(1): 22–30.

Al-Rawi, Farouk N. H., and Andrew R. George
  1994   Tablets from the Sippar Library III: Two Royal Counterfeits. *Iraq* 56: 135–148.

Bordreuil, Pierre, Felice Israel, and Dennis Pardee
  1996   Deux ostraca paléo-hébreux de la collection Sh. Moussaïeff. *Semitica* 46: 49–76.
  1998   King's Command and Widow's Plea: Two New Hebrew Ostraca of the Biblical
         Period. *Near Eastern Archaeology* 61: 2–12.

Brownlee, William H., and George E. Mendenhall
  1970   An Announcement Published by the Department of Antiquities of Jordan and the
         Archaeologists Dr William H. Brownlee and Dr George E. Mendenhall Regarding
         the Decipherment of Carian Leather Manuscripts Found in 1966 in the Hebron
         Area, the Hashemite Kingdom of Jordan. *Annual of the Department of Antiquities
         of Jordan* 15: 39–40.

Childs, Brevard
  1979   *Introduction to the Old Testament as Scripture*. Fortress Press, Philadelphia.

Cohen, Chaim
  2007   Biblical Hebrew Philology in the Light of Research on the New Yeho'ash Royal
         Building Inscription. In *New Seals and Inscriptions, Hebrew, Idumean and Cuneiform*,
         edited by Meir Lubetski, pp. 222–284. Sheffield Phoenix Press, Sheffield.

Coleman, Christopher B.
  1922   *The Treatise of Lorenzo Valla on the Donation of Constantine*. Renaissance Society of
         America Reprint Texts Vol. 1. University of Toronto, Toronto.

Coleman-Norton, Paul
  1950   An Amusing Agraphon. *Catholic Biblical Quarterly* 12: 439–449.

Cross, Frank Moore
  1968   The Phoenician Inscription from Brazil: A Nineteenth-Century Forgery. *Orientalia*
         37: 437–460.
  2003   Notes on the Forged Plaque Recording Repairs to the Temple. *Israel Exploration
         Journal* 53: 119–123.

Ehrman, Bart
  2011   *Forged: Writing in the Name of God–Why the Bible's Authors Are Not Who We Think
         They Are*. HarperOne, New York.

Eph'al, Israel
  2003   "The Jehoash Inscription": A Forgery. *Israel Exploration Journal* 53: 124–128.

Eph'al, Israel, and Joseph Naveh
  1998   Remarks on the Recently Published Moussaieff Ostraca. *Israel Exploration Journal*
         48: 269–273.

Gelb, Ignace J.
  1949   The Date of the Cruciform Monument of Maništušu. *Journal of Near Eastern Studies*
         8: 346–348.

Gordon, Cyrus H.

    1968   The Authenticity of the Phoenician Text from Parahyba. *Orientalia* 37: 75–80.

Greenstein, Edward L.

    2003   Hebrew Philology Spells Fake. *Biblical Archaeology Review* 29(3): 28–30.

    2012   Methodological Principles in Determining that the So-Called Jehoash Inscription is Inauthentic. In *Puzzling Out the Past: Studies in Northwest Semitic Languages and Literatures in Honor of Bruce Zuckerman*, edited by Marilyn J. Lundberg, Steven Fine, and Wayne T. Pitard, pp. 83–92. Brill, Leiden.

Hackett, Jo Ann

    2002   Hebrew (Biblical and Epigraphic). In *Beyond Babel: A Handbook for Biblical Hebrew and Related Languages*, edited by John Kaltner and Steven L. McKenzie, pp. 139–156. Society of Biblical Literature Resources for Biblical Study Vol. 42. Society of Biblical Literature, Atlanta.

Haiying, Yan

    1998   The Famine Stela: A Source-Critical Approach and Historical-Comparative Perspective. In *Proceedings of the Seventh International Congress of Egyptologists*, edited by C.J. Eyre, pp. 515–521. Peeters, Leuven.

Hurowitz, Victor

    1986   Another Fiscal Practice in the Ancient Near East: 2 Kings 12: 5–17 and a Letter to Esarhaddon (LAS 277). *Journal of Near Eastern Studies* 45: 289–294.

Lichtheim, Miriam

    1980   *Ancient Egyptian Literature, Vol. III. The Late Period.* University of California, Berkeley.

Lidzbarski, Mark

    1898   *Handbuch der nordsemitischen Epigraphik.* Verlag von Emil Felber, Weimar, Germany.

Lindenberger, James M.

    2003   *Ancient Aramaic and Hebrew Letters.* Writings from the Ancient World Vol. 14. Society of Biblical Literature, Atlanta.

Mendenhall, George E.

    1971   The Philistine Documents from the Hebron Area: A Supplementary Note. *Annual of the Department of Antiquities of Jordan* 16: 99–102.

Metzger, Bruce Manning

    1972   Literary Forgeries and Canonical Pseudepigrapha. *Journal of Biblical Literature* 91: 3–24.

    1997   *Reminiscences of an Octogenarian.* Hendrickson, Peabody, Massachusetts.

Na'aman, Nadav

    2011   The "Discovered Book" and the Legitimation of Josiah's Reform. *Journal of Biblical Literature* 130(1): 47–62.

Naveh, Joseph

    1982   Some Recently Forged Inscriptions. *Bulletin of the American Schools of Oriental Research* 247: 53–58.

Oppenheim, A. Leo (editor-in-charge)

    1964   *The Assyrian Dictionary of the Oriental Institute of the University of Chicago*, Vol. 1(1): A Part I. The Oriental Institute, Chicago.

Pardee, Dennis
  2003   Hebrew Letters. In *The Context of Scripture III: Archival Documents from the Biblical World*, edited by William W. Hallo and K. Lawson Younger, Jr, pp. 77–87. Brill, Leiden.

Röllig, Wolfgang
  1999   The Phoenician Inscriptions. In *Corpus of Hieroglyphic Luwian Inscriptions, Vol. II: Karatepe-Aslantaş*, edited by Halet Çambel, pp. 50–81. DeGruyter, Berlin.

Rollston, Christopher
  2003   Non-Provenanced Epigraphs I: Pillaged Antiquities, Northwest Semitic Forgeries, and Protocols for Laboratory Tests. *Maarav* 10: 135–193.

  2004   Non-Provenanced Epigraphs II: The Status of Non-Provenanced Epigraphs within the Broader Corpus of Northwest Semitic. *Maarav* 11: 57–79.

  2005   Navigating the Epigraphic Storm: A Paleographer Reflects on Inscriptions from the Market. *Near Eastern Archaeology* 68: 69–72.

Schleiermacher, Friedrich
  1807   *Ueber den sogenannten ersten Brief des Paulos an den Timotheos: Ein kritisches Sendschreiben an J.C. Gass, Consisorialassessor und Feldprediger zu Stettin.* Realschulbuchhandlung, Berlin.

Schlottmann, Konstantin
  1874   Die sogenannte Inschrift von Parahyba. *Zeitschrift der Deutschen Morgenländischen Gesellschaft* 28: 481–487.

Shanks, Herschel
  2003   Is it or Isn't it? King Jehoash Inscription Captivates the Archaeological World. *Biblical Archaeology Review* 29(2): 22–23, 69–70.

Smend, Rudolf
  1906   *Die Weisheit des Jesus Sirach.* Georg Reimer, Berlin.

Sollberger, Edmond
  1967–1968   The Cruciform Monument. *Jaarbericht van het Voorasiatisch-Egyptisch Genootschap Ex Oriente Lux* 20: 50–70.

WikiLeaks, Text, and Archaeology:
The Case of the Schøyen Incantation Bowls

NEIL J. BRODIE AND MORAG M. KERSEL

Do ancient texts speak for themselves? Does the historical interpretation of an inscribed artifact suffer without knowledge of its archaeological context? How can the Assyriologist, papyrologist, or epigrapher ever be truly confident that the artifact under study is genuine when its complete history is unknown? These questions address the often debilitating effects of missing provenance and provenience on archaeological and textual scholarship.

Provenance is usually defined as the ownership history of an artifact, including its known archaeological findspot, while provenience is its findspot only. Thus provenance encompasses provenience, although the terms are often used synonymously and interchangeably. Archaeologists and epigraphers engaged in the debate over the publication of unprovenanced artifacts are usually at odds on the topics of missing provenience and the loss of archaeological context. They agree that textual material can carry historical information that is to some extent independent of archaeological context, though they often disagree as to what extent. Archaeologists who are interested in the antiquities trade, however, are also concerned about issues relating to the broader provenance, or ownership history, of objects once they are out of the ground. Using Aramaic incantation bowls as an example, in this chapter we explore the multivalence of inscribed artifacts and show how scholarly disagreement over the importance of provenance, including provenience, has degenerated into an ongoing, often vitriolic debate, with occasional legal consequences. We will use the release on WikiLeaks of a previously sequestered report into the provenance of a collection of incantation bowls belonging to the Norwegian collector Martin Schøyen as a point of entry into a broad-ranging discussion that touches upon the nature of historical knowledge, intellectual access, and issues of provenance and evidence.

Provenance as Evidence

Provenance is ownership history, but often it is something less: it is a datum, recording the location of an artifact at a single point in time. Sometimes provenance is a publication, sometimes provenance comprises a named previous owner, and sometimes provenance is merely an auction sale – the auction catalogue entry is the concrete datum. Nevertheless, even limited provenance information of this sort can contribute towards a greater understanding of an artifact's recent biography – its history on the market, its authenticity, and its legal status. An irrefutable dated record of past ownership and/or legal exportation from a country of origin is believed to increase significantly the monetary and perhaps symbolic value of an artifact. There is no real consensus as to what constitutes good provenance in the antiquities marketplace – but when provenance is assured, the market responds positively, as it did with the sale of the so-called Guennol Lioness in December 2007.

In the private collection of Alistair Bradley Martin since 1948, this 5,000-year-old Mesopotamian limestone sculpture, standing only three and a quarter inches high, was bought by an anonymous British buyer at Sotheby's New York for almost $57.2 million, a record price at the time for any sculpture sold at auction (Porada 1950; Sotheby's Antiquities, December 5, 2007, Lot 30). Jane Levine, Senior Vice President and Worldwide Director of Compliance for Sotheby's, asserted that the solid provenance for the Lioness definitely contributed to the record-breaking hammer price (Kersel 2012; Levine 2009). Unfortunately, Levine was not clear about what exactly she thought constitutes solid provenance. She might have had in mind the "1970 rule," the idea that any artifact that can be documented as having been outside of its country of origin by 1970, or legally exported since that date, should be considered as legitimately available on the market (Brodie and Renfrew 2005). Nevertheless, even though the 1948 date for the Lioness from the Martin collection satisfies the "1970 rule," it does not predate the enactment of the 1936 national ownership law in Iraq. Article 3 of Iraq's 1936 Antiquities Law states: "All antiquities in Iraq whether moveable or immoveable that are now on or under the surface of the soil shall be considered to be the common property of the State," thus vesting the ownership of all antiquities found after 1936 in the State (*Republic of Iraq Antiquities Law No. 59 of 1936*). Was the Lioness illegally excavated and exported from Iraq in the period between 1936 and 1948? Quite possibly we will never know, and in any case, any Iraqi claim for recovery would probably be precluded by the lapsed interval of time. And even with a provenance (of sorts), there is still no provenience or record of archaeological context. We do not know where the Lioness was found, or anything about the associated architecture (funerary, religious, domestic, etc.) or artifacts (other limestone sculptures, human remains, inscriptions, etc.). Is the Lioness to be regarded purely as an objet d'art and valued on account of its art-historical worth?

What about unprovenanced texts when their archaeological contexts are unknown? Their artistic merits are not normally regarded as anything special, but textual content can sometimes impart a different kind of value on the antiquities market. What are the implications of their lost archaeological contexts, and of their missing ownership histories? In what follows, we consider these questions by way of a peculiar episode in the life of Martin Schøyen's collection of Aramaic incantation bowls.

The Strange Case of University College London and a Collection of Aramaic Incantation Bowls

In 1996 the Department of Hebrew and Jewish Studies at University College London (UCL) agreed to house 654 Aramaic incantation bowls from the collection of Martin Schøyen for the purposes of study and research by Shaul Shaked of the Hebrew University of Jerusalem (Shaked et al. 2013). Aramaic incantation bowls date to between the fifth and eighth centuries A.D. Typically, they are hemi-spherical or flat-bottomed ceramic bowls with inscriptions written in ink on their inner surfaces, frequently but not always spiraling outward from the center (e.g., Figure 11.1). Each inscription is in some dialect of Aramaic (or in a pseudoscript) and records an incantation intended to protect the client and ward off malevolent forces. The first mention of these bowls in an archaeological context was by Austen Henry Layard, who discovered them in 1850 at Babylon and Nippur, although the British Museum had already acquired two bowls several years earlier in 1841 (Layard 1853, II: 509–526). John Punnett Peters' (1897: 182–194) report on the University of Pennsylvania expedition to Nippur remains the best documented archaeological context for the bowls. During the mission to Nippur incantation bowls were found in the structural remains of houses that were uncovered immediately below the surface. A house might contain one or more incantation bowls, alongside domestic artifacts such as grinding stones and pottery. The bowls were found placed upside down under thresholds or under the floor in room corners and were thought to have functioned as apotropaic charms (e.g., Müller-Kessler 2005: 205). At least two thousand Aramaic incantation bowls are known, but to date only a few hundred have been published, and of that number only a few were recovered from a documented archaeological context, all of which were recovered from Iraq (Brodie 2008: 46, 50–51, table 2). These issues of archaeological findspot

Figure 11.1.   Aramaic incantation bowl (BM 103359, Segal 2000: 033A), ca. A.D.
              sixth–eighth century, top view of the bowl's interior (diameter: 14 cm,
              depth: 6.3 cm) © Trustees of the British Museum.

and country of origin are crucial to the following discussion of provenance
and the Schøyen collection.

From the mid-1990s to the mid-2000s, Shaked continued his work
translating and publishing the Schøyen bowls without public incident
or interference, until September 2004 when a Norwegian Broadcasting
Corporation (NRK) television documentary on the Schøyen Collection
claimed to have uncovered evidence that the Schøyen bowls had been
discovered in Iraq during looting in the aftermath of the 1991 Gulf War
(Lundén 2005; NRK 2005). Bowls were becoming increasingly common on
the open market during the uneasy conditions that followed the war, and
Kersel has observed personally that in the years following the 2003 invasion
of Iraq a significant quantity of incantation bowls appeared on the shelves
of licensed antiquities dealers in Israel (see Figures 11.2–11.3). The NRK
program alleged that, before he had acquired them, Schøyen's bowls had been
taken illegally out of Iraq and passed through a trade network that included
stops in Amman and London.

If this account is correct, the trade of the bowls would have been in
direct contravention of the August 6, 1990 United Nations Security Council
Resolution 661 (*UNSCR* 1990), which imposed a trade embargo on all

Figure 11.2.   Incantation bowl for sale in Antiquities Shop, Jerusalem
               (photograph: M.M. Kersel).

Figure 11.3.   Incantation bowl for sale in Antiquities Shop, Jerusalem
               (photograph: M.M. Kersel).

goods in and out of Iraq. The embargo applied to antiquities as much as
to any other class of material, although between the 1990s and early 2000s
a seemingly uninterrupted flow of artifacts (including incantation bowls)
out of Iraq onto the international market was evident (Brodie 2006; Lawler

2001; Russell 2008: 31). The export of the bowls might also have been in contravention of Iraq's own 1936 Antiquities Law, if they were exported after that date as the NRK program claimed. However, Schøyen's representatives denied the NRK account and counter-claimed that the bowls had been out of Iraq since at least the 1960s (Lundén 2005: 6). In swift response to rumblings of protest from the academic community, UCL announced on October 10, 2004, that it had alerted the Metropolitan Police to the incantation bowls in its possession, and that it would review their provenance and rightful ownership, together with the university's future policies on the acquisition and study of unprovenanced cultural objects more generally. UCL also announced that "subject to obligations of confidence," the conclusions of the review would be published (UCL 2004).

UCL's decision to alert the police was required under United Kingdom (UK) law. Article 8(2) of the UK's Statutory Instrument 2003 no. 1519, The Iraq (United Nations Sanctions) Order (SI 1519), implementing UNSCR 1483, which had come into effect on June 14, 2003, reconfirmed the trade embargo on cultural objects first introduced in August 1990 by UNSCR 661, stating that:

> Any person who holds or controls any item of illegally removed Iraqi cultural property must cause the transfer of that item to a constable. Any person who fails to do so shall be guilty of an offence under this Order, unless he proves that he did not know and had no reason to suppose that the item in question was illegally removed Iraqi cultural property [SI 1519 2003: Article 8(2)].

This law reflects trade sanctions first placed on Iraq by UNSCR 661 in August of 1990. Thus if the Schøyen bowls were believed to have been illegally exported from Iraq after August 1990, UCL would be obliged to transfer them "to a constable." However, UCL's 2004 announcement also said that the police had advised UCL that there was "no reason to take the matter further and has no objection to the return of the material to Mr. Schøyen."

UCL found itself in the uncomfortable position of arbitrator as regards ownership of the bowls. The simple solution would have been to return them to Schøyen, but the 2004 statement went on to say that "UCL's possession has now entered the post-2002 era when new principles and policies have emerged and attitudes have changed." The significance afforded to the 2002 date was probably because it was in that year that the British Government had acceded to the 1970 UNESCO Convention on the Means of Prohibiting and Preventing the Illicit Import, Export and Transfer of Ownership of Cultural Property (1970 UNESCO Convention). However, the 2002 adoption of the 1970 UNESCO Convention had no retroactive force in British law: because the bowls had been in the United Kingdom since 1996, its requirements as regards the return of stolen cultural objects would not have applied to the incantation bowls, even if they could have been shown to have been taken out of Iraq illegally. But by 2004 in Britain, both the Museums Association and the British Museum had formulated acquisitions and loans policies based on principles enshrined in the 1970 UNESCO Convention that prohibited the acquisition of any object that could not be shown to have been exported from its country of origin before 1970, or exported legally after that date (the "1970 rule" mentioned above). Thus if UCL wanted to adhere to what had by 2004 become best practice in British museums and other collecting institutions (which would include UCL), it would have to consider the implications of holding material that did not meet the 1970 threshold.

The question of an original Iraqi provenience (findspot) became crucial not only to Schøyen's claim to ownership, but also to UCL's disposal of the bowls. If Schøyen's incantation bowls were most probably found in Iraq, and if Schøyen could not document legal export, then UCL might decide to return them to Iraq. If, on the other hand, it could be shown that a substantial number of incantation bowls had been found in archaeological contexts outside of Iraq, then the claim of an Iraqi origin for Schøyen's bowls would be more difficult to sustain, and the evidence would favor their return to Schøyen. The problem arising for Schøyen in this situation was that with no hard evidence of provenance, especially provenience, it would be difficult for him to counter expert opinion that all bowls with a verifiable findspot had been found in Iraq. Even if his bowls had been found outside Iraq, it would be a difficult circumstance for him to prove.

In May of 2005, UCL announced that an independent committee of inquiry had been established in March of that year (with the cooperation and consent of Schøyen) to investigate the provenance (complete object history including previous owners and archaeological findspot) of the bowls. Members of the committee included lawyer David John Freeman, Professor Emeritus of Archaeology at the University of Cambridge, Colin Renfrew, and Director of the UCL Museums and Collections, Sally MacDonald. Their mission was twofold: (1) to determine (if possible) the provenance of the incantation bowls and the ethical, legal, and professional implications arising from UCL's possession of them; and (2) to make recommendations regarding ethical policies for future acquisition and study of cultural objects by UCL and UCL staff.

In July 2006, the UCL committee submitted its report and a copy was made available to Schøyen, though at that time the findings were not made public. In March 2007, Schøyen initiated legal proceedings against UCL for return of the bowls, claiming that the "Schøyen Collection has become frustrated with the waste of time and money caused by a lengthy and inconclusive inquiry into their provenance" (Schøyen Collection 2007a). In June 2007, a joint UCL/Schøyen Collection press release stated that after "investigation by an eminent panel of experts, and further enquiries of its own, UCL is pleased to announce that *no adverse* claims to the Schøyen Collection's right and title have been made or intimated" (Schøyen Collection 2007b, emphasis added). The press release went on to state, "UCL has now returned the Bowls to the Schøyen Collection and has agreed to pay a sum in respect of its possession of them" (Schøyen Collection 2007b). The agreement for the payment and the return of the bowls appears to have been brokered as part of an out-of-court settlement with Schøyen, in return for which he ended legal proceedings. Not only were the bowls returned to Schøyen, UCL in effect paid a type of "rent" for keeping possession of the bowls while the question of their disposition was settled. Despite repeated appeals from various scholars, and the refusal of a *Freedom of Information Act* (FOI) request submitted by Brodie, UCL refused to release the committee of inquiry's report, having signed a non-disclosure agreement with Schøyen.

However, in a *Science* article in October 2007 (Balter 2007) some of the report's contents were leaked, and it was claimed that while the committee of inquiry had found nothing to suggest that Schøyen had any knowledge of the bowls' origins or had acted dishonestly in acquiring the bowls, the committee had concluded that "on the balance of probabilities" the bowls had been removed illegally from Iraq sometime after August 1990. This finding should have prompted UCL to return the bowls to Iraq, not to Schøyen. When asked to comment on the withheld report, committee member Renfrew is quoted as saying, "UCL tried to do the right and ethical thing by setting up a committee of inquiry. Then, when threatened with a lawsuit, in my view, it gave way under pressure" (Balter 2007: 554). In response to the *Science* article and stung by the criticism that the bowls had been looted, Schøyen (Schøyen Collection 2007c) issued a statement that focused on the provenance of the bowls and denied allegations that the bowls had been looted, claiming that the material had been exported from Jordan prior to 1988 – the issue of country of origin and the incantation bowls arising once more. The *Science* article leak was a mere teaser, however, providing very few details from the approximately 100-page report. The report itself was still inaccessible – that is, until WikiLeaks.

Enter WikiLeaks

WikiLeaks (http://wikileaks.org/) is a not-for-profit organization that aims to obtain and make publicly available original source material on sensitive and otherwise secret issues in order to "reveal unethical behavior by governments and corporations" (New York Times 2010). Founded in December 2006,

WikiLeaks is now regarded as one of the most famous (or infamous) "whistle-blower" websites on the Internet, having exposed internal memos about the dumping of toxic waste off the coast of Africa, the U.S. military blueprint for operations at Guantanamo Bay, and, of primary interest here, the UCL committee of inquiry report into the provenance of some 654 Incantation Bowls from the private collection of Martin Schøyen. In November 2009 the UCL inquiry committee's report was placed in the House of Lords Library and subsequently found its way onto WikiLeaks, where it was made available for universal access.

The report confirms claims previously made by Balter (2007) in his *Science* article that

> the committee did believe that, on the balance of probabilities, the bowls were removed from Iraq and that their removal was illegal under Iraqi law; that it was probable that their removal took place after August 1990, post-dating UNSCR 661; that their removal from Iraq was illegal even if they came out of Iraq before 1990, given the national Antiquities Laws of Iraq of 1924 and 1936; that UCL should, within one month from the date of publication of this report (July 2006), *return* or *cause the return* of the 654 incantation bowls to the Department of Antiquities of the State of Iraq [Balter 2007, emphasis in original].

Recall that in fact – and counter to the committee's recommendation – UCL returned the bowls not to Iraq, but to Schøyen, in the out-of-court settlement in June 2007.

But our interest in the report does not end with the committee's recommendations; we are also interested in other possible information contained in the report that might be relevant to our interest in provenance, and that might otherwise be unavailable to public investigation or scholarly research.

As an example of information suppressed with the report, we want to highlight the issue of the Jordanian export documentation. Brodie has long been in possession of information relating to this documentation. The committee found "no direct evidence that positively contradicts or impugns Mr. Schøyen's honesty" in his account of how he acquired the bowls (Balter 2007: 554), and we are not contesting that conclusion. We do believe, however, that he may have been less than diligent in investigating the full provenance of the bowls, seemingly satisfied by the assurances of Jordanian dealer Ghassan Rihani, who was their ultimate supplier.

In testimony before the panel, Martin Schøyen and his two London antiquities dealers claimed that the bowls came from the Rihani family collection in Amman, Jordan (Freeman et al. 2006). The antiquities dealers were under the impression that the Jordanian collection was in existence prior to 1965 – Schøyen claimed that the collection was founded around 1935. Now, 1935 is a very curious date indeed. It antedates the enactment of the Antiquities Law of 1936, No. 59 – the wide-ranging statute that legislated the discovery and possession of moveable antiquities from Iraq. As evidence, Schøyen offered the panel documents that included an export license from the Jordanian Department of Antiquities, thus providing the ownership history and legal exportation of the bowls in question: they had been in Jordan since the 1960s and were later exported legally from Jordan in the 1980s.

We believe that Rihani did supply Schøyen with copies of two documents purporting to be Jordanian export licenses – an Arabic original dated September 19, 1988 and an English translation dated October 12, 1992 (copies in Brodie's possession). These documents are potentially important, not because they validate a Jordanian findspot for the bowls (they do not), but because they should establish the date by which the bowls were out of Iraq. Unfortunately, the documents in question are ambiguous. The export license refers only to 2,000 pottery vases, not specifically to incantation bowls, and there is no way of establishing whether Schøyen's bowls were included in that number. For example, there are no photographs attached, a requirement actually stipulated on the license itself. Furthermore, although the license was granted in 1988, it constitutes permission to export, but is not a record of exportation. The actual export would appear to have taken place in 1992, the date of the English translation. Thus the export documents do not irrefutably establish a date for the export of the bowls from Jordan but do suggest that it was 1992. The bowls could have left Iraq any time before that date, and thus potentially after August 6, 1990, the date of UNSCR 661.

We believe that Rihani also provided Schøyen with a copy of a document dating to 1965 stating that Rihani had made a gift of a collection of antiquities to the Jerash and Irbid Archaeological Museum in Jordan, and, furthermore, testifying that at the time he (Rihani) owned a collection of cylinder seals, cuneiform tablets, and incantation bowls (a copy of this document is in Brodie's possession). The authenticity of this document is questionable, however, as it is written in English and not signed. Even if it is genuine, there is no necessary link between the incantation bowls mentioned in a 1965 document and those acquired by Schøyen in the 1990s. Misrepresenting the country of origin (here Jordan is listed as the country of origin) on the import/export documentation is an often-used ploy in the antiquities market to "launder" illegally excavated artifacts (for examples, see Mackenzie 2002).

Schøyen may have turned a blind eye to the issue of provenance, but he is not alone in the archaeological marketplace. In his analysis of the international trade in antiquities, criminologist Simon Mackenzie concludes:

The market interview sample displayed a high level of desire to buy unprovenanced antiquities, a perception of adverse consequences (penal and other) at or approaching nil, and a routine approach to the purchase of unprovenanced antiquities which suggested that the act had an established place in their [the collectors'] "comfort zone" of action [Mackenzie 2005: 213].

Collectors are comfortable legally, morally, and socially with purchasing undocumented artifacts without knowledge of their origin, and it is this willingness to participate in the market that ultimately supports the ongoing illegal excavation of artifacts and their eventual sale without complete object histories.

Schøyen's ongoing assertions of good provenance show that he is unwilling or unable to engage in a critical consideration of provenance and of the possible harmful consequences of his actions. He has been helped in his endeavor by UCL's refusal to publish the report. By not publishing the report, and thereby keeping secret negative evidence relating to the provenance of the bowls, UCL has made it easier for Schøyen to remain in his comfort zone. The panel of inquiry concluded that UCL and Schøyen were guilty of not showing enough curiosity about the source of the bowls. In a sense, they took a "don't ask, don't tell" approach to purchasing artifacts.

In 2009, in culmination of the second part of the committee of inquiry's mission, UCL published a new Cultural Property Policy, offering guidance on the acquisition of cultural objects and the study of cultural objects in non-UCL ownership. It advised against working with cultural objects of questionable provenance.

Ancient Texts Speak

Schøyen seems to believe that, by acquiring unprovenanced objects, he is "rescuing" them for historical research, thereby acting in the public good and promoting scholarship. Westenholz (2010: 263), for example, describes how Schøyen's dedication to collecting texts is enmeshed with the idea that "his collection might make a difference for the writing of history." But do ancient documents speak for themselves? Does the contextual information provided by their archaeological recovery make them less or more instructive?

Mark Geller, who was at UCL's Department of Hebrew and Jewish Studies when the bowls were first accepted on loan, wrote in 2005 that

Many of the sites in Iraq have Jewish Aramaic incantation bowls as surface finds, and these magic bowls date from the period of the Babylonian Talmud, ca. 400–700 CE. These bowls reveal a great deal of useful social history about the Jewish community of Babylonia in late antiquity [Geller 2005].

He went on to say that

> Within the past decade, hundreds of Aramaic incantation bowls have appeared
> on the antiquities market, collected from archaeological sites; there is no
> evidence that these objects have been stolen from a museum. As such there is
> no identifiable owner.

Schøyen has also claimed that his bowls were "chance/surface finds" (Schøyen
Collection 2007c).

The idea that the bowls are surface finds probably reflects the fact that
many of them have been found on or close to the surface in the upper strata
of archaeological sites. That is not to say that they are altogether without
context, however, as Peters showed back in 1897 at Nippur. Even findspot
co-ordinates constitute minimal context and in aggregate can reveal spatial
patterning of historical significance, as data collected in England and Wales
by the Portable Antiquities Scheme is beginning to show (Bland 2012: 5).
And there always remains the possibility of a unique and important, though
previously unknown, context for the bowls, and one that remains hidden
from scholarship because of the clandestine nature of the bowls' recovery.
It is fallacious to believe that simply because all bowls so far known with a
documented provenience and context were found close to the surface, then all
bowls without provenance must also have been found close to the surface.

Nevertheless, when all is said and done, the mystery remains – are Aramaic
incantation bowls found only in Iraq, or are they also found in other modern
Middle Eastern countries? Would knowledge of an archaeological findspot of
these bowls outside of Iraq cause the scholarly world to rethink their meaning
and historical associations? We may never know.

Conclusion

In his contribution to the Festschrift honoring David Owen, Westenholz
(2010: 260) asserts, "The truth is, you cannot have it both ways. An
unprovenanced object… is either a relic of the past or a stolen good." This is
perhaps an inflammatory and polarizing statement to make, underestimating
the complexity of object provenance, and may be the reason for the
persistence of the current seemingly intractable debate. The absence of
provenance does not always mean that the object is looted and/or stolen and,
while an inscribed object is a material relic of the past, there is no reason
why it cannot also be a stolen good. These attributions are not mutually
exclusive – it is almost 30 years since Kopytoff (1986) and Appadurai (1986)
reminded us that objects have social lives and can take on various identities
throughout their existence. And does scholarly interest in an artifact erase

its identity as a stolen good? Surely not. Epigraphers such as Westenholz (2010: 260) may regard as "facile" suggestions such as the one made by the American Schools of Oriental Research (see Gerstenblith 2014; Cherry 2014 [Chapters 12 and 13 in this volume]) that unprovenanced textual materials should only be studied after they have been returned to their rightful owner, but it seems to us to be a realistic attempt to recognize the dual nature of artifacts and reconcile conflicting claims of access and ownership in the interest of equitable scholarship.

Acknowledgements

Neil Brodie acknowledges the European Research Council funding under the EU's Seventh Framework Programme (FP/2007–2013)/ERC Grant Agreement no. 283873 GTICO, which has supported his writing of this paper. Morag M. Kersel would like to thank the Joukowsky Institute for Archaeology and the Ancient World, Brown University, for supporting this research and the associated symposium on the Archaeologies of Text. Preliminary research on this topic was conducted while Kersel was a Social Sciences and Humanities Research Council of Canada (SSHRCC) postdoctoral fellow at the University of Toronto.

References

Appadurai, Arjun
    1986   Introduction: Commodities and the Politics of Value. In *The Social Life of Things: Commodities in Cultural Perspective*, edited by Arjun Appadurai, pp. 3–63. Cambridge University Press, Cambridge.

Balter, Michael
    2007   University Suppresses Report on Provenance of Iraqi Antiquities. *Science* 318: 554–555.

Bland, Roger
    2012   The Treasure Act and Portable Antiquities Scheme in Britain. *Art and Cultural Heritage Law Newsletter* 4(1): 1, 3–6.

Boardman, John
    2007   Comment on Irreconcilable Differences? *Papers from the Institute of Archaeology* 18: 10–11.

Brodie, Neil J.
    2006   Iraq 1990–2004 and the London Antiquities Market. In *Archaeology, Cultural Heritage and the Antiquities Trade*, edited by Neil J. Brodie, Morag M. Kersel, Christina Luke, and Kathryn Walker Tubb, pp. 206–226. The University Press of Florida, Gainesville.
    2008   The Market Background to the April 2003 Plunder of the Iraq National Museum.

In *The Destruction of Cultural Heritage in Iraq*, edited by Peter G. Stone and Joanne Farchakh Bajjaly, pp. 41–54. Boydell Press, London.

Brodie, Neil J., and Colin Renfrew

2005   Looting and the World's Archaeological Heritage: The Inadequate Response. *Annual Review of Anthropology* 34: 343–361.

Cherry, John F.

2014   Publishing Undocumented Texts: Editorial Perspectives. In *Archaeologies of Text: Archaeology, Technology, and Ethics*, edited by Matthew T. Rutz and Morag M. Kersel, pp. 227–244. Joukowsky Institute Publication 6. Oxbow, Oxford.

Freeman, David John, Sally MacDonald, and Colin Renfrew

2006   *An Inquiry into the Provenance of 654 Aramaic Incantation Bowls Delivered into the Possession of UCL by, or on the Instruction of Mr. Martin Schøyen.* Inquiry established by the Provost of UCL. Report deposited July 27, 2006.

Geller, Mark

2005   Spies, Thieves and Cultural Heritage. Electronic document, http://groups.yahoo.com/group/Unidroit-L/message/499, accessed July 21, 2012.

Gerstenblith, Patty

2014   Do Restrictions on Publication of Undocumented Texts Promote Legitimacy? In *Archaeologies of Text: Archaeology, Technology, and Ethics*, edited by Matthew T. Rutz and Morag M. Kersel, pp. 214–226. Joukowsky Institute Publication 6. Oxbow, Oxford.

Kersel, Morag M.

2012   The Power of the Press: The Effects of Press Releases and Popular Magazines on the Antiquities Trade. In *Archaeology, Politics and the Media* edited by Carol Meyers and Eric Meyers, pp. 72–82. Eisenbrauns, Winona Lake, Indiana.

Kopytoff, Igor

1986   The Cultural Biography of Things: Commodization as a Process. In *The Social Life of Things: Commodities in Cultural Perspective,* edited by Arjun Appadurai, pp. 64–94. Cambridge University Press, Cambridge.

Lawler, Andrew

2001   Destruction in Mesopotamia. *Science* 293: 32–35.

Layard, Austen Henry

1853   *Discoveries in the Ruins of Nineveh and Babylon.* 2 vols. John Murray, London.

Levine, Jane

2009   Heritage Issues in the Middle East. Panel presentation at the Boston University Art Law Society and the Lawyers' Committee for Cultural Heritage Preservation, Boston.

Lundén, Staffan

2005   TV Review: NRK (Norway) Skriftsamleren [The Manuscript Collector]. *Culture Without Context* 16: 3–11.

Mackenzie, Simon

2002   Regulating the Market in Illicit Antiquities. *Trends and Issues in Crime and Criminal Justice* 239: 221–240.

    2005   *Going, Going, Gone: Regulating the Market in Illicit Antiquities*. Institute of Art and Law, Leicester.

Müller-Kessler, Christa
    2005   *Die Zauberschalentexte in der Hilprecht-Sammlung, Jena, und weitere Nippur-Texte anderer Sammlungen*. Texte und Materialen der Frau Professor Hilprecht Collection of Babylonian Antiquities im Eigentum der Friedrich-Schiller-Universität, Jena, Vol. 7. Harrassowitz Verlag, Wiesbaden, Germany.

New York Times
    2010   The War Logs – An Archive of Classified Military Documents Offers Views of the Wars in Iraq and Afghanistan. Electronic document, http://www.nytimes.com/interactive/world/war-logs.html, accessed November 10, 2010.

NRK
    2005   Skriftsamleren. TV program, 7, 14 September. Norwegian Broadcasting Corporation, Oslo.

Peters, John P.
    1897   *Nippur, or, Explorations and Adventures on the Euphrates: The Narrative of the University of Pennsylvania Expedition to Babylonia in the Years 1888–1890*. G. P. Putnam and Sons, New York.

Porada, Edith
    1950   A Leonine Figure of the Protoliterate Period of Mesopotamia. *Journal of the American Oriental Society* 70: 223–226.

Republic of Iraq
    1936   *Republic of Iraq Antiquities Law No. 59 of 1936*.

Russell, John M.
    2008   Efforts to Protect Archaeological Sites and Monuments in Iraq, 2003–2004. In *Catastrophe! The Looting and Destruction of Iraq's Past*, edited by Geoff Emberling and Katharyn Hanson, pp. 29–44. The Oriental Institute of the University of Chicago, Chicago.

Schøyen Collection
    2007a   Schøyen Collection Sues University College London for Recovery of Incantation Bowls. Press Release, March 9, 2007. Electronic document, http://www.schoyencollection.com/news_articles/UCL-090307.html, accessed November 10, 2010.
    2007b   The Schøyen Collection of Aramaic Incantation Bowls. Press Release, June 26, 2007. Electronic document, http://www.schoyencollection.com/news_articles/bowlsreturned-260607.html, accessed November 10, 2010.
    2007c   Correction of Media Innuendo Concerning Alleged "Looted" Provenance of Incantation Bowls. Press Release, October 14, 2007. Electronic document, http://www.schoyencollection.com/news_articles/bowlscorrect-141007.htm, accessed November 10, 2010.

Segal, Judah B.
    2000   *Catalogue of the Aramaic and Mandaic Incantation Bowls in the British Museum*. With a contribution by Erica C.D. Hunter. British Museum Press, London.

Shaked, Shaul, James Nathan Ford, and Siam Bhayro
    2013   *Aramaic Bowl Spells, Jewish Babylonian Aramaic Bowls Vol. 1*. With contributions

from Matthew Morgenstern and Naama Vilozny. *Magical and Religious Literature of Late Antiquity*, Vol. 1. Brill, Leiden.

University College London (UCL)

2004   Incantation Bowls: Statement by UCL (University College London). Press Release, October 10, 2004.

United Kingdom Statutory Instrument (SI 1519)

2003   The Iraq (United Nations Sanctions) Order (SI 1519), 2003.

United Nations Educational, Scientific and Cultural Organization (UNESCO)

1970   UNESCO Convention on the Means of Prohibiting and Preventing the Illicit Import, Export and Transfer of Ownership of Cultural Property.

United Nations Security Council Resolution (UNSCR)

1990   United Nations Security Council Resolution 661, August 6, 1990.

2003   United Nations Security Council Resolution 1483, June 14, 2003.

Westenholz, Aage

2010   Illicit Cuneiform Tablets: Heirlooms or Stolen Goods? In *Why Should Someone Who Knows Something Conceal It? Cuneiform Studies in Honor of David I. Owen on his 70th Birthday*, edited by Alexandra Kleinerman and Jack M. Sasson, pp. 257–272. CDL Press, Bethesda, Maryland.

Do Restrictions on Publication
of Undocumented Texts Promote Legitimacy?

Patty Gerstenblith

It is generally accepted among archaeologists and anthropologists, as well as their professional societies, that the looting of archaeological sites is, for the most part, motivated by the desire to obtain artifacts for sale on the international art market and to reap the economic benefits from such sales. The looting of sites causes significant losses to our ability to understand and reconstruct the past, which imposes negative externalities on all of society. Under the basic economic law of supply and demand, if the demand for looted objects decreases, then the supply should contract in response and the incentive to loot sites will diminish. In many market nations, legal consequences are therefore imposed on those who purchase undocumented antiquities that turn out to have been recently looted from sites. These consequences can range from criminal prosecution for trafficking in stolen property to civil forfeiture of the artifacts with loss of their value for smuggling and misdeclaration of objects upon import.

Scholars of ancient languages do not necessarily agree with these basic propositions. While some dispute the connection between the monetary incentive of the international market and the looting of sites, the more prevalent view is that ancient texts and other epigraphic material can be read and understood, regardless of whether they have an archaeological context (Owen 2009). While acknowledging that loss of context is a serious issue for the understanding of archaeological (i.e., non-epigraphic) remains, text scholars have at times taken the view that more is lost if such materials are not studied, as their authenticity can be determined without context and the texts contain much inherent information and scholarly value.

In response to the detriment caused to the archaeological record through the looting of sites, archaeological organizations, particularly the Archaeological Institute of America (AIA) and the American Schools of Oriental Research (ASOR), adopted policies to restrict or prohibit the publication and announcement at their annual meetings through the presentation of papers of artifacts that are considered to be undocumented. When these policies began to have an impact on the publication of undocumented texts, some scholars of ancient languages reacted in considerable and vociferous opposition to these policies, often without even understanding exactly what they permitted or prohibited.

Developing a Publication Policy Concerning Undocumented Archaeological Objects

When a professional organization considers the adoption of a publication or other policy with respect to undocumented antiquities, two facets must be kept in mind: first, what is the goal of such a policy and what values is the policy intended to promote; and, second, what is the appropriate terminology to use in developing such a policy? These two tasks are often more difficult than they may seem. Terms are often used loosely, and it is not always easy to craft a policy that dovetails as closely as one might wish with the goals that the policy purports to promote.

Terminology

Three terms are often used interchangeably in reference to antiquities: looted, illegal, and undocumented. These terms are not synonymous, although the categories may overlap. Because these terms often appear in the publication policies of professional organizations, it is necessary first to clarify what they mean and how they should be used, at least for the purposes of the following discussion.

A *looted* antiquity is one recovered from the ground in an unscientific manner. The antiquity is decontextualized, and what it can tell us about the past is limited to the information intrinsic within the object itself, rather than what might have been learned from the object's full associated context. Looting also jeopardizes the object's physical integrity because the process of looting often destroys or damages fragile objects and those not desired by the market.

An *illegal* antiquity is one whose history or its handling involves some violation of law. The antiquity may be characterized as stolen property if it is removed from its country of modern discovery in violation of a national law vesting title to antiquities in the nation (see United States v. Schultz, 333 F.3d 393 [2d Cir. 2003], and Government of the Islamic Republic of Iran v. The Barakat Galleries Ltd., [2007] E.W.C.A. Civ. 1374; [2008] 1 All E.R. 1177). An illegal antiquity may also be contraband if it has been imported in violation of an import restriction or was not properly declared upon entry.

An *undocumented* antiquity is one that has poor or only recent evidence of its ownership history (provenance) and how it was obtained. The term is also often used more specifically in voluntary codes of museums and professional associations to indicate an antiquity whose existence out of the country of discovery is not documented before 1970 (the date of adoption of the 1970 UNESCO Convention on the Means of Prohibiting and Preventing the Illicit Import, Export and Transfer of Ownership of Cultural Property) or which was not legally obtained and exported from its country of discovery after 1970.

Objects often fit into all three of these categories, but an object can also, for example, be looted but documented (if its ownership history is known for a sufficiently long period of time) or legal (depending on the laws of the country of discovery and those of the country where the antiquity is currently located). A documented history back to 1970 is often used as a proxy to indicate legality or to indicate that any initial looting happened long enough ago that its acquisition will not provide further financial incentive to the contemporary looting of sites. However, one should keep in mind that this is only a proxy, and a documented history for the object to 1970 does not ensure that the object was legally obtained; equally, lack of a documented history to 1970 does not guarantee that the object is illegal.

Values Underlying a Publication Policy

There are three values that a professional organization's policies should try to promote. The first of these is to reduce the loss of knowledge caused by the looting of archaeological sites. When a site is looted the original stratigraphic context of artifacts, linking them to each other and to architectural and natural geographic features, as well as floral and faunal remains, is lost. This original context can never be retrieved or reconstructed if it is not recorded when the object is first removed from the ground. Not only is the original context destroyed, but many artifacts that are considered less saleable on the market are lost, while other artifacts are substantially distorted to enhance their market appeal. This last phenomenon is seen in the damage that was done to the pre-Iconoclastic Byzantine mosaics looted from the Kanakariá Church in northern Cyprus (Sease and Thimme 1995) and to Neo-Assyrian reliefs looted from Nineveh (Russell 1998).

Along with loss of original context and damage done to individual artifacts, acceptance in the market of undocumented antiquities allows the introduction of possibly forged artifacts into the historical record. As Gill and Chippindale have pointed out, the acceptance of undocumented antiquities has a "conservatizing" influence in that objects that look like those that are previously known from excavated contexts are accepted, while those that look anomalous are often rejected as presumed fakes (Chippindale and Gill 2000: 504–505). Thus, whether authentic objects are rejected or forged ones are accepted, the presence of undocumented antiquities, and the looting of sites of which such objects are the products, results in the corruption of the historical record.

While the codes of conduct of many archaeological organizations prohibit or discourage the involvement of a professional archaeologist in the antiquities trade by, for example, placing values on antiquities for market purposes, whether publication and related policies serve this same purpose is unclear. It is not clear whether there is a connection between the scholarly publication of a particular undocumented artifact and the encouragement of the market in undocumented artifacts in general. However, the scholarly publication of a particular artifact certainly increases the market value of that artifact, and if the artifact is on the market, then the market will benefit from the publication. One can further posit that the publication of undocumented antiquities indicates the scholarly community's stamp of approval for undocumented antiquities and that this, in turn, signals to the market and collectors that they should grant greater acceptability to undocumented antiquities as well.

A second value that a publication policy concerning undocumented antiquities should promote is recognition of the rights of the country of origin with respect to objects that are found within its borders. Many nations that are rich in archaeological resources enacted laws, known as national ownership laws, from the beginning of the twentieth century and earlier. These laws vest ownership of such resources in the nation (Gerstenblith 2009). Critics have castigated the notion that a modern nation has the right to own such artifacts based merely on the accident of geography that placed a particular ancient culture within the boundaries of a particular modern nation. Critics also rely on perceived discontinuities in culture, ethnicity, and/or religion between the ancient peoples and modern nation in their effort to denigrate recognition of such laws as creating ownership rights in the courts of market nations (Cuno 2008).

Regardless of whether there is cultural continuity between the ancient past and the modern inhabitants of a nation (and regardless of how one would measure or determine such continuity or lack thereof), it is undoubtedly the right of nations to declare ownership of property located within their boundaries. As a matter of comity, respect for national sovereignty, and dignity, nations can draw the lines between private and public property as they see fit and as is consonant with their own particular legal system (Gerstenblith 2001: 228–241). It is a well-accepted legal principle that one looks to local law to determine the nature of initial ownership of the property involved. To encourage the sale of antiquities removed from a nation without its permission is to encourage disrespect for the legal rights of that nation as well as denial of its right to cultural self-determination.

A third value to promote, and one that is closely linked to the second, is legality and respect for the law. Regardless of whether a scholar believes that national ownership laws should be regarded as creating ownership in antiquities, this is now an accepted legal principle in the United States and the United Kingdom, as the *Schultz* and *Barakat* decisions demonstrate. To intentionally ignore the legal (or illegal) nature of such objects makes the scholar who handles and studies them an intentional or knowing violator of the law. While no scholar has yet been prosecuted on this basis, one can recall that dealers, such as Frederick Schultz, have been prosecuted and his knowledge or intent (criminal state of mind) to violate the law was established through his willful avoidance of learning the true background of the artifacts in which he conspired to traffic.

Despite the potential for a variety of legal consequences, ranging from civil forfeiture to criminal prosecution, the burden of proof to establish the necessary elements, to varying standards, remains on the government that initiates a legal action or on the would-be claimant nation that seeks to recover its stolen artifacts. Because of this placement of the burden of proof and the difficulty of tracing the history of a particular object, it is relatively easy for those who deal in and handle undocumented objects to escape the law. While the law sets a minimum standard of behavior and its efficacy is limited by the placement of burdens of proof, voluntary codes of conduct adopted by professional organizations can close the loopholes that the law allows. Finally, professional associations may adopt voluntary codes of conduct that set a standard higher than the law, for the simple reason that they feel that this accords with the dignity, self-respect, and principles of their profession.

Publication Policies Concerned with Ancient Texts

Some scholars, particularly those who work with epigraphic and textual material, oppose restrictions on publication of archaeological and other ancient materials. Their reasons for this opposition vary. Some are opposed to what they view as censorship of knowledge (Boardman 2009: 117–119; Owen 2009: 125–126). Others imply that the amount of knowledge lost when antiquities are recovered unscientifically is less than that gained by publication of unprovenanced antiquities (Boardman 2009).

In 2006, a group of scholars, led by the Harvard archaeologist Lawrence Stager, endorsed a "statement of concern" protesting the publication policies adopted by the Archaeological Institute of America and the American Schools of Oriental Research (Stager 2006). The statement is remarkable in its failure to acknowledge that there is a connection between looting and the market; rather, the statement describes the market as playing an important role as "often the means by which [such objects] are rescued." Although many objects that are ripped from their context lose their value, the statement holds that other objects, particularly textual and epigraphic materials, retain much of their scholarly value. Perhaps the most interesting commentary in the statement follows:

> The real objection to the antiquities market and unprovenanced material is that it somehow sullies our hands by participation in an illegal enterprise. But we believe a more refined judgment is called for. Yes, it would be nice if we always had professionally excavated materials to study and publish. But that is not the situation. Our choice is either to study unprovenanced material or to ignore it. Given that choice, we prefer to study unprovenanced material. The sweeping exclusion of unprovenanced material from scholarly consideration results only in a loss to scholars, to scholarship and ultimately to the public [Stager 2006: Para. 10].

The statement is sufficiently unclear that one cannot be certain whether these scholars meant to ignore the potential illegality of such artifacts, asserting that they could bring a more nuanced or superior judgment to the issue; but this is how the statement seems to read. In its final paragraph, the statement purports to express no opinion on legal issues.

One of the most peculiar of arguments against a publication policy concerning unprovenanced antiquities is the statement that objects cannot be illegal or tainted (Owen 2009: 141). The writings of John Boardman are particularly interesting and display a considerable lack of understanding of how the law works in this regard. He wrote:

> What can be made of a law that regards objects with no apparent pedigree, or rather those who handle and study them, to be guilty until proven innocent? That is not natural justice. Objects cannot be "tainted" or "illicit," but only be so described by scholars who do not understand them, or by legislators. Objects are testaments of antiquity, whether handled by a thief or scholar; their integrity must be respected and their safety assured [Boardman 2009: 117–118].

As a general matter, particularly in the area of criminal law, the burden of proof remains on the government to establish the necessary facts. Only in the case of the special legislation enacted by the United Kingdom was the burden placed on one who deals in Iraqi cultural materials to establish that he or she had no reason to suspect that the materials had been illegally removed from Iraq after 1990 (Gerstenblith 2006: 330–332). But there is confusion between what the law requires and what professional organizations have chosen to adopt as voluntary conduct. His argument gets even more convoluted when he states, "theft from a museum or registered site is criminal activity. It can be prosecuted as such in many countries, and should be" (Boardman 2009: 108). However, he fails to explain why theft from an unregistered site is less destructive to the historical and cultural record than theft from a registered site. And later, he writes:

> But, yes, there has grown up an ugly private market in major antiquities deliberately looted. This is criminal and should be treated as such. Where a site is deliberately targeted for the market, and especially if any collector is involved in contracting such work, criminality is at work and should be dealt with as such [Boardman 2009: 114].

Of greater import is the argument that textual materials carry more intrinsic information than do other types of artifacts and that they are therefore worth studying, regardless of whether they have a documented history or not. An extension of this argument is that it is more difficult to produce forgeries that will pass the scrutiny of scholars and experts. As Westenholz (2010: 260) wrote, "Though undeniably a part of illicit trade merchandise, objects with inscriptions are indeed different from other 'works of art' – they are not easily faked, and they hold information more or less independent of their archaeological context."

Both these arguments have some validity. However, there has been a recent plethora of inscriptions and textual material that are now generally regarded as forgeries (or the inscription on the object is regarded as a forgery, even if the object itself is authentic), such as the ivory pomegranate in the collection of the Israel Museum, several Iron Age ostraca, and the Jehoash inscription, as well as the inscription on the James ossuary about which considerable disagreement persists and whose authenticity will likely never be conclusively determined (Goren 2004; Rollston 2003, 2004, 2009).[1] To this extent, at least some epigraphic material shares the same fate as other forms of undocumented ancient materials. As Christopher Rollston has proposed, unprovenanced epigraphic materials must be subjected to rigorous scholarly and laboratory scrutiny; they should be kept distinct from the provenanced corpus, with their lack of provenance noted, which implies questions about authenticity, and this information should follow the objects permanently into their subsequent scholarly history (Rollston 2009).

One can also point out that decontextualized written materials bear a greater resemblance to other forms of undocumented artifacts than is often acknowledged. When any type of object is looted, the context is destroyed. If a looter is searching for cuneiform tablets, the entire context of an ancient Mesopotamian site may be destroyed or compromised. Textual materials are equally subject to national ownership laws as are other forms of ancient objects and therefore, when taken without permission, they would be characterized as stolen property in the United States and the United Kingdom. The fact that it is often easier to determine the place of modern discovery of written materials makes it is easier also to discern the legal status of the object. Finally, as with other types of antiquities, more can be learned about some types of texts and their associated history can be more fully reconstructed, if the text is scientifically excavated.

Examples of Publication Policies

Policies of the Archaeological Institute of America

In November 1970, UNESCO adopted its Convention on the Means of Prohibiting and Preventing the Illicit Import, Export and Transfer of Ownership of Cultural Property. Among others, the American archaeologist Clemency Coggins, who specialises in the Maya world of Central America and documented the destruction of large stone stelae and other architectural pieces for the sake of feeding the antiquities market in the United States, played a crucial role in encouraging the adoption of the Convention and in its ultimate acceptance by the United States. Fairly soon after, the largest American archaeological organization, the Archaeological Institute of America (AIA), began to urge ratification of the Convention by the United States.

The AIA Council endorsed ratification of the Convention at its December 1970 meeting, and in December 1973 the Council adopted a resolution stating that its Annual Meeting "should not serve for the announcement or initial scholarly presentation of objects in conflict with the Resolution on antiquities" (Norman 2005: 135). In 1978, the then-editors of the *American Journal of Archaeology* (*AJA*), Brunilde S. Ridgway and Tamara Stech Wheeler, extended the same policy to the editorial policy of the *AJA*. As Norman explained, "[t]he clear intent of the policy was not to enhance the market value or importance of these objects by giving them the imprimatur of the AIA by publishing them for the first time in the *AJA*" (Norman 2005: 135). The policy means that the *AJA* will not be the place of first publication of an antiquity acquired after December 1973 that cannot be shown to have left the country of origin legally.

Over time, several questions and ambiguities in the wording of the policy have arisen and, from time to time, the *AJA* has sought to resolve these. For example, in 1990, the then-*AJA* Editor-in-Chief, Fred Kleiner, sought to clarify what type of prior publication would qualify so as to allow a subsequent publication of the object in the *AJA*. Kleiner wrote that a "proper 'scholarly presentation'" would be defined as "something other than an annual report or catalogue" (Norman 2005: 136). The subsequent *AJA* Editor-in-Chief, Naomi Norman, was somewhat critical of this because it raised questions of subjectivity in determining what was a proper scholarly publication and because, in her view, this was the "point at which the original intent of the resolutions and the policy begin to fade from consciousness" (Norman 2005: 136).

Norman pointed out that the policies themselves would not stop the trade in undocumented antiquities or the looting of sites; neither the AIA Council nor the *AJA* editors, which adopted and enforced these policies, expected that the policies would do so. "Nevertheless, the resolutions and the publication policy do cast a bright spotlight on the problem and take an unequivocal stand against the illegal export and exchange of ancient artifacts and the destruction of the archaeological record that such trade causes" (Norman 2005: 136).

This was a prelude to the announcement of a further refinement to the publication policy intended to bring the focus back to the problem of undocumented and likely looted artifacts. This revised policy now permits even the initial publication of undocumented antiquities, so long as that lack of documentation is made clear in the discussion of the piece and "emphasize[s] the loss of archaeological context" (Norman 2005: 135). In addition, reviews of exhibitions, catalogues, and publications that do not acknowledge the presence of unprovenanced material "should state that the exhibition or publication in question includes material without known archaeological findspot." As Norman explained, "[t]he intent here is to keep the checkered past of an object out in the open and part of the continuing scholarly discussion of that piece" (Norman 2005: 136). The revised policy is intended to accomplish the original purpose of the AIA resolutions by continuing to keep the spotlight on a particular object's questionable past, even after the object has entered into the scholarly canon.

ASOR's Policy on Publication of Cuneiform Tablets from Iraq: An Attempt to Recognize and Resolve the Conflicting Interests

The American Schools of Oriental Research (ASOR) adopted a brief publication policy in 1995 within the context of a broader statement concerning professional conduct. This policy states:

> ASOR members should refrain from activities that enhance the commercial value of [illegally excavated or exported] artifacts and thus contribute indirectly to the illicit market, for example, publication, authentication, or exhibition. ASOR publications and its annual meeting will not be used for presentations of such illicit material [Seger 1995].

There was remarkably little comment on the adoption of this policy for close to 10 years – until the invasion of Iraq in 2003 and the looting of the Iraq Museum in Baghdad and of archaeological sites throughout the country. The concern with this massive looting and the call for legal intervention to prevent trade in such looted materials indirectly brought attention to the looting of sites in Iraq that had been ongoing from the time of the First Gulf War in 1991 until 2003 (Gerstenblith 2006: 278–286) and the large numbers of artifacts, including cuneiform tablets, that were allegedly brought into the United States.

This led to an unexpected conflict when it was realized that the *Journal of Cuneiform Studies*, an ASOR journal, would be unable to publish articles that discussed cuneiform texts of uncertain provenance. Many text scholars lamented that there would be much significant information contained in these cuneiform tablets that would never be made available for study or dissemination. A further concern was that publication of these texts would be left to scholars of lesser ability or with greater ethical challenges. In response to this conflict, ASOR convened a committee to study the situation and to attempt to devise a solution.

This committee proposed, and the ASOR Board of Trustees subsequently adopted, a compromise position that could, under the right circumstances, serve as a model not only for other publication policies, but also for the disposition of so-called "orphan" artifacts that do not fit the criteria for acquisition by a museum. This policy allows for the publication of undocumented texts under the following conditions: (1) the Iraq State Board of Antiquities and Heritage (SBAH) consents; (2) the materials to be published are returned to Iraq and are in the ownership and custody of the SBAH, and (3) any ASOR-sponsored publication of the material must include a statement indicating that the texts are unprovenanced and any additional facts concerning the acquisition of the texts and their appearance in the United States should be included in the publication. Further, the policy defined "returned to Iraq" as including "temporary placement of the material on loan with an academic research institution in the United States which is approved by the SBAH, does not acquire undocumented antiquities, and commits in writing to transfer such material to Iraq at any time upon request from the SBAH" (American Schools of Oriental Research 2004). The texts would be given an Iraq Museum inventory number and photographed, and the image and number relayed to the Iraq Museum. Such materials could not be transferred or sold to any institution outside of Iraq. Finally, the ASOR Baghdad Committee would determine when conditions would permit the return of these materials to Iraq.

While there is much about the policy to make it attractive as a compromise between those concerned that the acquisition and publication of undocumented materials (including texts) would provide impetus for further looting of sites, and those concerned about the loss of information and knowledge caused by a stringent publication policy, it seems that the policy has never been used. This is likely because the private owner of cuneiform tablets would have little or no incentive to turn over the tablets to an institution for restitution to Iraq, merely to achieve the benefit of publication. The private owner would not be able to realize the economic value of such tablets, either through sale or through a deduction from income for the value of the charitable donation when the U.S. institution would not be taking title to the tablets. In addition, other avenues of publication, for example in books and monographs, which are not subject to publication restrictions, remained viable alternatives to private collectors.

The policy can also be evaluated in terms of the goals that any publication policy should promote. Its most explicit accomplishment is its acknowledgment, in the words of the introduction to the policy, of "the intellectual and ownership interests of Iraq in its cultural heritage" (American Schools of Oriental Research 2004). The recognition of Iraq's interests is made simpler because it is often possible to trace cuneiform tablets to their place of likely discovery. The recognition of Iraq's ownership should make the texts legal within the United States and other market nations. The policy is also successful in recognizing that undocumented materials should be treated with caution when they are introduced into the historical and archaeological record. Again, with cuneiform tablets, this is an easier task because it is more difficult to produce forgeries that would pass muster with scholars. In addition, the circumstances surrounding the publication of such texts would likely keep questions about their origins and authenticity in the minds of future scholars as well.

The goal that the policy is perhaps less successful in promoting is separation in time between purchase of the undocumented object and the likely looting that produced the object. The policy has potential to reduce the market value of such objects, although the failure of collectors to take advantage of this opportunity to have their collection published in a prominent journal like the *Journal of Cuneiform Studies* may indicate that the policy would have no effect on the market value of such objects. It is also difficult to evaluate whether this policy had a market effect in light of the stringent legal provisions that were swiftly put into place among many market nations to prohibit trade in illegally removed Iraqi cultural materials (Gerstenblith 2006: 328–334); these prohibitions likely reduced the market value of antiquities with origins in Iraq, unless they could be proved to have left Iraq before 1990 (Brodie 2006: 217–221).

While this policy was unused because of lack of financial incentive for the collector, this policy may provide a model for the disposition of objects with insufficient provenance history and that therefore cannot be acquired by

American museums, according to the guidelines of the American Association of Museum and the Association of Art Museum Directors. The voluntary placement of such objects with museums that are committed to returning them upon request and presentation of some degree of proof of country of origin provides a less contentious method of enabling restitution of undocumented antiquities currently held by private collectors. Nonetheless, it remains a disappointment that collectors have not yet chosen to take advantage of this policy and its potential efficacy as a model remains unclear.

Note

1. Oded Golan was acquitted of the criminal charge of forgery of portions of the ossuary's inscription in March 2012 (Vergano 2012). However, the judge was careful to point out that while the government had failed to prove the forgery charge beyond a reasonable doubt (the standard of proof required for a criminal conviction), acquittal did not establish that the inscription was authentic. The Israel Antiquities Authority stated, in a press release, that the prosecution had had the positive effect of discouraging sales of undocumented epigraphic materials, which, in turn, led to a dramatic decrease in site looting.

References

American Schools of Oriental Research
    2004 New Policy on Cuneiform Texts from Iraq. Electronic document, http://www.asor.org/excavations/textpolicy.html, accessed March 5, 2011.

Boardman, John
    2009 Archaeologists, Collectors, and Museums. In *Whose Culture? The Promise of Museums and the Debate over Antiquities*, edited by James Cuno, pp. 107–124. Princeton University Press, Princeton.

Brodie, Neil
    2006 The Plunder of Iraq's Archaeological Heritage, 1991–2005, and the London Antiquities Trade. In *Archaeology, Cultural Heritage, and the Antiquities Trade*, edited by Neil Brodie, Morag M. Kersel, Christina Luke, and Kathryn Walker Tubb, pp. 206–226. University Press of Florida, Gainesville.

Chippindale, Christopher, and David W. J. Gill
    2000 Material Consequences of Contemporary Classical Collecting. *American Journal of Archaeology* 104: 463–511.

Cuno, James
    2008 *Who Owns Antiquity? Museums and the Battle Over Our Ancient Heritage*. Princeton University Press, Princeton.

Gerstenblith, Patty
    2001 The Public Interest in the Restitution of Cultural Objects. *Connecticut Journal of International Law* 16: 197–246.

2006 From Bamiyan to Baghdad: Warfare and the Preservation of Cultural Heritage at the Beginning of the 21st Century. *Georgetown Journal of International Law* 37: 245–351.

2009 *Schultz* and *Barakat*: Universal Recognition of National Ownership of Antiquities. *Art Antiquity and Law* 14: 29–57.

Goren, Yuval

2004 The Jerusalem Syndrome in Archaeology: Jehoash to James. Electronic document, http://www.bibleinterp.com/articles/Goren_Jerusalem_Syndrome.shtml, accessed March 5, 2011.

Norman, Naomi

2005 Editorial Policy on the Publication of Recently Acquired Antiquities. *American Journal of Archaeology* 109: 135–136.

Owen, David I.

2009 Censoring Knowledge: The Case for the Publication of Unprovenanced Cuneiform Tablets. In *Whose Culture? The Promise of Museums and the Debate over Antiquities*, edited by James Cuno, pp. 125–142. Princeton University Press, Princeton.

Rollston, Christopher A.

2003 Non-Provenanced Epigraphs I: Pillaged Antiquities, Northwest Semitic Forgeries, and Protocols for Laboratory Tests. *Maarav* 10: 135–193.

2004 Non-Provenanced Epigraphs II: The Status of Non-Provenanced Epigraphs within the Broader Corpus of Northwest Semitic. *Maarav* 11: 57–79.

2009 Modern Epigraphic Forgeries. Electronic Document, http://www.rollstonepigraphy.com/?p=5, accessed March 5, 2011.

Russell, John M.

1998 *The Final Sack of Nineveh*. Yale University Press, New Haven, Connecticut.

Sease, Catherine, and Danaë Thimme.

1995 The Kanakariá Mosaics of Cyprus: The Conservators' View. In *Antiquities Trade or Betrayed: Legal, Ethical and Conservation Issues*, edited by Kathryn W. Tubb, pp. 122–130. Archetype, London.

Seger, Joe D.

1995 ASOR Policy on Preservation and Protection of Archaeological Resources. Electronic document, http://www.bu.edu/asor/excavations/policy.html, accessed March 4, 2011.

Stager, Lawrence E.

2006 Statement of Concern. Electronic document, http://groups.yahoo.com/group/ANE-2/message/1289, accessed March 4, 2011.

Vergano, Dan

2012 "James Ossuary" Verdict Adds to Burial Box Furor. *USA Today*, March 18. Electronic document: http://usatoday30.usatoday.com/tech/science/columnist/vergano/story/2012-03-17/james-ossuary-jesus/53578490/1, accesssed on August 20, 2014.

Westenholz, Aage

2010 Illicit Cuneiform Tablets: Heirlooms or Stolen Goods? In *Why Should Someone Who Knows Something Conceal It? Cuneiform Studies in Honor of David I. Owen on his 70th Birthday*, edited by Alexandra Kleinerman and Jack M. Sasson, pp. 257–272. CDL Press, Bethesda, Maryland.

— 13 —

Publishing Undocumented Texts:
Editorial Perspectives

John F. Cherry

Introduction

Let's begin with a short version of a very long story (Parker 2010). Sometime before the terrorist attacks of September 11, 2001, a large group of cuneiform tablets and plaques was looted from somewhere in southern Iraq, probably Nippur (the religious capital of Sumer) or some other settlement close by. Knowledge of them surfaced only in March 2001 when U.S. Customs authorities, investigating a New York gallery suspected of illicit antiquities dealing, followed a tip concerning a shipment from Dubai to Newark airport of two boxes containing "clay objects." Upon inspection, these proved to be cuneiform clay tablets and plaques, some 362 items in all, and after seizure they were taken where all such materials used to go: the basement of the United States Customs House at 6 World Trade Center in New York City. This building, as is well known, was one of those destroyed in the 9/11 attacks: debris from the collapse of adjacent structures punched a massive hole right down to the basement level, which was then flooded by burst pipes and fire-fighters' hoses. When officers of the Immigration and Customs Enforcement Agency were able to re-enter the remains of the building a few weeks later to retrieve the guns, drugs, and money they routinely stored there, they also brought out the two water-logged boxes of tablets. They were moved to another secure storage location and not re-opened until late 2004. But by then they were terribly fractured, because the soaking they had received caused the salts in the unbaked clay to come to the surface.

The tablets of course needed to be repatriated to Iraq; and indeed, along with a larger group of objects, they were formally returned to the Government of Iraq in a ceremony held at the Iraqi embassy in Washington D.C. in September 2008. But both instability in Iraq and the state of the tablets themselves made their physical return inadvisable, and – on the initiative of John Russell (Massachusetts College of Art and Design), with Iraqi permission, and ca. $100,000 of State Department funding – an effort was meanwhile mounted to restore them. So a team of private artifact conservators, Dennis and Jane Drake Piechota, worked on them for 18 months until March 2010, a process involving baking, desalinization, cleaning, and painstaking re-mending. Their academic study was entrusted to the Harvard Assyriologist Benjamin Studevent-Hickman, who has determined that the tablets represent part of an archive of a head administrator of the temple of Ninurta, a god whose main cult center was in Nippur; the central figure in these texts is a man named Arad-mu, very possibly the same individual who is known to have been a very major state official during the Third Dynasty of Ur (Studevent-Hickman, personal communication 2010). Finally, on September 7, 2010, the tablets, now in stable condition, were handed back physically in a ceremony at the Iraq National Museum in Baghdad (Myers 2010).

For these Arad-mu tablets, further facts about the circumstances of their discovery and looting a decade or more ago, let alone reliable information about their precise findspot, can no longer be expected. What has been lost for good is their archaeological provenance, "the scholar's most basic and valuable tool in establishing an object's date, its function within a systemic context, and ultimately, its authenticity" (Reichel 2008: 55). This makes it next to impossible now to resolve some "known unknowns" about them (to use Donald Rumsfeld's infamous phrase). For example, while the internal evidence of the texts themselves would suggest that they might stem from "downtown" Nippur, there are said to be no reports of looting there prior to the 9/11 attacks, at least in the area where the temple of Ninurta might be expected to have been (Studevent-Hickman, personal communication 2010) – nor, incidentally, does this site seem to have been heavily plundered subsequently, at least compared to many others in southern Iraq (Stone 2008).

Nonetheless, in light of (1) their sheer number, (2) their "surfacing" together as a group in the illicit antiquities trade, (3) the coherence as a partial archive that their study has revealed, (4) the fact that they can be pinned down closely in terms of date and place, (5) their historical significance, as dealing with a key figure in the Ur III administration, and, above all, (6) the miserable fate they have suffered in modern times, these documents surely deserve to be published. Is the situation not rather like that of a dog which has been stolen, abused, nursed back to health, found a safe home – and now deserves a little love?

The Problem: Texts as Super-artifacts

Whether such material should in fact be published, and, if so, under what conditions, has of course been the focus of a great deal of acrimonious discussion in recent years, greatly exacerbated by the two wars in Iraq since 1991 – discussion that Westenholz (2010: 264) characterizes as "a dirty war within the scholarly community, full of intolerance, mudslinging, name-calling, and mutual incriminations," involving archaeologists, Assyriologists, museum directors, politicians, and collectors. The problem, while probably incapable of finding a satisfactory resolution any time soon, is nonetheless straightforward to frame.

The moral and ethical arguments are complex (Hollowell 2006), but some archaeologists evince empathy for the social and political circumstances that may drive poor villagers into "subsistence digging" – that is, the exploitation of local sites to find archaeological objects for sale, in order to use the proceeds to support a subsistence lifestyle (e.g., Matsuda 1998). Most, however, maintain strongly that "collectors are the real looters" (Elia 1993), in the sense that, by purchasing undocumented antiquities,[1] they keep the looting going, and feed the international trade in illicit antiquities. At the very heart of the archaeologists' position is the notion that artifacts robbed of their archaeological context have little scholarly value, and furthermore that a documented context of discovery is the best (in fact, ultimately the *only*) guarantee of authenticity. The latter is an increasingly important element of the argument, because it is now very clear that, as Eric Meyers (2005) puts it, "in addition to promoting illicit trade in antiquities the publishing of unauthenticated and unprovenanced material also has promoted an entire industry, namely the forgery business." Furthermore, irrespective of whether an artifact has been ripped from the ground illegally or taken from a museum, and taking a skeptical view of suspicious guarantees of authenticity and origin ("from an old private collection in Munich"), new undocumented materials reaching the market are in all likelihood stolen goods, since they lack export licenses and thus are in violation of the patrimony laws that have long been in place in most Mediterranean and Near Eastern nations.

Textual specialists, and some museum directors, have countered these sorts of arguments by casting scorn on the "context is everything" position. Thus, James Cuno (2008: 9) writes:

> Sometimes archaeologists argue that antiquities have no meaning outside their archaeological context... But of course antiquities have meaning outside their specific archaeological context, all kinds of meanings: aesthetic, technological, iconographic, even, in the case of those with writing on them, epigraphic.

> Indeed, most of what we know about the Ancient Near East we know from unprovenanced cylinder seals and cuneiform tablets.

This last sentence is, manifestly, an exaggeration that willfully overlooks the products of two centuries of legitimate excavation in the Middle East. Nonetheless, scholars must adopt a stance in the face of the fact that potentially important documents, such as the Gospel of Judas, lack any clear provenance history (Eakin 2006a).

One argument is that both legitimate, scientific excavation and entirely undocumented site looting involve destruction, and neither can be justified except via full publication. Another asserts that ignoring such works that have come to light through illicit activities may be even more damaging than the destruction caused by the original looting, an argument that represents the publication of undocumented texts as a form of justifiable "rescue" operation. Other scholars speak of "scare tactics" or the "censoring of knowledge," (Owen 2009) and assert that publishing restrictions amount to forcing them to "close their eyes to important information" (Eakin 2006b). Most prominently, a statement drafted by Lawrence Stager of Harvard University, signed by over 100 scholars worldwide, and posted on the website of the *Biblical Archaeology Review* (*BAR*) (but now, apparently, taken down), espoused the view that much of the history of the Near East would be shut to us if we cannot use these unprovenanced items, and that "looted artifacts, especially inscriptions, often have much of value to impart." *BAR* has gone out of its way to post articles proclaiming the valuable contributions of supposedly "worthless" unprovenanced artifacts (Resig 2009), with claims that a history of the ancient Near East is impossible without relying on unprovenanced textual material.

Texts, of course, are also artifacts. Scholars who object so strenuously to publication restrictions generally deny that publication, or even the authentication of material in dealers' hands, has any effect in enhancing the value of texts. Nor do they recognize the widely held view of archaeologists that *any* involvement in publishing undocumented materials merely reinforces the cycle of looting, or – as Elizabeth Stone put it – "if you publish, you are contributing to the illegal market" (Eakin 2006a). In other words, they are unwilling to accept any line drawn in the sand where undocumented texts are concerned, because, for them, texts are in effect "super-artifacts" – that is, artifacts with added-value that gives them intrinsic scholarly importance, even in the absence of any known context, and makes them deserving of study and publication no matter what the circumstances.

Both camps in this tricky ethical dilemma have adopted entrenched positions. It seems most unlikely that there can be any softening of opinion or convergence of viewpoints any time soon. In this light, it is interesting, then, to take a look at how matters are actually playing out in terms of publishing practices.

An Informal Survey of Editorial Practices

When the editors approached me to participate in the conference on which this book is based, they indicated that they would welcome my thoughts on the subject of the publication of undocumented texts from the perspective of a long-time journal editor. It is true that I have been involved in academic editing for many years – 10 years as co-editor of *World Archaeology*, five as co-editor of book reviews for the *American Journal of Archaeology*, 24 as co-editor of the *Journal of Mediterranean Archaeology*, as well as founding two monograph series and currently serving on the editorial boards of several other archaeological journals. All this has certainly given me plentiful experience of the issues with which editors in our field must often deal. On the other hand, none of these journals serves as the venue for the publication of texts, or at least not for their *primary* publication (which is the crux of the matter). Consequently, in all these years of journal work I have never faced an editorial problem concerning undocumented texts, and only once, if truth be told, with unprovenanced artifacts.

This lack of direct personal experience suggested that it might be more useful to conduct an informal survey of current editorial policies and practices across a range of different types of Mediterranean and Near Eastern journals, asking a series of pointed questions (Table 13.1). The editors of some 19 journals were

---

1. Does your journal have a published ethics policy?
    - If so, is this the creation of the journal's sponsoring body, or of the editors themselves?
    - If not, are there *tacit* ethical principles that guide your editorial decisions?

2. How often, in practice, have you faced an ethical decision about the publication of undocumented artifacts? With what outcomes?

3. Has your journal faced any problems relating specifically to the publication of *texts*? How often? Are these problems increasing?

4. Has your journal's editorial policy been influenced by, for instance:
    - the 2004 ASOR resolution to endorse the publication in its journals, under very strict rules, of undocumented texts likely emanating from Iraq?
    - the 2007 ASP resolution concerning the illicit trade in papyri?

Table 13.1.   Sample questions posed to editors about their journals' publication policies.

Journals	Editors
American Journal of Archaeology	Naomi Norman*
Anatolian Studies	Roger Matthews, Gina Coulthard
Bulletin of the American Schools of Oriental Research	James Weinstein*
Hesperia	Tracey Cullen*
Israel Exploration Journal	Shmuel Ahituv, Amihai Mazar
Journal of Ancient Near Eastern Religion	Seth Sanders
Journal of Biblical Literature	James VanderKam*
Journal of Cuneiform Studies	Piotr Michalolowski
Journal of Field Archaeology	Curtis Runnels*
Journal of Mediterranean Archaeology	Bernard Knapp, Peter van Dommelen, John Cherry
Journal of Near Eastern Studies	Christopher Woods, Robert Biggs*
Journal of Roman Archaeology	John Humphrey
Journal of the Canadian Society for Mesopotamian Studies	Robert Chadwick*, Paul-Alain Beaulieu
Journal of the Economic and Social History of the Orient	Norman Yoffee*
Levant	Graham Phillip
Mesopotamia	Carlo Lippolis
Near Eastern Archaeology	Ann Killebrew*
Palestine Exploration Quarterly	David Jacobson
Tel Aviv	Israel Finkelstein

* = Former editor of the journal

Table 13.2.　Journals included in the survey and their editors.

duly contacted by e-mail (Table 13.2); gratifyingly, all of them responded, in some cases with detailed responses that signaled their genuine concern about these issues. Obviously, it cannot be claimed that this is a thorough, or even representative, sample of all the key journals.[2] It is decidedly Anglophone; it omits certain areas altogether (e.g., Egypt); and it deliberately excludes certain journals already well known as being open to the publication of undocumented artifacts, including texts, and even possible forgeries. Still, this at least offers a snapshot of some current practices and editorial opinions. In what follows, I survey and offer a rough classification of the responses received, in three groups.

Journals with an Explicit Published Ethics Policy

Some journals, of course, are wholly constrained by their sponsoring institutions' ethics policies, in most cases willingly embraced by their editors. For example, *Hesperia*, *Hesperia* supplements, and all the many other monograph series of the American School of Classical Studies at Athens are bound by the School's strictly-enforced ethics policy, which states:

> The American School of Classical Studies at Athens will not knowingly print in any of its publications the announcement or initial scholarly presentation of any object acquired after December 30, 1970, by any means other than through an officially sanctioned excavation or survey, unless the object was part of a previously existing collection or was legally exported from the country of origin [ASCSA 1998].

Thus, if there is ever the slightest doubt about the provenance of the main subject of a *Hesperia* article (whether text or object), the author is asked to provide a letter from the dealer, collector, or museum, clarifying when the object was purchased and under what circumstances. One casualty of this policy, for example, was a publishable manuscript about a rare Greek and Roman bilingual dedication on a votive relief of a Thracian rider, withdrawn by its author who was unable to document when it entered the private collection in which it is held.

Equally explicit and firm are the policies of the *American Journal of Archaeology* and *Archaeology* magazine, which conform to the ethical stance of the Archeological Institute of America; since 1978, *AJA* has adopted what is perhaps the clearest position on no first publication of recently acquired material without context, and successive editors-in-chief have reiterated and refined this policy, among them Ridgway and Stech (1978), then Kleiner (1990), and most recently Norman (2005). The latest 2005 revision of the policy in fact allows quite a bit of leeway in considering publication of looted or illegally acquired material *if* one of the primary purposes of the article is to spotlight the problem of provenance itself, by articulating the history of acquisition and noting how that history complicates our understanding of the material:

> As a publication of the Archaeological Institute of America, the *American Journal of Archaeology* will not serve for the announcement or initial scholarly presentation of any object in a private or public collection acquired after December 30, 1973, unless its existence is documented before that date, or it was legally exported from the country of origin. An exception may be made if, in the view of the Editor, the aim of publication is to emphasize the loss of archaeological context. Reviews of exhibitions, catalogues, or publications that do not follow these guidelines should state that the exhibition or publication in question includes material without known archaeological findspot [Norman 2005: 135].

The former editor-in-chief of *AJA*, Naomi Norman, reports that she never had to turn away a manuscript because of non-compliance with the journal's stated policy: that, presumably, is because it is so widely known, prominently advertised, and rigorously upheld. *AJA*'s very effectiveness in policing submissions seems to be the reason why the *Journal of Near Eastern Studies* has also recently decided to adopt the same policy, prompted directly by recent difficulties over articles dealing with Iranian texts of dubious origin, and in anticipation of more problems down the road with texts flowing out of Iraq and philologists bolder about seeking to publish them. *Anatolian Studies*, which has encountered virtually no ethical publication problems over the past decade, despite having no published policy on the matter, appears to be heading in the same direction and, according to its Executive Editor (in 2010), is also about to adopt one.

Likewise, the journals issued under the aegis of the American Schools of Oriental Research (*BASOR, Near Eastern Archaeology, Journal of Cuneiform Studies*) are bound by comparably strict policies. Of special relevance here, of course, is the adoption at the 2004 ASOR meeting of an *exception* to its policies, to permit the publication in ASOR journals and books and the presentation at its meetings of undocumented cuneiform texts from Iraq, albeit under strictly limited circumstances (American Schools of Oriental Research 2004):

- The State Board of Antiquities and Heritage (SBAH) of Iraq has given its consent.
- Materials to be published are returned to Iraq and are in the ownership and custody of the SBAH. (Because of current conditions in Iraq, however, "return to Iraq" allows for temporary placement, under strict conditions, in an approved academic research institution in the United States.)
- In addition, the ASOR-sponsored publication and any future ASOR-sponsored publication of this material must include a reference to the fact that the published texts are unprovenanced. Additional facts that are known concerning the acquisition or appearance of the texts in the US should also be included.

It was the heated discussions leading up to this resolution that for the first time clearly revealed the bitter split in the scholarly community discussed in the previous section, and the flames were further fanned by the considerable coverage given to this ethics debate in the popular press. ASOR publications now conform to this policy – even though in one instance (*Journal of Cuneiform Studies*) it is alleged that its present editor, Piotr Michalowski, does not entirely agree with it (Owen 2009: 132, n. 5).

Journals without a Written Ethics Policy, but Material Must Come from Authorized Fieldwork, or with Certified Provenance

Another group of journals comprises those that, while having no official policy either printed in the journal or disseminated via the internet, nonetheless in practice operate more or less like the ones discussed above. Thus, the editor of *Mesopotamia*, Carlo Lippolis, writes:

> We do not have a precise or written "publication policy" about this matter, but up to now we have not had any problem with publishing unprovenanced material… If there is any doubt, we do not accept the study [C. Lippolis to J.F. Cherry, e-mail, 25 October 2010]).

Similarly, Robert Chadwick, the former editor of the *Journal of the Canadian Society for Mesopotamian Studies*, says:

> I am fairly certain we have never published any unprovenanced materials, and would never do so. During my years as editor I was never aware of any texts that would contravene the 1973 UNESCO cut-off date, nor do I believe that any of our contributors ever used such texts [R. Chadwick to J.F. Cherry, e-mail, 21 October 2010].

The *Journal of Field Archaeology* and the *Journal of Mediterranean Archaeology* would also fall under this rubric.

Levant does not as a rule publish undocumented artifacts or texts; but it deliberately declines to post an ethics statement on its website, in light of the politically-charged nature of the region this journal covers. Its editor, Graham Phillip, reports that a small proportion of all submissions are rejected because of ethical concerns; these concerns, however, mainly relate not to undocumented texts or artifacts, but rather to fieldwork carried out in occupied territory, which the journal does not publish. Other journals also wrestle with this issue: for example, Robert Biggs, the long-term former editor of the *Journal of Near Eastern Studies*, noted problems with articles concerning objects excavated during the Israeli occupation of Sinai, and *BASOR* too will not consider manuscripts dealing with such material. This is a slightly different ethical twist, since the problem here is not that objects have no documented context, but rather that the circumstances of their discovery might well be regarded as illicit. The *Palestine Exploration Quarterly* appears to have fewer qualms in this respect.

Journals that Generally Refrain from Publishing Undocumented Materials, but that Would Consider Publication, Depending on the Circumstances

A final group of journals encompasses those claiming that they generally refrain from publishing undocumented materials, including texts, but that are willing, at least, to consider publication, depending on the specific circumstances. The *Journal of Roman Archaeology*, for example, has no announced policy on materials lacking a secure provenance, and each submission is considered on its merits. The editor serves, as it were, as his own journal's investigative policeman, and has sometimes published items lacking secure provenance, if in his view the good outweighs the harm of so doing. A noteworthy example is the publication, as *JRA Supplement* 12.1 in 1994, of the inscribed, Sevso Treasure of Roman silver plate, which is both unprovenanced and hotly disputed as regards ownership (Mundell Mango and Bennett 1994).

Tel Aviv has published some undocumented texts, most notably a Neo-Hittite stele (Singer 1988–1989), although its inclination is to judge each case on its merits; thus, fairly recently, it declined to publish an article dealing with some important Persian-period inscribed metal bowls. Its editor, Israel Finkelstein, rightly emphasizes that in Israel, especially, there is another important angle to the problem – namely, forged items. But the journal's response is caution, not outright prohibition on publication. Thus, for example, in a recent issue there appeared an article (Schipper 2010) on the history of the southern Levant in the seventh century B.C., which draws on seals and seal-impressions which originated in the antiquities market and are suspected of being forgeries; the only condition imposed on the author was that a footnote be added to warn the reader about their authenticity.

The *Israel Exploration Journal* claims that it refrains from publishing unprovenanced artifacts, especially if they have not been previously published. At the same time, its editors would have no problems in publishing what they deem to be highly valuable texts, such as Judaean desert documents on papyrus or parchment that still occasionally appear on the market. Certainly, *IEJ* has published papers on at least three undocumented texts over the past several years: an inscribed lead weight seized from looters by the Israeli Antiquities Authority (Zissu and Ganor 2006), a fragmentary Roman inscription of unknown origin, now in the Islamic Museum of the Haram ash-Sharif in Jerusalem (Grüll 2006), and the "Gabriel Revelation" stone which surfaced in the antiquities market (Goren 2008). It also now seems to be the go-to journal for discussions relating to the authenticity of certain inscriptions, again based on the editors' estimation of their importance. Examples include the "Jehoash inscription" (Eph'al 2003), a forged plaque recording repairs to the Temple (Cross 2003), two forged Iron Age ostraca from the Moussaieff Collection (Goren et al. 2005a), and the inscribed pomegranate purchased by the Israel Museum in 1989 (Ahituv et al. 2007; Goren et al. 2005b; Lemaire 2006).

Lastly, I include in this group the *Journal of Biblical Literature*, although with some hesitation, since it has no explicit written policy regarding undocumented texts, and it has not been shy in the past about serving as an outlet through which editions of texts obtained through the market have first seen the light of publication (e.g., a manuscript from the Dead Sea Scrolls, as well as an article – but not its first publication – on a new text whose authenticity is questionable). Editor James VanderKam kindly indicated to me the sorts of approaches he would adopt, were he to be faced with an undocumented text submitted for publication: they include (a) asking whether it has been subjected to scientific tests to confirm its antiquity, (b) inviting the author to emphasize that the text lacks a known provenance, and (c) consulting experts in the field, to see if more information exists about the text and the circumstances under which it came to light. These may well be sensible steps; but, as an editor myself, I do not think it is our role to do this sort of detective work in order to clear a manuscript for publication. With a history of publishing texts acquired through the market, its lack of an explicit publication policy one way or another, and yet a clear concern for matters of authenticity and provenance, *JBL* occupies a somewhat awkward position between the *laissez-faire* attitudes of (e.g.) *Biblical Archaeology Review* and the more circumspect guidelines of most of the other journals discussed above.

Discussion

Insofar as this informal survey of editorial practices is at all representative, it would appear that many of these journals do not, and will not, publish undocumented texts. Equally, the others that at least do not *officially* preclude such a possibility do not seem to be doing so very much. Of course, the sample is biased, in that it does not include a number of journals that were not contacted, since their answers to my questions were already apparent from their actual publication decisions, which reveal an evident lack of any scruples about handling material of this sort.

As several editors asked me, "If it's not appearing in our pages, where *is* all the illicit and undocumented material being published?" One answer is that just indicated. If an unprovenanced object of any potential historical significance comes on the antiquities market or shows up in the hands of a private collector or enters a museum not governed by strict acquisition policies, it is quite likely to be published in a journal such as *Biblical Archaeology Review* (if it has implications for Biblical history), or in any of the various European and Middle Eastern journals that have no restrictions on publishing objects or texts lacking known provenance. These include, but are not limited to, *Journal of the American Oriental Society*, *Orientalia*, *Revue d'Assyriologie*, *Studi Epigrafici e Linguistici*, *Zeitschrift für Assyriologie*, and *Kaskal: Rivista di storia, ambienti e culture del Vicino Oriente Antico*.[3]

This, however, is to focus on journals alone. While the matter is difficult to quantify, one has the sense that the less receptive atmosphere now presented by many top-tier periodicals is making it more attractive to place articles dealing with undocumented texts not in journals, but rather in edited books or monographs, and – perhaps especially in the field of Near Eastern Studies – in *Festschriften* and other types of honorary volumes. A single example of the latter will suffice: the recently published volume for Professor David Owen, who through purchases has established the third-largest university collection of cuneiform tablets in the world at Cornell University, and who is outspoken in his defense of the right and necessity to publish any and all ancient texts (e.g., Owen 2005, 2009). The volume is tellingly entitled *Why Should Someone Who Knows Something Conceal It?* (Kleinerman and Sasson 2010), mirroring Owen's (2005: 1816) own view that "as scholars, our primary purpose is to preserve and disseminate knowledge, not to suppress and ignore it." Its final paper, appropriately, is an impassioned (though sometimes illogical) tirade against archaeologists who have seen fit to question the motives of "enlightened collectors" of cuneiform materials and those scholars who collaborate with them (Westenholz 2010: 265).

Still, if my hunch is correct that much stiffer publication policies at many journals have simply driven those bound on publishing undocumented texts into the arms of other types of outlets, it of course raises the question whether the firm stances adopted by ASOR, the AIA, the American Papyrological Society, the Deutsches Archäologisches Institut, and several other bodies have had any practical impact at all on reducing the number of publications of materials without provenance, and thus helping stem the circulation of illicit antiquities (whether they bear texts or not). Yet even to ask such a question raises another one, to which clear answers do not seem to exist: just how big a problem do we face here?

Perhaps influenced by images of the destruction of the Iraq Museum in Baghdad and the devastating looting of Mesopotamian sites, as so vividly documented in the Oriental Institute's exhibition and publication *Catastrophe! The Looting and Destruction of Iraq's Past* (Emberling and Hanson 2008), we have readily accepted the notion that there is a veritable tsunami of undocumented cuneiform texts flowing out of Iraq. The ASOR resolution of November 2004, certainly, was in direct response to that fear. But do we have any reliable figures? Here is a quotation from a report on the heated debates at the 2005 Rencontre Assyriologique Internationale (held at the Oriental Institute of the University of Chicago, 17–23 July, 2005):

> Today, as many as 100,000 tablets a year are being ripped out of archaeological sites in war-torn Iraq and put on the international market, according to U.S. government estimates. By comparison, only 300,000 to 400,000 likely existed in libraries and private collections prior to 1990, say scholars [Lawler 2005: 869].

Eric Meyers (ASOR 2004) put the figure even higher, at 150,000. We might compare that statement, however, with the evaluation of David Owen: monitoring of the internet since 2003 by CDLI (the Cuneiform Digital Library Initiative) has turned up fewer than 500 genuine tablets, "a far cry from the hundreds of thousands of tablets that certain archaeologists allege to have been smuggled out of Iraq" (Owen 2009: 131, n. 3). I too, in an amateur fashion, have been inspecting e-Bay in recent months and find that genuine tablets are much scarcer there than popular opinion has it (many are declared as replicas, and some are obvious fakes). Indeed, those in the market to purchase cuneiform texts would do better going to established auction houses, where what is on sale is often described, predictably, as coming from "a well-known European collection." In short, as with so many aspects of the arguments concerning undocumented objects, reliable quantified data are hard to come by.

It is encouraging to see the extent to which professional associations, as well as some individual scholars – whether cuneiformists, papyrologists, or epigraphers, have begun to assume responsibility for advocating for the bodies of ancient material that are in fact the very *raison d'être* of their own disciplines. For example, the 2007 Resolution of the American Society of Papyrologists now explicitly recognizes:

> that papyri and other inscribed objects are part of the archaeological record and that their historical value is diminished significantly when they have been stripped from their original contexts in the course of illicit and undocumented excavations; and that the looting of archaeological sites destroys the original contexts of *all* forms of material culture and permanently diminishes our ability to reconstruct and understand the past [ASP 2007].

This stance is very different from that of scholars who would maintain, with Owen (2005: 1816), that "our field is built upon the tens of thousands of unprovenanced tablets that make up the majority of collections in museums, universities, and private collections the world over," or agree, with Cuno (2008: 9), that "most of what we know about the Ancient Near East we know from unprovenanced cylinder seals and cuneiform tablets." To adopt such views involves according absolute primacy to the decipherment and study of ancient texts as our *entrée* to the ancient world, undervaluing the role of material culture in all its forms, and ignoring all arguments about the critical importance of context.

One cannot help being struck by the extent to which cuneiform studies, papyrology, and Greek and Roman epigraphy do in practice work with material lacking secure, detailed archaeological contexts. For instance, the archaeological journal *Hesperia* has for many years been a regular publisher of epigraphic articles.

Some of these, certainly, are reports of fresh material from well-documented excavations in, especially, the Athenian agora; but many are re-examinations of texts first published long ago in the many fascicles of *Inscriptiones Graecae*, coming from inscriptions recorded by 19th-century travelers and scholars as *spolia* built into churches, chapels, and even private houses, and thus lacking any meaningful primary archaeological context whatsoever. The latter types of study are certainly useful, sometimes even of high historical significance: few indeed would try to deny that objects without context, perhaps especially inscriptions, do often have much of scholarly importance to impart. That, however, is not what the arguments are about.

The shriller voices in Assyriology maintain that "archaeologists" (generally depicted as a unified bloc) wish to redouble the tragedy of looting by now seeking to suppress knowledge of looted or undocumented texts via the promulgation of ethical codes that restrict their publication. The reality, of course, is that there exist tens of thousands of unstudied and unpublished cuneiform texts still awaiting proper attention in older collections around the world; the Persepolis Fortification Archive, discussed elsewhere in this volume, is a good instance of how much material still requires scholarly attention, and how long that generally takes. What drives archaeological opinion is concern about the massive growth in the value of the market for illicit antiquities in the latter decades of the 20th century, now greatly exacerbated and facilitated by the various wars waged in the Middle East early in the 21st century. There exists no animus against those who work on what we might term "legacy collections," nor (contrary to some assertions in the literature) any wish to impose a blanket ban on publication of all unprovenanced material. But in order to confront current realities a line has to be drawn in the sand, no matter how arbitrary – and that line is the 24 April 1972 date upon which the *UNESCO Convention on the Means of Prohibiting and Preventing the Illicit Import, Export, and Transfer of Ownership of Cultural Property* entered into force, the deadline widely acknowledged in most ethical codes and various pieces of legislation. One can only repeat: the fact that artifacts ripped from their context by looters often lose much of their meaning, and so can provide only part of their story, is precisely the ground on which so many archaeologists object to the publication of undocumented materials. Scholars who publish materials that are clearly (or even probably) in violation of the UNESCO convention refuse to acknowledge that their actions, however indirectly, make them complicit in the looting cycle. Archaeologists, on the other hand, have yet to hear any persuasive logical, legal, ethical, or scholarly arguments why undocumented texts should be allowed to evade international conventions and be given a free pass.

Epilogue

Finally, what of those poor tablets with which I began? The Arad-mu archive will apparently be published, as a planned monograph in the *Journal of Cuneiform Studies Supplemental Serie*s. This is entirely above board: it has the approval of the State Board of Antiquities and Heritage of Iraq, and the tablets themselves are physically back in Iraqi hands. In other words, the publication process abides by the rules, or at least conforms to the special exception enshrined in the 2004 ASOR resolution concerning cuneiform materials from Iraq. Thus, a relevant code of ethics will have been followed, one representing a compromise that explicitly attempts to acknowledge the conflicting interests that exist in such circumstances. Yet, as Patty Gerstenblith (this volume) asks: Do such codes of ethics on publication of undocumented texts in fact promote legitimacy? That is an unresolved question, both ethically and practically, and likely to remain so for many years to come.

Acknowledgements

I am indebted to my fellow journal-editors, all of whom responded promptly and sometimes at length to my pesky inquiries. Benjamin Studevent-Hickman was most generous in sharing information about his study of the Arad-mu archive, as well as his views about the problems and ethics of publishing undocumented texts. Lastly, thanks to my colleagues Matthew Rutz and Morag Kersel for inviting my participation in what proved to be a stimulating and thought-provoking conference, and for being diligent editors of a volume in the series for which I serve as General Editor.

Notes

1. I use the term *undocumented* in the same sense as Patty Gerstenblith (Ch. 12, this volume) to refer to an artifact that has limited, or only recent, information about its ownership history and how it was obtained; such an object may, of course, also be looted (unscientifically excavated and lacking context) and/or illegal (involving some violation of law).

2. For example, it was only at a late stage in the research for this paper that it was drawn to my attention that the American Society of Papyrologists had also approved a resolution in June 2007 concerning the illicit trade in papyri and other archaeological objects. It includes a declaration that "the publication, presentation, and/or exhibition of such material shall not occur under the Society's auspices (for example, in its *Bulletin* or at its Annual Meeting) unless the author, speaker, or curator includes a frank and thorough discussion of the provenance of every item" (ASP 2007).

3. I am informed by one of the co-editors of this volume that to this list should also be added the Cuneiform Digital Library Initiative's *Journal*, *Bulletin*, and *Notes* (http://cdli.ucla.edu/?q=publications).

References

Ahituv, Shmuel, Aaron Demsky, Yuval Goren, and André Lemaire
    2007 The Inscribed Pomegranate from the Israel Museum Examined Again. *Israel Exploration Journal* 57: 87–95.

American Society of Papyrologists (ASP)
    2007 ASP Resolution Concerning the Illicit Trade in Papyri. Electronic document, http://tebtunis.berkeley.edu/ASPresolution.pdf, accessed 19 September 2013.

American School of Classical Studies at Athens (ASCSA)
    1998 Ethics Policy. Electronic document, http://www.ascsa.edu.gr/index.php/publications/author-Ethics-Policy, accessed 19 September 2013.

American Schools of Oriental Research (ASOR)
    2004 New Policy on Cuneiform Texts from Iraq. Electronic document, http://www.asor.org/excavations/textpolicy.html, accessed 19 September 2013.

Cross, Frank M.
    2003 Notes on the Forged Plaque Recording Repairs to the Temple. *Israel Exploration Journal* 53: 119–122.

Cuno, James
    2008 *Who Owns Antiquity? Museums and the Battle over Our Ancient Heritage*. Princeton University Press, Princeton.

Eakin, Hugh
    2006a Must Looted Relics Be Ignored? *The New York Times*, Arts Section, 2 May. Electronic document, http://www.nytimes.com/2006/05/02/arts/02publ.html?pagewanted=all, accessed September 19, 2013.
    2006b Looted Relics Inflame Scholars' Ethics Debate. *The New York Times*, Arts Section, 3 May. Electronic document, http://www.nytimes.com/2006/05/03/arts/03iht-loot.html?scp=13&sq=Judas%20Kiss&st=Search, accessed September 19, 2013.

Elia, Ricardo
    1993 A Seductive and Troubling Work. *Archaeology* 46 (January/February 1993): 64–69.

Emberling, Geoff, and Katharyn Hanson (editors)
    2008 *Catastrophe! The Looting and Destruction of Iraq's Past*. Oriental Institute Museum Publication No. 28. The Oriental Institute of the University of Chicago, Chicago.

Eph'al, Israel
    2003 The "Jehoash Inscription": A Forgery. *Israel Exploration Journal* 53: 123–128.

Goren, Yuval
    2008 Micromorphological Examination of the "Gabriel Revelation" Stone. *Israel Exploration Journal* 58: 220–229.

Goren, Yuval, Miryam Bar-Matthews, Avner Ayalon, and Bettina Schilman
    2005a Authenticity Examination of Two Iron Age Ostraca from the Moussaieff Collection. *Israel Exploration Journal* 55: 21–34.

Goren, Yuval, Shmuel Ahituv, Avner Ayalon, Miryam Bar-Matthews, Uzi Dahari, Michal Dayagi-Mendels, Aaron Demsky, and Nadaü Levin
    2005b A Re-examination of the Inscribed Pomegranate from the Israel Museum. *Israel Exploration Journal* 55: 3–20.

Grüll, Tibur
    2006 A Fragment of a Monumental Roman Inscription at the Islamic Museum of the Haram ash-Sharif, Jerusalem. *Israel Exploration Journal* 56: 183–200.

Hollowell, Julie
    2006 Moral Arguments on Subsistence Digging. In *The Ethics of Archaeology: Philosophical Perspectives on Archaeological Practice*, edited by Chris Scarre and Geoffrey Scarre, pp. 69–93. Cambridge University Press, Cambridge.

Kleiner, Fred S.
    1990 On the Publication of Recent Acquisitions of Antiquities. *American Journal of Archaeology* 94: 525–527.

Kleinerman, Alexandra, and Jack M. Sasson (editors)
    2010 *Why Should Someone Who Knows Something Conceal It? Cuneiform Studies in Honor of David I. Owen on his 70th Birthday.* CDL Press, Bethesda, Maryland.

Lawler, Andrew
    2005 Looted Tablets Pose Scholars' Dilemma. *Science* 309 no. 5736 (5 August 2005): 869.

Lemaire, André
    2006 A Re-examination of the Inscribed Pomegranate: A Rejoinder. *Israel Exploration Journal* 56: 167–177.

Matsuda, David J.
    1998 The Ethics of Archaeology, Subsistence Digging, and Artifact "Looting" in Latin America: Point, Muted Counterpoint. *International Journal of Cultural Property* 7: 87–97

Meyers, Eric
    2005 Should Scholars Authenticate and Publish Unprovenanced Finds? Electronic document, http://www.bibleinterp.com/articles/Meyers_scholars_publish.shtml, accessed February 26, 2011.

Mundell Mango, Marlia, and Anna Bennett
    1994 *The Sevso Treasure: Art Historical Description and Inscriptions, and Methods of Manufacture and Scientific Analyses.* Journal of Roman Archaeology Supplement 12.1. Journal of Roman Archaeology, Portsmouth, Rhode Island.

Myers, Steven L.
    2010 Iraqi Treasures Return, but Questions Remain. *New York Times*, 8 September. Electronic document, http://www.nytimes.com/2010/09/08/world/middleeast/08iraq.html, accessed September 19, 2013.

Norman, Naomi J.
    2005 Editorial Policy on the Publication of Recently Acquired Antiquities. *American Journal of Archaeology* 109: 135–136.

Owen, David I.

　2005　An Archaeological Dilemma. *Science* 309 (16 September 2005): 1816.

　2009　Censoring Knowledge: The Case for the Publication of Unprovenanced Cuneiform Tablets. In *Whose Culture? The Promise of Museums and the Debate over Antiquities*, edited by James Cuno, pp. 125–142. Princeton University Press, Princeton and Oxford.

Parker, Ashley

　2010　Detoured by 9/11 Attack, 4,000-year-old Tablets Make it Back to Iraq. *New York Times*, Arts section, 16 September. Electronic document, http://www.nytimes.com/2010/09/16/arts/design/16tablets.html, accessed September 19, 2013.

Reichel, Clemens

　2008　Cataloging the Losses: The Oriental Institute's Iraq Museum Database Project. In *Catastrophe! The Looting and Destruction of Iraq's Past*, edited by Geoff Emberling and Katharyn Hanson, pp. 51–63. Oriental Institute Museum Publication No. 28. The Oriental Institute of the University of Chicago, Chicago.

Resig, Dorothy D.

　2009　The Valuable Contribution of "Worthless" Artifacts. *Biblical Archaeological Review*. Electronic document, http://www.bib-arch.org/e-features/unprovenanced-objects.asp, accessed September 19, 2013.

Ridgway, Brunhilde S., and Tamara S. Stech

　1978　Editorial Statement. *American Journal of Archaeology* 82: 1.

Schipper, Bernd U.

　2010　Egypt and the Kingdom of Judah under Josiah and Jehoiakim. *Tel Aviv* 37: 200–226.

Singer, Itamar

1988–1989　A New Stele of Hamiyatas, King of Masuwari. *Tel Aviv* 15/16: 184–192.

Stone, Elizabeth C.

　2008　Archaeological Site Looting: The Destruction of Cultural Heritage in Southern Iraq. In *Catastrophe! The Looting and Destruction of Iraq's Past*, edited by Geoff Emberling and Katharyn Hanson, pp. 65–80. Oriental Institute Museum Publication No. 28. The Oriental Institute of the University of Chicago, Chicago.

Westenholz, Aage

　2010　Illicit Cuneiform Tablets: Heirlooms or Stolen Goods? In *Why Should Someone Who Knows Something Conceal It? Cuneiform Studies in Honor of David I. Owen on his 70th Birthday*, edited by Alexandra Kleinerman and Jack M. Sasson, pp. 257–266. CDL Press, Bethesda, Maryland.

Zissu, Boaz, and Amir Ganor

　2006　A Lead Weight of Bar Kokhba's Administration. *Israel Exploration Journal* 56: 178–182.

Index